THE LITTLE BROWN HOUSE.

FERN LEAVES
FROM
FANNY'S PORTFOLIO
SECOND SERIES
N. ORR. Sc. N.Y.
AUBURN & BUFFALO:
Miller, Orton & Mulligan.

EIGHTEENTH THOUSAND.

Fern Leaves

FROM

FANNY'S PORT-FOLIO.

SECOND SERIES.

With Original Designs by Fred. M. Coffin.

AUBURN AND BUFFALO:
MILLER, ORTON & MULLIGAN.
LONDON:
SAMPSON LOW, SON & CO.,
1854.

Published first in England by International Arrangement with the American Proprietors, and entered at Stationers' Hall.

AUBURN:
MILLER, ORTON & MULLIGAN
STEREOTYPERS AND PRINTERS.

TO

MY TRUEST FRIEND,

OLIVER DYER,

WHOSE FRIENDSHIP NEVER FALTERED, IN ADVERSITY;

WHOSE SYMPATHY AND ENCOURAGEMENT CHEERED ME,

WHEN NO BOW OF PROMISE WAS SET IN MY SKY;

This Book is Gratefully Dedicated,

BY

THE AUTHOR.

PREFACE.

To my Readers:

Six months since, I was in a deplorable state of ignorance as to the most felicitous style of Preface; at this lapse of time, I find myself not a whit the wiser. You will permit me, therefore, in pressing again your friendly hands, simply to say, that I hope my second offering of "Fern Leaves" will be more worthy of your acceptance, than the first.

Fanny Fern.

CONTENTS.

Illustrations.

Fern Leaves—Second Series.

SHADOWS AND SUNBEAMS.

CHAPTER I.

I CAN see it now: the little brown house, with its sloping roof, its clumsy old chimneys, and its vine-clad porch; where the brown bee hummed his drowsy song, and my silver-haired old father sat dozing the sultry summer noons away, with shaggy Bruno at his feet. The bright earth had no blight or mildew then for me. The song of the little birds, resting beneath the eaves, filled my heart with a quiet joy. It was sweet, when toil was over, to sit in the low door-way, and watch the golden sun go down, and see the many-tinted clouds fade softly away (like a dying saint) into the light of heaven, and evening's glittering star glow, like a seraph's eye, above them. 'Twas sweet, when Autumn touched the hill-side foliage with rainbow dyes, to see the gorgeous leaves come circling down on the soft Indian-summer breeze. 'Twas sweet, when the tripping, silver stream lay still and cold in Winter's icy clasp, and the flowers fainted beneath his chilly breath, and the leafless trees stretched out their imploring arms, and shook off, impatiently, their snowy burthen, and the heavy wagon-wheels went creaking past, and the ruddy farmer struck his brawny arms across his ample chest, for warmth, and goaded the lazy, round-eyed oxen up the icy hill. Even then, it was sunshine still, in the little brown house: in the ample chimney glowed and crackled the blazing faggots; rows of shining pans glittered upon the shelves; the fragrant loaf steamed in the little oven; the friendly tea-kettle, smoking, sang in the chimney corner, and by its side still sat the dear old father, with the faithful newspaper, that weekly brought us news from the busy world, from which our giant forest-trees had shut us out.

Ah! those were happy days: few wants and no cares: the patriarch's head was white with grave blossoms, yet his heart was fresh and green. Alas! that, under the lowliest doorway, as through the loftiest portal, the Guest unbidden cometh. The morning sun rose fair, but it shone upon silver locks that stirred with no breath of life, upon loving lips forever mute, upon a palsied, kindly hand that gave no returning pressure. Soon, over the heart so warm and true, the snow lay white and cold; the winter wind sang its mournful requiem, and from out the little brown house, the orphan passed with tearful gaze and lingering footstep.

CHAPTER II.

Oh, the bitter, bitter bread of dependence! No welcome by the hearth-stone: no welcome at the board: the mocking tone, the cutting taunt, the grudged morsel. Weary days, and sleep less, memory-torturing nights.

"Well, Josiah's dead and gone," said my uncle, taking down his spectacles from the mantel, to survey me, as I sank on the settle, in the chimney corner. "Take off your bonnet, Hetty. I suppose we must give you house-room. Josiah never had the knack of saving anything — more's the pity for *you*. That farm of his was awfully mismanaged. I could have had twice the produce he did off that land. Sheer nonsense, that shallow ploughing of his, tiring the land all out; he should have used the sub-soil plough. Then he had no idea of the proper rotation of crops, or how to house his cattle in winter, or to keep his tools where they wouldn't rust and rot. That new barn, too, was a useless extravagance. He might have roofed the old one. It's astonishing what a difference there is in brothers, about getting beforehand in the world. Now I've a cool thousand in the bank, all for taking care of little things. (There, Jonathan! Jonathan! you've taken the meal out of the wrong barrel: it was the damaged meal I told you to carry to Widow Folger.)

"Well, as I was saying, Hetty, in the first place, your father didn't know how to manage; then he didn't know how to say No. He'd lend money to anybody who wanted it, and pay his workmen just what they took it into their heads it was right to ask. Now, there's Jonathan, yonder; a day or two since, he struck for higher wages. Well, I *let* him strike, and got an Irishman in his place. This morning he came whining back, saying that his wife was sick, and his youngest child lay dead in the house, and that he was willing to work on at the old wages. That's the way to do, Hetty. If Jonathan chose to saddle himself with a wife and babies, before he was able to feed them, I don't see the justice of my paying for it. But it's time for family prayers: that will be something new to you, I suppose. I don't want to judge *any* body: I hope your father has gone to Heaven, but I'm afraid he didn't let his light shine. Don't whimper, child; as the tree falls so it must lie. You must see that you do *your* duty: make yourself useful here in my house, and try to pay your way. Young people of your age consume a great deal in the way of food and clothes."

Oh, the monotony of those weary days! how memory lingered over the sunny past: how thought shrank back affrighted from the gloomy future: how untiringly and thanklessly I strove to cancel the debt for daily bread, and how despairingly I prayed for relief from such bitter thraldom.

CHAPTER III

"Make up the bed in the north room, Hetty," said my aunt; "it's our turn to board the schoolmaster this week. You needn't put on the best sheets: these book-learning folks are always wool-gathering. He never'll know the difference. What a hungry set these schoolmasters are, to be sure: it keeps a body all the time cooking. A bushel of doughnuts is a mere circumstance. When the last master was here, our winter barrel of cider went off like snow in April. I hope Jonathan learned enough at school to pay for it, but I have my doubts: he trips in the multiplication table yet. Your uncle and I think that this boarding schoolmasters is a poor business — a losing bargain. He says I must put less on the table, but it is no use to try that game with George Grey. He's as independent as Adam in Eden, before the serpent and his wife got in. He'd just as lief call for anything he wanted as not, and somehow or other, when he does, I always feel as if I had no choice about bringing it. That eye of his always makes me think of forked lightning; and yet he's kindly spoken, too. He is as much of a riddle to unravel, as one of Parson Jones' doctrinal sermons. But, go make his bed, Hetty, and mind you stuff a few rags in that broken pane of glass over it. I spoke to your uncle about getting it mended, but he said warm weather would be along in three months, and that's very true, Hetty. Hist! your uncle is calling you. He says he is going out in the barn to thresh, and if Peter Tay comes up the road, and stops in here again, for him to subscribe towards the minister's new cloak, you must say that he has gone to Jifftown, and will not be home for a week at least. Now don't forget, Hetty: people seem to think one earns money now-a-days on purpose to give away. A new cloak! humph! I wonder if the Apostle Paul's hearers ever gave him a new cloak? I wonder if John the Baptist ever had a donation party? Don't the minister have his salary, two hundred dollars a year — part in produce, part in money; paid regularly, when the times ain't too hard?

Go make the school-master's bed now, Hetty. One pillow will do for him. Goodness knows he carries his head high enough when he is awake. I should n't wonder if he had been captain or colonel, or something, some muster day."

The schoolmaster! Should I be permitted to go to school? or should I be kept drudging at home? Would this Mr. Grey think me very ignorant? I began to feel as if his forked-lightning eyes were already on me. My cheeks grew hot at the idea of making a blunder in his awful presence. What a miserable room my aunt had provided for him! If I could but put up some nice white curtains at the window, or get him a cushioned chair, or put in a bureau, or chest of drawers. It looked so comfortless—so different from the welcome my dear old father was wont to give to "the stranger within the gates;" and now memory pictured him, as he sat in the old arm chair, and I knelt again at the low foot-stool at his feet, and his hand strayed caressingly over my temples, and I listened to old continental stories, till the candle burned low in the socket, and only the fire-light flickered dimly on the old portrait of General Washington, and on my father's time-worn face.

My aunt's shrill voice soon roused me from my reverie. Dinner time had come, and with it Mr. Grey—a gentlemanly young man, of about two and twenty, with a bright, keen, blue eye, and a frank, decided, off-hand manner, that seemed to me admirably in keeping with his erect, imposing figure and firm step. Even my uncle reefed in a sail or two in his presence, and my aunt involuntarily qualified her usual bluntness of manner. I uttered a heartfelt thanksgiving when dinner was over

CHAPTER IV.

"Hetty," said my uncle, as the door closed upon Mr. Grey, "I suppose you must go to school, or the neighbors will say we don't treat you well. You ought to be very thankful for such a home as this, Hetty; women are poor miserable creatures, left without money. I wish it had pleased Providence to have made you a boy. You might then have done Jonathan's work just as well as not, and saved me his wages and board. There's a piece of stone wall waiting to be laid, and the barn wants shingling. Josiah now would be at the extravagance of hiring a mason and a carpenter to do it.

"Crying? I wonder what's the matter now? Well, it's beyond me to keep track of anything in the shape of a woman. One moment they are up in the attic of ecstasy; the next, down in the cellar of despondency, as the Almanac says; and it is as true as if it had been written in the Apocrypha. I only said that it is a thousand pities that you were not a boy; then you could graft my trees for me, and hoe, and dig, and plant, and plough, and all that sort of thing. This puttering round, washing dishes a little, and mopping floors a little, and wringing out a few clothes, don't amount to much toward supporting yourself. Let me see, you have had, since you came here" — and my uncle put on his spectacles, and pulled out a well-thumbed pocket memorandum — "You've had t-w-o p-a-i-r-s of shoes, at t-h-r-e-e s-h-i-l-l-i-n-g-s a pair, and nine yards of calico, for a dress, at s-i-x c-e-n-t-s a yard. That 'mounts up, Hetty, 'mounts up. You see it costs something to keep you. I earned *my* money, and if you ever expect to have any, you must earn yours" — and my uncle took out his snuff-box, helped himself to a pinch, and, with the timely aid of a stray sunbeam, achieved a succession of very satisfactory sneezes.

The following day, under the overwhelming consciousness of my feminity and consequent good-for-nothingness, I made my debut at Master Grey's school.

It was a huge barn of a room, ill lighted, ill warmed, and worse ventilated, crowded with pupils of both sexes, from the little, chubby A B C D-arian, to the gaunt Jonathan of thirty, who had begun to feel the need of a little ciphering and geography, in making out his accounts, or superscribing a business letter. There were rows of awkward, mop-headed, freckled, red-fisted boys; and rosy-cheeked, buxom lasses, bursting out of their dresses, half-shy, half-saucy, who were much more conversant with "apple bees," and "husking frolics," than with grammar or philosophy. There was the parson's son, and the squire's and the blacksmith's son, besides a few who hadn't the remotest idea whose sons they were, having originally been indentured to their farming masters, by the overseers of the county alms-house.

Amid these discordant elements, Master Grey moved as serenely as the August moon of a cloudless night; now patting some little curly head, cruelly perplexed by "crooked S;" now demonstrating to some slow, older brain, a stumbling block in Euclid; now closing the creaking door after an ill-mannered urchin; now overlooking the pot-hooks and trammels of an unsophisticated scribe, who clutched the pen as if it were a hoe-handle; now feeding the great, draftless Behemoth of a stove with green hickory knots, and vainly attempting to thaw out his own congealed fingers.

In a remote corner of the school-room sat Zeb Smith, the village blacksmith's son, who came into the world with his fists doubled up, and had been pugilist–ing ever since. It was Zeb's proud boast that "he had whippped every schoolmaster who had ever appeared in Frog-town," and in his peaceful retreat from under his bent brows, he was now mentally taking the measure of Master Grey, ending his little reverie with a loud, protracted whistle.

Master Grey turned quickly round, and facing his overgrown pupil of thirty, said in a voice clear as the click of a pistol, "You will be pleased not to repeat that annoyance, Mr. Smith." Zeb bent his gooseberry eyes full upon the master, and gave him a blast of "Yankee Doodle."

All eyes were bent on Master Grey. The guantlet of defiance was thrown in his very teeth. Zeb had a frame like an ox, and a fist like a sledge-hammer, and he knew it. Master Grey was slight, but panther-y; to their unscientific eyes, he was already victimized.

Not a bit of it! See! Master Grey's delicate white fingers are on Zeb's check shirt-collar; there is a momentary struggle: lips grow white; teeth are set; limbs twist, and writhe, and mingle, and now Zeb lies on the floor with Master Grey's handsome foot on his brawny chest. Ah, Master Grey! science is sometimes a match for bone and muscle. Your boxing master, Monsieur Punchmellow, would have been proud of his pupil.

Peace restored, Master Grey shakes back from his broad forehead his curly locks, and summons the first class in geography. A row of country girls, round as little barrels and red as peonies, stand before him, their respect and admiration for "the master" having been increased ten per cent. by his victory over Zeb. Feminity pardons any thing in a man sooner than lack of courage. The recitation goes off very well, with the exception of Miss Betsey Jones, who persists in not reciting at all. Master Grey looks at her: he has conquered a *man*, but that's no reason why he should suppose he can conquer a *woman*. He sees that written in very legible characters in Miss Bessie's saucy black eye. Miss Bessy is sent to her seat, and warned to stay after school, till her lesson is learned and recited perfectly. With admirable nonchalance, she takes her own time to obey, and commences drawing little caricatures of the master, which she places in her shoe, and passes round under the desk, to her more demure petticoat neighbors.

School is dismissed: the last little straggler is kicking up his heels in the snow drifts, and Master Grey and Miss Bessie are left alone. Master Grey inquires if the lesson is learned, and is told again by Miss Bessie, with a toss of her ringlets, that she has no intention of learning it. Master Grey again reminds her that the lesson must be recited before she can go home. Bessie looks mischievously at the setting sun, and plays with the master's commands and her apron strings. An hour passes, and Bessie has not opened the book. Master Grey consults his watch, and reminds her "that it is growing dark." Bessie smiles till the dimples play hide and seek on her cheek, but she says nothing. Another hour: Master Grey bites his lip, and, replacing his watch in his pocket, says, "I see your intention, Miss Betsey. It is quite impossible, as you know, for us to remain here after dark. To-morrow morning, if your lesson is not learned, I shall punish you in the presence of the whole school. You can go."

"Thank you, sir," says Bessie, with mock humility, as she crushed her straw hat down over her bright ringlets.

"Mischief take these women," Master Grey was heard to utter, as he went through the snow by starlight to a cold supper. "Shall I conquer Zeb, to strike my colors to a girl of sixteen?"

There was plenty to talk about over the brown bread and milk, at the farmers' tea-tables that night; the youngsters all made up their minds that if there was "a time to play," it was not in Master Grey's school-room, and the old farmers said they were glad the District had a schoolmaster at last that was good for something, and that they should think better of city chaps in future for his sake. Even Zeb himself acknowledged, over his father's forge, as he mended his broken suspenders, that Master Grey was a "trump."

The nine o'clock bell summoned again the Frog-town pupils to the District School. Master Grey in vain looked in Bessie's face for any sign of submission. She had evidently made up her mind to brave him. After the usual preliminary exercises, she was called up to recite. Fixing her saucy black eyes upon him, she said, "I told you I would *not* learn that lesson, and I have not learned it." "And I told *you*," said Master Grey, (a slight flush passing over his forehead) that I should punish you if you did not learn it? Did I not?" Bessie's red lip quivered, but she deigned him no reply.

"You will hold out your hand, Betsey," said Mr. Grey, taking up a large ferule that lay beside him. The color left Bessie's cheek, but the little hand was extended with martyr-like determination, and amid a silence that might be felt, the ferule came down upon it, with justice as unflinching as if it were not owned by a woman. Betsey was not proof against this humiliation; she burst into tears, and the answering tear in Master Grey's eye showed how difficult and repugnant had been the task.

From that day, Master Grey was "monarch of all he surveyed," and, truth compels me to own, by none better loved or more implicitly obeyed, than by Miss Bessie.

Master Grey's "boarding week" at my uncle's had now expired. What a change had it effected in me! Life was no longer aimless: the old, glad sparkle had come back to my heavy eye; I no longer dreaded the solitude of my own thoughts. The dull rain dropping on my chamber roof had its music for my ears; the stars wore a new and a glittering brightness, and Winter, with his snowy mantle, frosty breath, and icicle diadem, seemed lovelier to me than violet-slippered Spring, with roses in her hair. I still saw Master Grey each day at school. How patiently he bore with my multiplied deficiencies, and with what a delicate and womanly appreciation of my extreme sensitiveness, he soothed my wounded pride.

No pale-eyed flower fainting beneath the garish noonday heat, ever so thirsted for the cool dews of twilight, as did my desolate heart for his soothing tones and kindly words.

CHAPTER V.

"Betsey," said my uncle, "we shall want you at home now. It will be impossible for me to get along without you, unless I hire a hand, and times are too hard for that: so you must leave school. You've a good home here, for which you ought to be thankful, as I've told you before; but you must work, girl, work! Some how or other the money goes;" (and he pulled out the old pocket-bock;) "here's my grocer's bill — two shillings for tea, and three shillings for sugar; can't you do without sugar, Hetty? And here's a dollar charged for a pair of India rubbers. A dollar is a great deal of money, Hetty; more than you could earn in a month. And here's a shilling for a comb; now that's useless, you might cut your hair off. It won't do — won't do. I had no idea of the additional expense when I took you in. Josiah ought to have left you something no man has a right to leave his children for other people to support; 't isn't Christian. I've been a professor these twenty years, and I ought to know. I don't know as you have any legal claim on me because you are my niece. Josiah was thriftless and extravagant. I suppose 't is in your blood, too, for I can't find out that you have begun to pay your way by any chores you have done here. If you must live on us, (and I can't say that I see the necessity,) I repeat, I wish you had been born a boy."

"But as I am not a boy, Uncle, and as I do not wish to be a burthen to you, will you tell me how to support myself?"

"Don't ask me. I'm sure I don't know. That is your business. I have my hands full to attend to my own affairs. I am deacon of the church, beside being trustee of the Sandwich Island Fund. I don't get a copper for the office of deacon; nobody pays *me* for handing round the contribution box; not a cent of the money that passes through my hands goes into my till; not a *mill* do I have by way of perquisite, for doling it out to bed-ridden Widow Hall, or asthmatic Mr. Price. Not a penny the richer was I, for that twenty dollars I collected in the contribution box at last communion: no, I am a poor man, comparatively speaking. I may die yet in the almshouse; who knows? You must work, girl, work; can't have any drones in my hive."

A shadow just then passed the window. I should know that retreating footstep! Could it be that Master Grey had come to the door with the intention of calling, and overheard my uncle? At least, then, I was spared the humiliation of exposing his parsimony.

CHAPTER VI.

It was the night for the weekly vestry lecture. I was left quite alone in the old kitchen. My uncle had extinguished the lamp in leaving, saying that it was "a waste to burn out oil for me." The fire, also, had been carefully taken apart, and the brands laid at an incombustible distance from each other. The old clock kept up a sepulchral, death-watch tick, and I could hear the falling snow drifting gloomily against the windows.

I drew the old, wooden settle closer between the tall andirons, and sat sorrowfully gazing into the dying embers. What was to become of me? for it seemed impossible to bear longer the intolerable galling of my yoke. Even the charity of strangers seemed to me preferable to the grudging, insulting tolerance of my kindred. But, with my sixteen years' experience of quiet valley-life, where should I turn my untried footsteps? To Him who guideth the little bird through the pathless air, would I look.

Weeping, I prayed.

"My poor child," said a voice at my side; and Master Grey removed my hands gently from my tear-stained face, and held them in his own. "My poor Hetty, life looks very dark to you, does it not? I know all you suffer. Don't pain yourself to tell me about it; I overheard your uncle's crushing words. I know there are none to love you — none to care for you — none on whom you can lean. It is a bitter feeling, my poor child. I, too, have passed through it. You would go from hence, but where? Life is full of snares, and you are too young, and too inexperienced to brave them.

"Hetty," and Master Grey drew me gently toward him,—"Hetty, could you be happy with me?"

Is the ship-wrecked mariner happy, who opens his despairing eyes at length in the long looked for, long prayed for, home?

Is the little bird happy, who folds her weary wings safe from the pursuer's talons, in her own fleece-lined nest?

Is the little child happy, who wakes, sobbing, in the gloomy night, from troubled dreams, to find his golden head still safely pillowed on the dear, maternal bosom?

CHAPTER VII.

It was very odd and strange to me, my new home in the great, busy city; with its huge rows of stores and houses, its myriad restless feet, and anxious, care-worn faces; its glittering wealth, its squalid poverty; the slow moving hearse, and the laughing harlequin crowd; its noisy Sabbaths, and its gorgeous churches, with its jeweled worshippers, and its sleepy priests; its little children, worldly-wise and old, and its never-ceasing, busy hum, late into the day's pale light. I had no acquaintances: I needed none; for I moved about my pretty little home as in a glad dream. My husband was still "Master Grey," but over a private school of his own, bounded by no "District," subject to the despotic dictation of no "Committee." In his necessary absence, I busied myself in arranging and re-arranging his books, papers and wardrobe, thinking the while such *glad* thoughts! And when the little mantel clock chimed the hour of return, my cheek flushed, my heart beat quick, and my eyes grew moist with happy tears, at the sound of the dear, loved footstep.

How very nice it seemed to sit at the head of that cheerful little table — to make, with my own hands, the fragrant cup of tea — to grow merry with my husband, over crest-fallen Zeb, and poor, stubborn little Bessie, and my uncle's time-worn bugbear of a memorandum book!

And how proud I was of him, as he sat there correcting some school-boy's Greek exercise, while I leaned over his shoulder, looking attentively at his fine face, and at those unintelligible hieroglyphics, and blushing that he was so much wiser than his little Hetty.

This thought sometimes troubled me. I asked myself, will my husband never weary of me? I even grew jealous of his favorite authors, of whom he was so fond. Then I pondered the feasibility of pursuing a course of reading unknown to him, and astonishing him some day with my profound erudition. In pursuance of my plan, I would sit demurely down to some great, wise book; but I saw only my husband's face looking out at me from every page, and my self-inflicted task was sure to end in some blissful dreamy reverie, with which Cupid had much more to do than Minerva.

CHAPTER VIII.

"A proposition, Hetty!" said my husband, throwing aside his coat and hat, and tossing a letter in my lap. "It is from a widow lady, who desires that I should take charge of her little boy, and give him a home in my family, while she goes to the continent, to secure some property lately left her by a foreign relative. It will be advantageous to us, in a pecuniary way, to have him board with us, unless it should increase your cares too much. But, as you are so fond of children, it may, perhaps, after all, prove a pleasant care to you. She is evi dently a superior woman. Every line in her letter shows it."

My husband immediately answered in the affirmative. and the child arrived a week after. He was a fine, intelligent, gentlemanly boy of eight years, with large hazel eyes, and transparently beautiful temples: disinclined to the usual sports of childhood, sensitive, shy, and thoughtful beyond his years — a human dew-drop, which we look to see exhale. He brought with him a letter from his mother, which powerfully affected my husband. During its perusal he drew his hand repeatedly across his eyes, and sat a long while after he had finished reading it, with his eyes closed, in a deep reverie. By-and-by he said, handing me the letter, "there is genius there, Hetty. I never read anything so touchingly beautiful. Mrs. West must be a very talented and superior woman."

I glanced over the letter. It fully justified my husband's encomiums. It was a most touching appeal to him to watch with paternal care over her only child; but while she spoke with a mother's tenderness of his endearing qualities, she wished him taught implicitly, that first of all duties for the young, *obedience*. Then followed allusions to dark days of sorrow, during which the love of that cherished child, was the only star in her sky.

I folded the letter and sat very still, after my husband left, in my little rocking-chair, thinking. Such a gifted woman as that my husband should have married. One who could have sympathised with him and shared his intellectual pursuits; who would have been something besides a toy to amuse an idle hour, or to minister to his physical necessities. Perhaps it was of this that my husband was thinking, as he sat there with his eyes closed over the open letter. Perhaps he had wed me only from a generous impulse of pity, and that letter had suddenly revealed to him the happiness of which he was capable with a kindred spirit. I was very miserable. I wished the letter had never reached us, or that I had declined the care of the child. Other letters, of course, would come, and the boy would keep alive the interest in the intervals. I wept long and bitterly. At length I was aroused by the entrance of little Charley. A bright flush mounted to his forehead, when he saw my swollen eyes. He hesitated a moment, then gliding up to my side he said, sweetly, "Are you sick? Shall I bathe your head? I used to bathe mamma's head when it pained her."

I stood abashed and rebuked in the child's angel presence, and taking the boy, *her* boy, in my arms, I kissed him as tenderly as if I had been his mother; while in his own sweet way he told me with childish confidence of his own dead papa; how much he loved mamma; how many, many beautiful things he used to bring her, saying that they were not half good, or half handsome enough for her; how distressed he used to be if she were ill; how carefully he closed the shutters, and tip-toed about the house, with his finger on his lip, telling the servants to close the doors gently; and how he promised him little toys, if he would not disturb mamma's slumbers; and then, how like diamonds his eyes shone, when she got well; and what beautiful flowers he brought her for her vases; and what a nice, soft-cushioned carriage he brought for her to take the air; and how tenderly he wrapped the shawls about her, and how many charges he gave the coachman, to drive slowly and carefully. And then, how dear papa, at last, grew sick himself; and how mamma watched day and night beside his bed, forgetting to sleep, or eat, or drink; and how nobody dared to tell her that the doctor said he must die; and how papa grew fainter and weaker, and how he said, "Kiss me, Mary, and lay your cheek to mine; I can 't see you." And then, how mamma fainted and was carried out, and for many, many long days did n't know even her own little Charley; — and how dreadful it was when she first waked, and tried to remember what had happened; and how nobody could comfort her but Charley; and how he used often to wake up in the night, and find her with a lamp looking at him, because when he was asleep he looked so much like dear, dead papa; and how bitterly she would sob when she was sick, because papa was not there to pity her, and bathe her aching head; and how he (Charley) meant, when he grew up to be a man, to get a nice house for her, and put everything she wanted in it, and make her just as happy as he could.

Well has the Saviour said, "Of such is the kingdom of Heaven." That night I bent over little Charley's bed, blessing the little sleeper for his angel teachings, with a heart as calm and peaceful as the mirrored lake, reflecting only the smile of Heaven.

Time passed on. Life became earnest; for a little heart pulsated beneath my own, and a strange, sweet, nameless thrill sent to my chastened lips a trembling prayer. Tiny caps and robes, with many a hope and fear interwoven in their delicate threads, lay awaiting the infant's advent. I, myself should know the height, and breadth, and depth of a mother's undying love. What could come between me and *this* new found treasure?

Meantime letters continued to come from Charley's mother to her boy, and my husband. It was impossible for me to blind myself to his growing interest in them. On the days they were expected, (for she wrote at regular intervals,) he would be absent and abstracted, or if any delay occurred, almost irritable. When they were received, his eye kindled, his step became elastic, and his whole face grew radiant with happiness.

As the time drew near for the birth of my infant, I grew timid with sad forebodings. I was sitting, one evening at twilight, watching the setting sun, and thinking of the quiet grave it was gilding, where my silver-haired father slept, in the old church yard, when my husband entered. An expression of pain flitted over his features, as he looked at me, and taking my hand, he said, gently, *almost tenderly*, "You are less well than usual, Hetty; you must not sit here, moping, by yourself."

I laid my head upon his shoulder with a happiness I had not known for many months. "Listen to me, dear Grey," said I; "I have a confidence to repose in you that will ease my heart.

"It was pity, only, that drew your heart to mine; you do not love me. I have known it a long while since. At first, the discovery gave me a pang keener than death; but I have had a long and bitter struggle with myself, and have conquered. It is not your fault that you cannot love me. To the many voices of your heart, which cry, 'Give, give,' my response is weak and unsatisfying. Your wife should be gifted. She should sympathise with you in your intellectual pursuits. She should stimulate your pride, as well as your love. Such an one is Charley's mother. Your *heart* has already wed her, and as God is my witness, I have ceased to blame you. We cannot help our affections. I cannot help loving you, though I know her mysterious power over your heart. I have seen your struggles, your generous self-reproaches, in some sudden outburst of kindness toward me, after the indulgence of some bright dream, in which I had no share. Dear Grey, she is worthy of your love. She has a heart, noble, good and true; a heart purified by suffering. I see it in every line she writes. Should I not survive the birth of my infant, I could give your happiness into her keeping without a misgiving, though I have never looked upon her face."

Little Hetty's noble heart has long since ceased to throb with joy or pain. To her husband's breast is folded the babe, for whose little life her own was yielded up. Threads of silver prematurely mingle amid his ebon locks; for memory writes only on bereaved hearts the virtues of the dead, while, with torturing minuteness, she pictures our own short-comings, for which, alas! we can offer no atonement but our tears.

AUNT HEPSY.

It was a comical little old shop, "Aunt Hepsy's," with its Lilliputian counter, shelves and stove, and its pigmy assortment of old-fashioned ginghams, twilled cambrics, red flannels, factory cotton and homespun calicoes; its miniature window, with its stock of horn-combs and candy, tin horses and peppermint drops, skeins of yarn and Godfrey's Cordial, gaudy picture books, and six-penny handkerchiefs, from whose center Lafayette and George Washington smiled approbatively upon the big A's and little A's printed round the border.

"Aunt Hepsy;" so every brimless-hatted urchin in the neighborhood called her, though it would have puzzled them worse than the multiplication table, had you asked them why they did so. Year in and year out, her ruddy English face glowed behind the little shop window. Sometimes she would be knitting a pair of baby's socks, sometimes inventing most astonishing looking bags out of rainbow fragments of silk or ribbon. Sometimes netting watch-guards, or raveling the yarn from some old black stocking, to ornament the "place where the wool ought to grow," on the head of some Topsy doll she was making. Sometimes comforting herself with a sly pinch of snuff, or, when sunbeams and customers were scarce, nodding drowsily over the daily papers.

Aunt Hepsy *had* been a beauty, and her pretty face had won her a thriftless husband, of whom champagne and cigars had long since kindly relieved her. And though Time had since forced her to apply to the perruquier, he had gallantly made atonement by leaving her in the undisputed possession of a pair of very brilliant black eyes. Add to this a certain air of coquetry, in the fanciful twist of her gay-colored turban, and the disposal of the folds of her lace kerchief over her ample English bust — and you have a faithful daguerreotype of "Aunt Hepsy."

From the window of her little shop she could look out upon the blue waters of the bay, where lay moored the gallant ships, from whose tall masts floated the stars and stripes, and whose jolly captains might often be seen in Aunt Hepsy's shop, exchanging compliments and snuff, and their heavy voices heard, recounting long Neptune yarns, and declaring to the buxom widow that nothing but the little accident of their being already spliced for life, prevented their immediately spreading sail with her for the port of Matrimony. Aunt Hepsy usually frowned at this, and shook her turbaned head menacingly, but immediately neutralized it, by offering to mend a rip in their gloves, or replace a truant button on their overcoats.

It was very odd, how universally popular was Aunt Hepsy. She had any number of places to "take tea," beside a standing invitation from half-a-dozen families, to Christmas and Thanksgiving dinners, and to New-Year's suppers. She had an eligible seat in church, gratis; an inexhaustible bottle of sherry for her often infirmities; fresh pies on family baking days, newspapers for stormy day reading; tickets to menageries, and invitations to picnics.

She always procured lodgings at a cheaper rate than anybody else; had the pleasantest room in the house at that, the warmest seat at table, the strongest cup of coffee, the brownest slice of toast, the latest arrival of buckwheats, the second joint of the turkey, and the only surviving piece of pie. To be sure, she always praised ugly babies, asked old maids why they *would* be so cruel as to persist in remaining unmarried, entreated hen-pecked husbands to use their powerful influence over their wives to secure to her their custom; begged the newly fledged clergyman to allow her a private perusal of his last Sunday's able discourse; complimented ambitious Esaus on the luxuriant growth of their very incipient, and microscopically perceptible whiskers; asked dilapidated, rejected widowers, when they intended taking their choice of a wife out of a bevy of rosy girls, and declared to Editors that she might as well try to get along without her looking glass, as without their interesting newspapers.

One day, the little shop was shut up. Nine o'clock came—eleven o'clock, and the shutters were still closed, and Aunt Hepsy so punctual, too! What *could* it mean? Old Mrs. Brown was ready to have fits because she could n't get another skein of yarn to finish her old man's stockings. Little Pat Dolan had roared himself black in the face, because he could n't spend his cent to buy some maple sugar; and the little match girl stood shivering at the corner for a place to warm her poor benumbed fingers, while the disappointed captains stamped their feet on the snow, stuffed their cheeks with quids, and said it was "deuced funny," and an old maid, opposite, who had long prayed that Aunt Hepsy's reign might be shortened, laid her skinny forefinger on her hooked nose, and rolled up the whites of her eyes like a chicken with the pip.

It was no great enigma, (at any rate not after you found it out!) Rich old Mr. Potts ventured into Aunt Hepsy's shop, one day, to buy a watch-ribbon. He was very deaf; so Aunt Hepsy had to come round the counter to wait upon him, and the upshot of it was, that she and Cupid together, hailed him through an ear-trumpet; and all I know about it is, that they have now a legalized right to a mutual pillow and snuff-box, and that the little shop window still remains unopened, while the old maid hisses between her teeth, as Aunt Hepsy rolls by in her carriage, "How do you suppose she did it?"

THOUGHTS AT CHURCH.

I HAVE an old-fashioned way of entering church, before the bells begin to chime. I enjoy the quiet, brooding stillness. I love to think of the many words of holy cheer that have fallen there, from heaven-missioned lips, and folded themselves like snow-white wings over the weary heart of despair. I love to think of the sinless little ones, whose pearly temples have here been laved at the baptismal font. I love to think of the weak, yet strong ones, who have tearfully tasted the consecrated cup, on which is written, "Do this in remembrance of me." I love to think of those self-forgetting, self-exiled, who, counting all things naught for Gethsemane's dear sake, are treading foreign shores, to say to the soul-fettered Pagan, "Behold the Lamb of God." I love to think of the loving hearts that at yonder altar have throbbed, side by side, while the holy man of God pronounced "the twain one." I love to think of the seraph smile of which death itself was powerless to rob the dead saint, over whose upturned face, to which the sunlight lent such mocking glow, the words, "Dust to dust," fell upon the pained ear of love. I love, as I sit here, to list through the half open vestry door, to the hymning voices of happy Sabbath scholars, sweet as the timid chirp of morn's first peeping bird. I love to hear their tiny feet, as they patter down the aisle, and mark the earnest gaze of questioning childhood. I love to see the toil-hardened hand of labor brush off the penitential tear. I love — "*our* minister." How very sad he looks to-day. Are his parish unsympathetic? Does the laborer's "hire" come tardily and grudgingly to the overtasked, faithful servant? Do censorious, dissatisfied spirits watch and wait for his halting?

Now he rises and says, slowly — musically, "The Lord is my shepherd, I shall not want." Why at such sweet, soul-resting words, do his tears overflow? Why has his voice such a heart quiver? Ah! there is a vacant seat in the pastor's pew. A little golden head, that last Sabbath gladdened our eyes like a gleam of sunlight, lies dreamlessly pillowed beneath the coffin lid: gleeful eyes have lost their brightness: cherry lips are wan and mute, and beneath her sable vail the lonely mother sobs. And so the father's lip quivers, and for a moment nature triumphs. Then athwart the gloomy cloud flashes the bow of promise. He wipes away the blinding tears, and with an angel smile, and upward glance, he says, "*Though he slay me, yet will I trust in Him.*"

THE BROTHERS.

Close the door. One would scarcely think, in this luxurious atmosphere, that we had left mid-winter behind us. The warm air is heavy with the odor of blossoming greenhouse plants, over whose fragrant clusters a tiny fountain tosses its sparkling spray: bright-winged, sweet-voiced canaries dart, like flashes of sunlight, through the dark green foliage: beautiful are those sculptured infants, cheek to cheek, over whose dimpled limbs the crimson drapery throws such a rosy glow: beautiful is that shrinking Venus, with her pure, chaste brow, and Eve-like grace: lovely those rare old pictures, to the artistic eye: beautiful that recumbent statuette of the peerless, proud "Pauline."

Hush! tread softly; on yonder couch a gentleman lies sleeping. His crimson velvet cap has fallen back from his broad white forehead; his long curving lashes droop heavily upon his cheek, and his Grecian profile is as faultless as a sculptor's dream. Pity, that the stain of sensuality should have left so legible an impress there.

A servant enters, bearing a note upon a silver tray. His master languidly opens a pair of large dark eyes, and beckons him to approach. As he breaks the seal, a contemptuous sneer disfigures his handsome lip, and an angry flush mounts to his brow. Motioning the servant away, he crushes the note between his fingers, muttering,—"No—no—as he has made his bed, so let him lie in it." Then walking once or twice rapidly across the room, he takes up a small volume, and throws himself again upon the velvet couch. He does not turn the leaves, and if you peep over his shoulder, you will see that the book is upside down. His thoughts are far away. He remembers a bright-eyed, open-browed, guileless-hearted brother, whom early orphanage had thrown upon his fraternal care; whose trusting nature he had perverted; whose listening ear he had poisoned with specious sophistries and worldly maxims; whom he had introduced to the wine party, where female virtue was held in derision, and to the "green room," where the foreign *danseuse* understood well how to play her part; whom he had initiated into modern follies and dissipations, and then launched upon the Charybdis of fashionable society, without chart, or rudder, or compass, other than his own headstrong passions and unbridled will.

Soon came a rumor, at first vague and undefined, and then voraciously seized upon and circulated by Paul Pry penny-a-liners, (who recked little, in their avidity for a paragraph, of broken-hearted mothers or despairing gray-haired fathers,) of a true heart that had been betrayed, of a disgraced household, of a fair brow that must henceforth walk the earth shame-branded. Then from his avenging pursuers the rash boy fled for refuge to him who had first turned his youthful footsteps aside from truth and honor. He was repulsed with scorn · not because he had wronged his own soul and hers whose star had forever set in night, but because he had not more skilfully and secretly woven the meshes for his victim.

Across the seas, amid the reckless debauchery of God-for getting Paris, the miserable boy sought oblivion; welcoming with desperate eagerness the syren Pleasure, in every chameleon shape that could stifle conscience or drown torturing memory. Sometimes by a lucky throw of the dice he was enabled to shine as the Adonis of some ball, or theatre, or gay saloon: sometimes destitute as the humblest *chiffonier*, who suns himself in the public square, and solicits charity of the indifferent passer-by. In the rosy glow of morning, the bright stars paled while Harry sat at the enticing gaming table, till even those accustomed to breathe the polluted atmosphere of those gates of perdition, turned shuddering away, from the fiendish look of that youthful face.

Nature revenged herself at last. Wearisome days of sickness came, and he who was nurtured in luxury, was dependent upon the charity of grudging strangers.

Oh! what a broad, clear beam eternity throws upon the crooked by-paths of sin! how like swift visions pass the long forgotten prayer at the blessed mother's knee; the long-forgot ten words of Holy Writ; the soothing vesper hymn, of holy time; the first cautious, retrograding step—the gradual searing of conscience, till the barrier between right and wrong is ruthlessly trampled under foot; the broken resolutions, the mis-spent years, the wasted energies; the sins against one's own soul, the sins against others; the powerless wish to pray, 'mid paroxysms of bodily pain; the clinging hold on life — the anxious glance at the physician — the thrilling question, "Doctor, is it life or death?"

Poor Harry! amid the incoherent ravings of delirium, the good little grisette learned his sad history. Her little French heart was touched with pity. Through her representations, on his partial restoration to health, a sufficient sum was subscribed by the American consul, and some of his generous countrymen, to give him the last chance for his life, by sending him to breathe again his native air. Earnestly he prayed that the sea might not be his sepulchre.

Tearfully he welcomed the first sight of his native shore. Tremblingly he penned those few lines to the brother whose face he so yearned to see — and on whose fraternal breast it would seem almost easy to die. Anxiously he waited the result, turning restlessly from side to side, till beaded drops of agony started from his pallid temples. Walter would not refuse his *last* request. No — no. The proud man would at least, at the grave's threshold, forget that "vulgar rumor" had coupled his patrician name with disgrace. Oh, why had the messenger such leaden footsteps? when life and strength like hour-glass sands, were fleeting! A step is heard upon the stairs! A faint flush, like the rosy tinting of a sea-shell, brightens the pallid face.

"No answer, sir," gruffly says the messenger.

A smothered groan of anguish, and Harry turns his face to the wall, and tears, such only as despair can shed, bedew his pillow.

"*Do* go, dear Walter; 'tis your own brother who asks it. If he has sinned, has he not also suffered? We all so err, so need forgiveness. Oh, take back those hasty words; let him die on your breast, for *my* sake, Walter," said the sweet pleader, as her tears fell over the hand she pressed.

"That 's my own husband," said the happy Mary, as she saw him relent. "Go *now*, dear Walter. Take away the sting of those cruel words, while yet you may, and carry him these sweet flowers, he used to love, from me. Quick, dear Walter."

"This way, sir, this way. Up another flight," said the guide, gazing admiringly at the fine figure before him, enveloped in a velvet Spanish cloak. "Second door to the left, sir. May-be the gentleman's asleep now; he 's been very quiet for some time. Seen trouble, sir, I reckon. 'Tis not age that has drawn those lines on his handsome face. He 's not long for this world, God rest his soul. That 's right, sir; that 's the door. Good day, sir."

Walter stood with his finger on the latch. He had at all times a nervous shrinking from sickness — a fastidious horror of what he termed "disagreeables." He half repented that he had suffered a woman's tears to unsettle his purpose. Perhaps Harry would reproach him. (His own conscience was prompter to that thought.) There he stood, irresolutely twirling Mary's lovely flowers in his nervous grasp.

If Harry should reproach him!

Slowly he opened the door. The flowers fell from his hand!

Was that attenuated, stiffened form his own, warm-hearted, bright-eyed, gallant young brother?

"Reproach?"

Oh, Walter, there is no "reproach" like that passionless upturned face; no words so crushing as the silence of those breathless lips; no misery like the thought that those we have injured are forever blind to our gushing tears, and deaf to our sobs of repentance.

CURIOUS THINGS.

CURIOUS: The exaggerated anxiety of wives to see the women who were formerly loved by their husbands.—*Exchange.*

WELL, yes — rather curious; there are a great many curious things in this world. Curious, your husband always perceives that you are "sitting in a draft," whenever one of your old lovers approaches you in a concert room; curious he insists upon knowing who gave you that pretty gold ring on your little finger; curious that you can never open a package of old letters, without having his married eyes peeping over your shoulder; curious he never allows you to ride on horseback, though everybody says you have just the figure for it; curious he always sends his partner on all the little business trips of the firm; curious such an ugly frown comes over his face when he sees certain cabalistic marks in a masculine hand, in the margin of your favorite poet; curious that he will not let you name your youngest boy Harry, unless you tell him your confidential reasons; curious he is always most gracious to the most uninteresting men who visit the house; and *very* curious, and decidedly disagreeable, that whenever you ask him for money, he is so busy reading the newspaper that he can't hear you.

THE ADVANTAGES OF A HOUSE IN A FASHIONABLE SQUARE.

"WHOM did you say wished to see me, Bridget?"

The broad-faced Irish girl handed her mistress a card.

"'Mrs. John Hunter!' was there *ever* anything so unfortunate? had she called on any other day in the week, I should have been prepared to receive her, but of a 'washing day,' when nothing but a calico wrapper stands Master George's clawings and climbings; when the nursery maid is in the kitchen, and the baby on my hands for the day; when my 'Honiton collar' is in soak, the parlor window curtains in the wash-tub, and the dimensions of the whole family, big and little, are flapping on the clothes-line, displaying their rents and patches in full view of the parlor windows! Was there ever anything so unfortunate? What *could* induce Mrs. John Hunter to call on a washing day?"

But what was "washing day" to Mrs. John Hunter, who lived in St. John's Square, kept four servants, and patronized a laundry? What did she know of Mondays' picked up dinners and littered parlors, cluttered china closet, and untidied nurseries? Mrs. John Hunter, who came down to breakfast every morning in a fawn-colored silk morning dress, trimmed with cherry, over an elaborately embroidered white skirt; in a cobweb lace cap, silk stockings, and the daintiest of Parisian toilette slippers; how could *she* see the necessity of going down cellar, after breakfast, to see if the pork was under brine, the pickle jar covered, and the preserves unfermented? What did *she* know about washing up breakfast-cups, polishing the silver sugar bowl, filling the astral lamp, counting up the silver forks and spoons, or mending that little threadbare place in the carpet, that would soon widen into an ugly rent, if neglected? What did she know about washing children's faces for school, or finding their missing mittens, or seeing that Webster's spelling book and a big apple were safely stowed away in their satchels? How did she (whose family broadcloth the tailor mended) know that Monday was always the day when husbands threw their coats into wives' lap "for just one stitch," (which translated, means new sleeve-linings, new facings for the flaps, a new set of buttons down the front, and a general resuscitation of dilapidated button-holes.) How did she know that the baby always got up a fit of colic on washing days, and made it a point to dispense with its usual forenoon nap?—that all the collectors for benevolent societies, and bores in general, preferred it to any other day in the calendar?—that school teachers always selected it to ferule children for sneezing without permission—that milkmen never could spare you, on that day, your usual share of milk by two quarts—that the coal, potatoes, starch, soap, molasses, and vinegar always gave out on Monday—that "the minister" always selected it for his annual call, and country cousins for a "protracted meeting?" How should the patrician, Mrs. John Hunter, know all that?

There she sat in the parlor taking notes, after the usual fashion of lady callers, while Mrs. John Smith hurriedly tied on her bonnet, to hide her disheveled tresses, threw on a shawl, and made her appearance in the parlor as if "just returned from a walk."

How their tongues ran! how fashions and gossip were discussed; how Mrs. Smith admired Mrs. Hunter's new dress hat; how the latter lady advised Mrs. Smith to "insist on her husband's moving from such an undesirable neighborhood into a more aristocratic locality;" and how Mrs. Smith wondered that the idea had never struck her before; and how Mrs. Hunter told her that of course Mr. Smith would refuse at first, but that she must either worry him into it, or seize upon some moment of conjugal weakness to extort a binding promise from him to that effect; and how the little wife blushed to find herself conniving at this feminine piece of diabolism.

Mrs. John Smith's husband commenced life in a provision store. He was well acquainted with cleavers, white aprons, and spare-ribs — was on hand early and late to attend to business — trusted nobody — lived within his income, and consequently made money.

Miss Mary Wood kept a dressmaker's establishment just over the way. Very industriously she sat through the long summer days, drooping her pretty golden ringlets over that never-ending succession of dresses. Patiently she "took in," and "let out," bias-ed, flounced, tucked, gathered and plaited, at the weathercock option of her customers. Uneasily she leaned her head against her little window at sundown, and earnestly Mr. John Smith wished he could reprieve forever from such drudgery those taper little fingers. Very tempting was the little basket of early strawberries, covered with fresh green leaves, that went across the way to her one bright summer morning — and as red as the strawberries, and quite as tempting, looked Miss Mary's cheek to Mr. John Smith, as she sat at the window, reading the little billet-doux which he slily tucked into one corner.

The milkman wondered why Mr. Smith had grown so particular about the flowers in the bouquets his little grand-daughter plucked for sale, and why there must *always* be "a rose-bud in it." Miss Rosa Violet could n't imagine what ailed her dressmaker, Miss Wood, (who was always so scrupulous in executing orders,) to make her boddice round, when she told her so particularly to make it pointed. The little sewing girls employed in Miss Wood's shop were "afraid she was getting crazy," she smiled so often to herself, broke so many needles, and made so many mistakes in settling up their accounts on pay day; and very great was their astonishment one day, after finishing a pretty bridal dress, to find that Miss Wood was to wear it herself to church the very next Sunday!

One bright June morning found the little dressmaker in a nice, two story brick house, furnished with every comfort, and some luxuries; for the warm-hearted John thought nothing half good enough for his little golden-haired bride. As time passed on, other little luxuries were added; including two nice, fat, dim pled babies; and within the last year John had bought the house they lived in, and at Mary's suggestion introduced gas, to lighten the labors of the servant, and also added a little bathing-room to the nursery. His table was well provided —the mother's and children's wardrobes ample, and not a husband in Yankee land was prouder or happier than John Smith, when on a sunshiny Sunday, he walked to church with his pretty wife, whose golden curls still gleamed from beneath her little blue bonnet, followed by Katy and Georgy with their shining rosy faces, and pretty Sunday dresses.

It was quite time the honeymoon should wane, but still it showed no signs of decrease. Little bouquets still perfumed Mary's room. John still sprung to pick up her handkerchief, or aid her in putting on her cloak or shawl. The anniversary of their wedding day always brought her a kind little note, with some simple remembrancer. Trifles, do you call these? Ah, a wife's happiness is made or marred by just such "trifles."

"Katy will make somebody's heart ache one of these days, said John Smith to his wife. Katy will be a beauty. Did you hear me, Mary?"

"Yes," said Mary, drooping her bright ringlets till they swept John's cheek, "and I was thinking how I hoped she would marry well, and whether it would not be better for us to move into a more genteel neighborhood, and form a new set of acquaintances."

"*My* little wife getting ambitious!" said John, smoothing her ringlets back from her white forehead; "and where would you like to live, Mary?"

"St. John's Square is a nice place," said the little wife, timidly.

"Yes; but my dear Mary, rents there are enormous, and those large houses require a greater outlay of money than you have any idea of. The furniture which looks pretty and in good taste here, would be quite shabby in such an elegant establishment. The pretty de laine, which fits your little round figure so charmingly, must give place to a silk or brocade. Katy and Georgy must doff their simple dresses, for velvet and embroidery; broad-faced, red-fisted Bridget must make way for a French cook. The money which I have placed in the bank for a nest-egg for you and the children in case of my death, must be withdrawn to meet present demands. But we will talk of this another time: good-by Mary, dear; not even your dear face must tempt me away from business; good-by," and he kissed his hand to her, as he walked rapidly out the door.

But somehow or other Mary's words kept ringing in John's ears. It was very true Katy must be married some day, and then he ran over the circle of their acquaintance; the Stubbses, and the Joneses, and the Jenkinses—good enough in their way, but (he confessed to himself) *not just the thing for his Katy.* John was ambitious too: Mary was right; they ought to con sider that Katy would soon be a woman.

It is not to be supposed because John Smith never sported white kids, save on his wedding day, that he was not a man of taste; by no means. Not an artistic touch of Mary's feminine fingers, from the twist of a ringlet or ribbon to the draping of a curtain, the judicious disposal of a fine engraving, or the harmonious blending of colors in a mantel bouquet, escaped him. It was his joy and pride to see her glide about his home, beautifying almost unconsciously everything she touched; and then, he remembered when she was ill, and Bridget had the oversight of the parlors—what a different air they had; how awkwardly the chairs looked plastered straight against the wall—how ugly the red cloth all awry on the centre table; what a string-y look the curtains had, after her clumsy fingers had passed over them. Yes, Mary would grace a house in St. John's Square, and if it would make her any happier to go there (and here he glanced at his ledger)—why, go she should—for she was just the prettiest, and dearest, and most loving little Mary who ever answered to that poetical name. What would full coffers avail him, if Mary should die?—and she might die first. His health was good—his business was good. Mary and Katy *should* live in St. John's Square.

Mary and Katy *did* live in St. John's Square. The upholsterer crammed as many hundreds as possible into the drawing rooms, in the shape of vis-a-vis antique chairs, velvet sofas, damask curtains, mirrors, tapestry, carpets, and a thousand other nick-nacks, too numerous to mention: then the blinds and curtains shut out the glad sunlight, lest the warm beams should fade out the rich tints of the carpets and curtains, and left it as fine and as gloomy as any other fashionable drawing room. There was a very pretty prospect from Mary's chamber windows, but she never allowed herself to enjoy it, after Mrs. John Hunter told her, that it was considered "decidedly snobbish to be seen at the front window." The Smiths took their meals in a gloomy basement, where gas was indispensable at mid-day. Mary was constantly in fear that the servants would spoil the pictures and statues in the parlor, so she concluded to sweep and dust it herself, before there was any probability of Mrs. John Hunter's being awake in the morning. As this was something of a tax, she and Mr. Smith and the children kept out of it, except on Sundays and when company called, burrowing under ground the residue of the time in the afore-mentioned basement.

Directly opposite Mrs. Smith lived Mrs. Vivian Grey, the leader of the aristocracy (so Mrs. Hunter informed her) in St. John's Square. It was a great thing to be noticed by Mrs. Vivian Grey. Mrs. Hunter sincerely hoped she would patronise Mrs. Smith. Mrs. Hunter, after a minute survey, pronounced Mrs. Smith's establishment quite *comme il faut*, but suggested that a *real* cachemire should be added as soon as possible to Mrs. Smith's wardrobe, as Mrs. Grey considered that article quite indispensable to a woman of fashion. She also suggested that Mrs. Smith should delicately hint to her husband the propriety of his engaging a man servant, which appendage was necessary to give a certain *distingué* finish to the establishment; an Irishman would do, if well trained, but a *black* man was more fashionable, provided he was not *green*— and Mrs. Hunter smiled at her own wit.

The cachemire was added — so was the black servant-man.

Katy no longer skipped and jumped, but minced in corsets and whalebone. She never *ate* unless at a private lunch with mamma. Mr. John Smith staid late at his counting-room, and looked anxious, and two ugly lines made their appearance on Mrs. Mary's fair forehead. The French cook gave away provisions enough to feed an entire family of French emigrants. The black man-servant pulled up his dicky and informed Mrs. Smith that it was at the price of his reputation to live with a family who dispensed with the use of finger bowls, and the house-maid (who had the honor of being descended from the establishment of Mrs. Vivian Grey) declined remaining with a family who did n't keep a private carriage.

Mrs. Vivian Grey was *not* baited by the real cachemire, and her son, little Julius Grey, a precocious youth of ten, told little George Smith that his mamma had forbidden him playing marbles with a boy whose father had kept a provision store.

A scurrilous penny paper published a burlesque of Mrs. Smith's first grand party, on the coming out of Miss Katy, in which, among other allusions to Mr. Smith's former occupation, the ball-room was said to be "elegantly festooned with sausages." This added "the last ounce to the camel's back;" even Mrs. Hunter's tried friendship was not proof against such a test.

A council of war was called. Mrs. Smith begged her husband, as her repentant arms encircled his dicky, to buy a place in the country. John very gladly consented to turn his plebeian back forever on the scene of their humiliation; and what with strawberries and cherries, peaches, pic-nics, early rising and light hearts, the Smith family have once more recovered their equanimity, and can afford to laugh when "St. John's Square" and Mrs. John Hunter are mentioned.

WINTER IS COMING.

WELCOME his rough grip! welcome, the fleet horse with flying feet, and arching throat, neck-laced with merry bells; welcome, bright eyes, and rosy cheeks, and furred robes, and the fun-provoking sleigh-ride; welcome, the swift skater who skims, bird-like, the silvery pond; welcome, Old Santa Claus with his horn of plenty; welcome, the "Happy New-Year," with her many-voiced echoes, and gay old Thanksgiving, with his groaning table, old friends and new babies; welcome, for the bright fireside, the closed curtains, the dear, unbroken home-circle, the light heart, the merry jest, the beaming smile, the soft "good-night," the downy bed, and rosy slumbers.

WINTER IS COMING.

ALAS for his rough grip! the barrel of meal is empty, and the cruse of oil fails. Sharp winds flutter thin rags 'round shivering limbs. There are pinched features, and benumbed feet, and streaming eyes, and repulsed hands, and despairing hearts; there are damp corners, and straw pallets, and hollow coughs, and hectic cheeks; there are dismantled roofs, through which the snow gently drops its white, icy pall over the wasted limbs of the dying; there are babes whose birthright is pov erty, whose legacy is shame, whose baptism is tears, *whose lit tle life is all winter.*

"THE OTHER SEX."

"Let cynics prattle as they may, our existence here, without the presence of the other sex, would be only a dark and cheerless void."

Which "other sex?" Don't be so obscure. Dr. Beecher says, "that a writer's ideas should stand out like rabbits' ears, so that the reader can get hold of them." If you allude to the female sex, I don't subscribe to it. I wish they were all "translated." If there is anything that gives me the sensations of a landsman on his first sea voyage, it is the sight of a bonnet. Think of female friendship! Two women joining the Mutual Admiration Society; emptying their budget of love affairs; comparing bait to entrap victims; sighing over the same rose leaf; sonnetizing the same moonbeam; patronizing the same milliner, and *exchanging female kisses!* (Betty, hand me my fan!)

Well, let either have one bonnet or one lover more than the other — or, if they are blue stockings, let either be one round the higher on Fame's ladder — bodkins and darning needles! what a tempest! Caps and characters in such a case are of no account at all. Oh, there never should be but one woman alive at a time. Then the fighting would be all where it belongs, — in the masculine camp. What a time there 'd be, though! Would n't she be a belle? Bless her little soul! how she would queen it. It makes me clap my hands to think of it. *The only woman in the world!* If it were I, should n't they all leave off smoking, and wearing those odious plaid continuations? Should they ever wear an outside coat, with the flaps cut off, or a Kossuth hat, or a yellow Marseilles vest? — or a mammoth bow on their neck-ties; or a turnover dickey; or a watch-chain; or a ring on the little finger? — or any other abomination or off-shoot of dandyism whatsoever? Should n't I politely request them all to touch their hats, instead of jerking their heads, when they bowed? Would n't I coax them to read me poetry till they had the bronchitis? Would n't they play on the flute, and sing the soul out of me? And then if they were sick, would n't I pet them, and tell them all sorts of comicalities, and make time fly like the mischief? Should n't wonder!

SOLILOQUY OF MR. BROADBRIM.

"There's another of Miss Fiddlestick's articles! She's getting too conceited, that young woman! Just like all newly-fledged writers — mistakes a few obscure newspaper puffs for the voice of the crowd, and considers herself on the top round of the literary ladder. It will take *me* to take the wind out of her sails. I'll dissect her, before I'm a day older, as sure as my name is Ezekiel Broadbrim. I don't approve her style; never did. It's astonishing to me that the editor of The Green Twig dare countenance it, when he knows a man of my influence could annihilate her with one stroke of my pen. She has talent of a certain inferior order, but nothing to speak of. She's an unsafe model to follow; will lead her tribe of imitators into tremendous mistakes. It's a religious duty for a conspicuous sentinel, like myself, on Zion's walls, to sound the blast of alarm;—can't answer it to my conscience to be silent any longer. It might be misconstrued. The welfare of the world in general, and her soul in particular, requires a very decided expression of my disapprobation. I'm sorry to annihilate her, but when Ezekiel Broadbrim makes up his mind what is the path of duty, a bright seraph could n't stop him. Perhaps I may pour a drop of the balm of consolation after wards, but it depends altogether upon whether I succeed in bringing her into a penitential frame of mind. It 's my private opinion she is an incorrigible sinner. Hand me my pen, John. Every stroke of it will tell."

WILLY GREY.

A STERN, unyielding, line-and-plummet, May-flower descend ant, was old Farmer Grey, of Allantown, Connecticut. Many a crop had he planted, many a harvest had he garnered in, since he first became owner of Glen Farm. During that time, that respected individual, "the oldest inhabitant," could not remem ber ever to have seen him smile. The village children shied close to the stone wall, and gave him a wide berth, when he passed. Even the cats and dogs laid their ears back, and crept circumspectly by him, with one eye on his whip-lash.

Farmer Grey considered it acceptable to the God who painted the rainbow, and expanded the lily, and tinted the rose, to walk the bright earth with his head bowed like a bulrush, and his soul clad in sackcloth. No mercy fell from the lips of *his* imaginary Saviour; no compassion breathed in His voice; no love beamed in His eye; His sword of justice was never sheathed.

The old farmer's wife was a gentle, dependent creature, a delicate vine, springing up in a sterile soil, reaching forth its tendrils vainly, for some object to cling to. God, in his mercy, twined them lovingly around a human blossom. Little Willy partook of his mother's sensitive, poetical nature. A yearning spirit looked out from the fathomless depths of his earnest eyes. Only eight short summers the gentle mother soothed her boy's childish pains, and watched his childish slumbers. While *he* grew in strength and beauty, *her* eye waxed dim, and her step grew slow and feeble.

And so sweet memories were only left to little Willy,—dear, loving eyes, whose glance ever met his on waking; a fair, caressing hand, that wiped away his April tears; a low, gentle voice, sweet to his childish ear as a seraph's hymning.

Willy's father told him that "his mother had gone to Heaven," John, the plough-boy, said "she was lying in the church-yard." Willy could not understand this. He only knew that the house had grown dark and empty, and that his heart ached when he stayed there; and so he wandered out in the little garden, (his mother's garden;) but the flowers looked dreary, too; and her pretty rose-vine lay trailing its broken buds and blighted blossoms in the dust.

Then Willy crept up to his father's side, and looked up in his face, but there was something there that made him afraid to lay his little hand upon his knee, or climb into his lap, or in any way unburden his little heart; so he turned away, more sorrowful than before, and wandered into his mother's chamber, and climbed up in her chair, and opened her drawer, to look at her comb and hair brush; and then he went to the closet, and passed his little hand, caressingly, over her empty dresses, and leaning his little curly head against them, sobbed himself to sleep.

By and by, as years passed on, and the child grew older, he

learned to wander out in the woods and fields, and unbosom his little yearning heart to Nature. Reposing on her breast, listening to the music of her thousand voices, his unquiet spirit was soothed as with a mother's lullaby. With kindling eye, he watched the vivid lightnings play; or, saw the murky east flush, like a timid bride, into rosy day; or, beheld the shining folds of western clouds fade softly into twilight; or, gazed at the Queen of Night, as she cut her shining path through the cloudy sky; or, questioned, with earnest eyes, the glittering stars.

All this but ill pleased the old farmer. He looked upon the earth only with an eye to tillage; upon the sloping hill, with its pine-crowned summit, only with an eye to timber; upon the changeful skies, only as reservoirs for moistening and warming his crops; upon the silver streams, that laced the emerald meadows, only as channels for irrigation; upon the climbing vine, as an insidious foe to joists, and beams, and timbers; and upon flowers, only as perfumed aristocrats, crowding and over-topping the free-soil democracy of cabbage, onions, and potatoes.

In vain poor Will tried to get up, "to order," an enthusiasm for self-acting hay-cutters, patent plows, rakes, hoes, and harrows. In vain, when Sunday came, and he was put "on the limits," did the old farmer, with a face ten-fold more ascetic than the cowled monk, strive to throw a pall of gloom over that free, glad spirit, by rehearsing, in his ear, a creed which would forever close the gate of heaven on every dissenter, or inculcate doctrines, which, if believed, would fill our lunatic asylums with the frantic wailings of despair.

Restlessly did Will, with cramped limbs and fettered spirit, sit out the tedious hours of that holy day, which should be the "most blessed of all the seven," and watch, with impatient eye, the last golden beam of the Sabbath sun sink slowly down behind the western hills.

Oh, well-meaning, but mistaken, parent! let but one loving smile play over those frigid lips: let but one tear of sympathy flood that stony eye: let but *one drop* from that overflowing fountain of love, that wells up in the bosom of the Infinite, moisten the parched soil of that youthful heart! Open those arms but once, and clasp him to the paternal heart; for even now, his chafed spirit, like a caged bird, flutters against its prison bars; even now, the boy's unquiet ear catches the far-off hum of the busy world: even now, his craving heart beats wildly for the voice of human love!

Weary feet, houseless nights, the scant meal, and the oft-repulsed request: what are *they* to the strong nerve, and bounding pulse, and hopeful heart of the young adventurer? Laurel wreaths, dizzy places on Ambition's heights, have not its aspirants reached them by just such rugged steps?

"Will" is in the city. Will sits upon the steps of the New York City Hall, reading a penny paper: he has begged it from a good-natured newsboy, who has also shared with him a huge slice of gingerbread. As Will's eye glances over the sheet, it falls upon the following paragraph:

"PROSPECTUS OF THE WEEKLY CHRONICLE.

"The Weekly Chronicle is a paper founded on the demands of the age for a first-class journal. It soars above all sectional and personal considerations, and fearlessly proffers its feeble aid, in developing the natural resources of the country, fostering the genius of the people, rewarding meritorious effort in every department of art, exalting virtue, however humble, and confounding vice, however powerful. The editor and proprietor of the Chronicle is Mr. Philanthropas Howard; office, No. 199 Cloud-street.

"Boy wanted immediately at the above office: one from the country would be preferred."

Will threw down the paper, and started to his feet: "199 Cloud-street?" He asked orange-women; he asked image-boys; he asked merchants; he asked clerks; he asked lawyers; he asked clients; he investigated cellars; he explored attics; he traveled through parks, and through alleys; till finally, he coaxed a graceless, bare-footed urchin to shew him the way.

Mr. John Howard, editor and proprietor of the Weekly Chronicle, went upon the principle of paying nothing where nothing would pay, and paying as little as possible where he could get something for next to nothing. It was a fixed principle and confirmed practice with him, never to pay anything for contributions to the Chronicle. He considered that the great advantage that would accrue to an author from having his or her articles in his paper, would be ample remuneration. At the moment Will's eye first fell upon him, he was reposing in a huge leathern arm chair, in the corner of his sanctum. His proportions very much resembled an apoplectic bag of flour, surmounted by an apple. His head was ornamented with sparse spires of fiery red hair; on his cheeks, a pair of cream-colored whiskers were feebly struggling into life; and sundry tufts of the same color, under his chin, shadowed forth his editorial sympathy with the recent "Beard Movement." Before him was a table, of doubtful hue and architecture, laden with manuscripts, accepted, rejected, and under consideration; letters of all sizes, opened and unopened, prepaid and unpaid, saucy and silly, defiant and deprecatory. There was also an inkstand, crusted with dirt and cobwebs; a broken paper weight, pinning down some bad money, paid by distant subscribers; a camphene lamp, with a broken pedestal, propped up by a Directory on one side, and Walker's Dictionary on the other; sundry stumps of cigars; a half-eaten apple; a rind of an orange; a lady's glove, and a box of bilious pills.

Will stepped before him, and made known his errand. Mr. John Howard looked at him, with a portentous scowl, inspected him very much as he would a keg of doubtful mackerel, and then referred him to the foreman of the office, Mr. Jack Punch. Jack had been victimized, in the way of office boys, for an indefinite period, with precocious city urchins, who smoked long nines, talked politics, discussed theatricals, and knew more of city haunts than the police themselves. Of course he lost no time in securing a boy to whose verdant feet the plow-soil was still clinging. Will's business was to open the office at half past six in the morning, sweep it out, make the fires, go to the post-office for letters and exchanges, wrap up papers for new subscribers, carry them to the post, and see that the mail was properly "got off." To all these requirements, Will immediately subscribed.

On Will's daily tramps to and from the office, he was obliged to pass Lithe & Co.'s magnificent show window, where the choicest pictures and engravings were constantly exposed for sale. There he might be seen loitering, entranced and spell-bound, quite oblivious of the Chronicle, hour after hour, weaving bright visions — building air castles, with which his over-seer, Mr. Jack Punch, had little sympathy. Yes; Will had at length found out what he was made for. He knew *now* why he had lain under the trees, of a bright summer day, watching the fleecy clouds go sailing by, in such a dreamy rapture; why the whispering leaves, and waving fields of grain, and drooping branches of graceful trees, and the mirror-like beauty of the placid lake, reflecting a mimic heaven; why the undulating hills, and mist-wreathed valleys, with their wealth of leaf, and buds and blossom, filled his eyes with tears and his soul with untold joy, and why, when slumber sealed each weary lid under the cottage eaves, he stood alone, hushing his very breath, awe-struck, beneath the holy stars.

Poor Will, his occupation became so distasteful! Poor Will, winged for a "bird of paradise," and forced to be a mole, burrowing under the earth, when he would fain try his new-found pinions! To Jack's intense disgust, he soon detected Will in drawing rude sketches on bits of paper, stray wrappers, and backs of letters; even the walls were "done in crayons," by the same mischievous fingers. His vision was so filled "with the curved line of beauty," that he was constantly committing the most egregious blunders. He misplaced the bundles of newspapers which he carried to the post-office; placing the "north" packages on the "south" table, the east on the north, the south on the east, &c.; mixing them up generally and indescribably and inextricably, so that the subscribers to the "Weekly Chronicle" did not receive their papers with that precision and regularity which is acknowledged to be desirable, particularly in small country places, where the blacksmith's shop, the engine house, and "the newspaper" form a trio not to be despised by the simple-hearted, primitive farmers.

Jack, whose private opinion it was that he should have been christened Job, being obliged to shoulder all the short-comings of his assistants, and being worked up to a pitch of frenzy by letters from incensed subscribers, which Mr. Howard constantly thrust in his face, very unceremoniously ejected Will from the premises, one morning, by a vigorous application of the toe of his boot.

The world was again a closed oyster to Will. How to open it? that was the question. Our hero thought the best place to consider the matter was at "Lithe & Co.'s shop-window. Just as he reached it, a gentleman passed out of the shop, followed by a lad bearing a small framed landscape. Perhaps the gentleman was an artist! Perhaps he could employ him in some way! Will resolved to follow him.

Up one street and down another, round corners and through squares—the gentleman's long legs seemed to be shod with the famed seven-leagued boots. At length he stopped before the door of an unpretending looking building, and handing the lad who accompanied him a bit of money, he took from him the picture, and was just springing up the steps, when he lost his balance, and the picture was jerked violently from his hand, but only to be caught by the watchful Will, who restored it to its owner uninjured.

"Thank you, my boy," said the gentleman, "you have done me a greater service than you think for;" at the same time offering him some money.

"No, I thank you," said Will, proudly. "I do not wish to be paid for it."

"As you please, Master Independence," replied the gentleman, laughing; "but is there no other way I can serve you?"

"Are you an artist?" asked Will.

"The gentleman raised his eyebrows, with a comical air, and replied, "Well, sometimes I think I am, and then, again, I don't know; but what if I were?"

"I should *so* like to be an artist," said Will, the quick flush mounting to his temples.

"You!" exclaimed the gentleman, taking a minute survey of Will's nondescript *toute ensemble*, "Do you ever draw?"

"Sometimes," replied Will, "when I can get a bit of charcoal, and a white wall. I was just kicked out of the Chronicle office for doing it."

"Follow me," said the gentleman, tapping him familiarly on the cheek.

Will needed no second invitation. Climbing one flight of stairs, he found himself in a small studio, lined on all sides by pictures; some finished and framed, others in various stages of progression. Pallets, brushes, and crayons, lay scattered round an easel; while in one corner was an artist's lay figure, which, in the dim light of the apartment, Will mistook for the artist's wife, whose presence he respectfully acknowledged by a profound bow, to the infinite amusement of his patron.

Mr. Lester was delighted with Will's naive criticisms on his pictures, and his profound reverence for art. A few days found him quite domesticated in his new quarters; and months passed by swift as a weaver's shuttle, and found him as happy as a crowned prince; whether grinding colors for the artist, or watching the progress of his pencil, or picking up stray crumbs of knowledge from the lips of connoisseurs, who daily frequented the studio; and many a rough sketch did Will make in his little corner, that would have made them open their critical eyes wide with wonder.

"What a foolish match!" Was an engagement ever announced that did not call forth this remark, from some dissenting lip? Perhaps it *was* a "foolish match." Meta had no dower but her beauty, and Will had no capital but his pallet and easel. The gossips said she "might have done much better." There was old Mr. Hill, whose head was snow white, but whose gold was as yellow and as plenty as Meta's bright ringlets; and Mr. Vesey, whose father made a clergyman of him, because he did n't know enough to be a merchant; and Lawyer Givens, with his carrotty head and turn-up nose, and chin that might have been beat; and Falstaff-ian Captain Reef, who brought home such pretty china shawls and grass cloth dresses, and who had as many wives as a Grand Turk. Meta might have had any one of these by hoisting her little finger. Foolish Meta! money and misery in one scale, poverty and love in the other. Miserable little Meta! And yet she does not look so *very* miserable, as she leans over her husband's shoulder, and sees the landscape brighten on the canvass, or presses her rosy lips to his forehead, or arranges the fold of a curtain for the desired light and shade, or grinds his colors with her own dainty little fingers; no, she looks anything but miserable with those soft eyes so full of light, and that elastic step, and voice of music, that are inspiration to her artist husband. No; she thinks the "old masters" were fools to her young master, and she already sees the day when his studio will be crowded with connoisseurs and patrons, and his pictures bring him both fame and fortune; and then, they will travel in foreign countries, and sleep under Italia's soft blue skies, and see the Swiss glaciers, and the rose-wreathed homes of England, and the grim old chateaux of France, and perhaps beard old Haynau in his den. Who knows? Yes; and Will should feast his eyes on beauty, and they 'd be as happy, as if care and sorrow had never dimmed a bright eye with tears, since the seraph stood, with a flaming sword, to guard the gate of Eden.

Hopeful, happy, trusting Meta! the bird's carol is not sweeter than yours;—and yet the archer takes his aim, and with broken wing it flutters to the ground.

Yes: Meta was an angel. Will said it a thousand times a day, and his eyes repeated it when his tongue was silent. Meta's brow, and cheek, and lips, and tresses were multiplied indefinitely, in all his female heads. Her dimpled hand, her round arm, her plump shoulder, her slender foot, all served him for faultless models.

Life was so beautiful to him now! his employment so congenial, his heart so satisfied. It *must be* that he should succeed. The very thought of failure— "but then, he *should not* fail!" Poor Will! he had yet to learn that garrets are as often the graves as the nurseries of genius, and that native talent goes unrecognized until stamped with *foreign* approbation. Happily — hopefully — heroically he toiled on; morning's earliest beam, and day's last lingering ray finding him busy at his easel. But, alas! as time passed, though patrons came not, creditors did; and one year after their marriage, Meta might have been seen stealthily conveying little parcels back and forth to a small shop in the neighborhood, where employment was furnished for needy fingers. It required all her feminine tact and diplomacy to conceal from Will her little secret, or to hide the tell-tale blush, when he noticed the disappearance of her wedding ring, which now lay glittering in a neighboring pawn-broker's window; yet never for an instant, since the little wife first slept on Will's heart, had she one misgiving that she had placed her happiness unalterably in his keeping.

Oh, inscrutable womanhood! Pitiful as the heart of God, when the dark cloud of misfortune, or shame, bows the strong frame of manhood; merciless—vindictive—implacable as the Prince of Darkness, towards thy tempted, forsaken and sorrowing sisters!

The quick eye of affection was not long in discovering Meta's secret; and now every glance of love, every caress, every endearing tone of Meta's, gave Will's heart a sorrow pang.

Meta! who had turned a deaf ear to richer lovers, to share *his* heart and home; Meta! whose beauty might grace a court, whose life should be all sunshine: that Meta's bright eyes should dim, her cheek pale, her step grow prematurely slow and faltering, for him!—the thought was torture.

"To-morrow, Will—you said to-morrow," said Meta, hiding her tears on her husband's shoulder; "the land of *gold* is also the land of *graves*," and she gazed mournfully into his face.

"Dear Meta," said her husband, "do not unman me with your tears; our parting will be brief, and I shall return to you with gold—gold! Meta; and you shall yet have a home worthy of you. Bear up, dear Meta—the sun will surely break through the cloud rift. God bless and keep my darling wife."

Poor little Meta! for hours she sat stupefied with sorrow, in the same spot where Will had left her. The sun shone cheerfully in at the little window of her new home, but its beams brought no warmth to Meta's heart. The clinging clasp of Will's arms was still about her neck: Will's kiss was still warm upon her lips, and yet — *she was alone.*

She thought, with a shudder, of the treacherous sea; of the pestilence that walketh in darkness; of a sick-bed, on a foreign shore; of the added bitterness of the death pang, when the eye looks vainly for the *one loved face*; and bowing her face in her hands, she wept convulsively.

"Dear heart! Goodness alive!" said Meta's landlady, peeping in at the door. "Do n't take on so; bless me, how long have you been married? you 're nothing better than a child *now.* Why did n't you go to Californy with your husband? Where 's your folks? — whose picter is that? Ah! I see now, it is meant for you. But why did n't you have on a gown, dear, instead of being wrapped up in them clouds? It makes you look like a sperit. Come now, don't sit moping here; come down stairs and see me work; it will amuse you like. I 'm going to make some brown bread. I dare say you never made a bit of brown bread in your life. I put a power of Ingin in mine. I learned that in the country. I was brought up in the country. I hate city folks; they 've no more heart than a sexton; much as ever they can stop frolicking long enough to bury one another. They 'll sleep, too, like so many tops, while the very next street is all of a blaze, and their poor destitute fellow-creatures are turned naked into the streets. They 'll plow right through a burying ground, if they take a notion, harrowing up dead folks, and *live* ones, too, *I* guess. And as to Sunday — what with Jews, and Frenchmen, and down Easters, and other foreigners, smoking and driving through the streets, 'tis n't any Sunday at all. Well, I never knew what Sodom meant till I came to the city. Why Lot's wife turned round to take a second look at it, is beyond me. Well, if you won't come down stairs I must leave you, for I smell my bread burning; but do cheer up — you look as lonesome as a pigeon on a spout of a rainy day."

A letter from the best beloved! How our eye lingers on the well-known characters. How we torture the words to extract hidden meanings. How tenderly we place it near the heart, and under the pillow. How lingeringly comes the daylight, when our waiting eyes would re-peruse what is already indelibly written on the heart!

Will's voyage had been prosperous — his health was good — his hope and courage unabated. Meta's eye sparkled, and her cheek flushed like a rose, as she pressed the letter again and again to her lips; but, after all, it was *only* a letter, and time dragged *so* heavily. Meta was weary of sewing, weary of reading, weary of watching endless pedestrians pass and repass beneath her window, and when *twilight* came, with its deepening shadows — that hour so sweet to the happy, so fraught with gloom to the wretched — and Meta's eye fell upon the little house opposite, and saw the little parlor lamp gleam like a beacon light for the absent husband, while the happy wife glided about with busy hands, and lightsome step, and when, at last, *he* came, and the broken circle was complete, poor Meta turned away to weep.

Joy, Meta, joy! dry your tears! Will has been successful. Will is coming home. Even now the Sea-Gull plows the waves, with its precious living freight. Lucky Will! he *has* "found gold," but it was dug from "the mine" of the artist's brain. Magical Will! the liquid eyes and graceful limbs of Senor Alvarez's only daughter are reproduced on canvas, in all their glowing beauty, by your magic touch! The Senor is rich — the Senor is liberal — the Senor's taste is as unimpeachable as his credit — the Senor has pronounced Will "a genius." Other Senors hear it; other Senors have gold in plenty, and dark-eyed, graceful daughters, whose charms Will perpetuates, and yet *fails to see*, for *a sweeter face which comes between.*

Dry your tears, little Meta — smooth the neglected ringlets — don *his* favorite robe, and listen with a flushed cheek, a beating heart and a love-lit eye, for the long absent but well remembered footstep.

Ah! Meta, there *are* meetings that o'erpay the pain of parting. But, dear Reader, you and I are *de trop.*

You should have seen how like a little brigand Will looked, with his bronzed face and fierce beard and mustache — so fierce that Meta was half afraid to jump into his arms; you should have seen Meta's new home to know what a pretty little nest love and taste may weave for a cherished bird; you should have seen with what a Midas touch Will's gold suddenly opened the eyes of people to his wonderful merit, as an artist; how "patrons" flocked in, now that he lived in a handsome house in Belgrave Square; how Mr. Jack Punch repented with crocodile tears, that he had ever kicked him out of "the Chronicle office," and how Will immortalized him on canvas, in the very act; not forgetting to give due prominence, in the foreground, to the figure of his philanthropic employer, Mr. John Howard, who, in the touching language of his Prospectus, always made it a point to "exalt virtue, however humble!"

TABITHA TOMPKINS' SOLILOQUY.

Have I, Tabitha Tompkins, a right to my share of fresh air uncontaminated? or have I not? I ask the question with my arms akimbo. I might as well say what I've got to say, pop-gun fashion, as to tiptoe round my subject, mincing and curtesying when I'm all ablaze with indignation.

I ask again: Have I a right to my share of fresh air uncontaminated? or have I not?

Do I go out for a walk? Every man I meet is a locomotive chimney. Smoke—smoke—smoke—smoke:—great, long tails of it following in their wake, while I dodge, and twist, and choke, trying to escape the coils of the stifling anaconda, till I'm black in the face. I, Tabitha Tompkins, whose grandfather was one of the "signers" of the Declaration of Independence! I feel seventy-six-y! I have borne it about as long as I can without damage to hooks and eyes.

If I try to escape it, by getting into an omnibus, there it is again! If it does not originate inside, some "gentleman" on the box or top, wafts it into the windows. If I take refuge in a ferry boat, I find "gentlemen requested not to smoke," (as usual) a dead letter,— no more regarded than is the law against gaming, or the Sunday liquor traffic. Do I go to a concert at

"Mr. Stubbs is earnestly requested to call and settle the above bill at his earliest convenience."

Castle Garden, and step out on the balcony between the performances for a breath of fresh air?—myriads of lighted Havannas send me dizzy and staggering back into the concert room. Does a gentleman call to see me of an evening?—the instant he shakes his "ambrosial curls," and gives "a nod," I have to run for my vinaigrette.

Do I advertise for lodgings; and after much inspection of rooms, and wear and tear of patience and gaiter boots, make a final selection? Do I emigrate with big trunk, and little trunk, and a whole nest of bandboxes? Do I get my rocking-chair, and work-table, and writing-desk, and pretty little lamp, all safely transported and longitudinized to my fancy? Do I, in a paradisaical state of mind, (attendant upon said successful emigration,) go to my closet, some fine morning, and take down a pet dress?—asafœtida and onions, what an odor! All the "pachouli" and "new mown hay" in New York would n't sweeten it. Six young men the other side of that closet, and all smokers!!! Betty, you may have that dress;—I would n't touch it with a pair of tongs.

Do I lend a masculine friend my copy of Alexander Smith's Poems?—can I ever touch it again till it has been through quarantine? Does he, by mistake, carry home my tippet in his pocket after a concert?—can I compute the hours it must hang dangling on the clothes line, before it can be allowed to resume its place round my neck?

Do I go to church on Sunday, with a devout desire to attend to the sermon?—my next neighbor is a young man, apparently seated on a nettle cushion: he groans and fidgets, and fidgets and groans; crosses his feet and uncrosses them; kicks over the cricket; knocks down his cane; drops the hymn-book, and finally draws from his coat pocket a little case; takes out one segar after another, transposes them, applies them to the end of his nose, and pats them affectionately; then he examines his watch; then frowns at the pulpit; then, glancing at the door, draws a sigh long enough and strong enough to inflate a pair of bellows, or burst off a vest button.

With a dolorous whine, this same young man deplores (in public) his inability to indulge in the luxury of a wife, "owing to the extravagant habits of the young ladies of the present day." I take this occasion to submit to public inspection a little bit of paper found in the vest pocket of this fumigated, cork-screwed, pantalooned humbug, by his washerwoman:

NEW YORK, October 1st, 1853.

MR. THADDEUS THEOPHILUS STUBBS,

TO JUAN FUMIGO, Dr.

To Sogars for Sept., 1853.	
Sept. 1—To 20 Trabucos, at 5c. - - - - - - -	$1 00
" To 12 Riohondas, at 6d. - - - - - -	75
" 3—To 12 Los Tres Castillos, at 6d. - - - - -	75
" To 12 La Nicotiana, at 6d. - - - - - -	75
" 4—(Sunday—for Segars for a party) 10 Palmettoes, 10 Esculapios, 12 La Sultanos, 12 El Crusados, 20 Norriegos, 16 L'Alhambros, at 4c.	3 20
" 6—To 50 L'Ambrosias, at 4c. - - - - - -	2 00
" 10—To 30 Cubanos, at 8c. - - - - - - -	2 40
" 12—To 50 Londres, at 4c. - - - - - - -	2 00
" 15—To 30 Jonny Linds, (for concert party,) at 8c. - -	2 40
" 24—To 50 Figaros, (for party to see Uncle Tom, at the National,) at 8c.	4 00
" 26—To 100 Mencegaros, (for party of country relations and friends,) at 2c. - - - - - - - - - -	2 00
" 30—To 40 Imperial Regalias, at 1s. - - - - -	5 00
	$26 25

Received Payment,

(Mr. Stubbs is earnestly requested to call and settle the above at his earliest con venience. J. F.)

Consistent Stubbs! But, then, his segar bill is not re ceipted!

SOLILOQUY OF A HOUSEMAID.

Oh, dear, dear!. Wonder if my mistress *ever* thinks I am made of flesh and blood? Five times, within half an hour, I have trotted up stairs, to hand her things, that were only four feet from her rocking-chair. Then, there's her son, Mr. George,—it does seem to me, that a great able-bodied man like him, need n't call a poor tired woman up four pair of stairs to ask "what's the time of day?" Heigho!—its "*Sally* do this," and "*Sally* do that," till I wish I never had been baptized at all; and I might as well go farther back, while I am about it, and wish I had never been born.

Now, instead of ordering me round so like a dray horse, if they would only look up smiling-like, now and then; or ask me how my "rheumatiz" did; or say good morning, Sally; or show some sort of interest in a fellow-cretur, I could pluck up a bit of heart to work for them. A kind word would ease the wheels of my treadmill amazingly, and would n't cost *them* anything, either.

Look at my clothes, all at sixes and sevens. I can't get a minute to sew on a string or button, except at night; and then I'm so sleepy it is as much as ever I can find the way to bed; and what a bed it is, to be sure! Why, even the pigs are now and then allowed clean straw to sleep on; and as to bed-clothes, the less said about them the better; my old cloak serves for a blanket, and the sheets are as thin as a charity school soup. Well, well; one wouldn't think it, to see all the fine glittering things down in the drawing-room. Master's span of horses, and Miss Clara's diamond ear-rings, and mistresses rich dresses. I *try* to think it is all right, but it is no use.

To-morrow is Sunday — "day of *rest*," I believe they *call* it. H-u-m-p-h! — more cooking to be done — more company — more confusion than on any other day in the week. If I own a soul I have not heard how to take care of it for many a long day. Wonder if my master and mistress calculate to pay me for *that*, if I lose it? It is a *question* in my mind. Land of Goshen! I aint sure I've got a mind — there's the bell again!

CRITICS.

"Bilious wretches, who abuse you because you write better than they."

SLANDER and detraction! Even I, Fanny, know better than that. *I* never knew an editor to nib his pen with a knife as sharp as his temper, and write a scathing criticism on a book, because the authoress had declined contributing to his paper. I never knew a man who had fitted himself to a promiscuous coat, cut out in merry mood by taper fingers, to seize his porcupine quill, under the agony of too tight a *self-inflicted* fit, to annihilate the offender. I never saw the bottled-up hatred of years, concentrated in a single venomous paragraph. I never heard of an unsuccessful masculine author, whose books were drugs in the literary market, speak with a sneer of successful literary feminity, and insinuate that it was by *accident*, not *genius*, that they hit the popular favor!

By the memory of "seventy-six," No! Do you suppose a *man's* opinions are in the market — to be bought and sold to the highest bidder? Do you suppose he would laud a vapid book, because the fashionable authoress once laved his toadying temples with the baptism of upper-tendom? or, do you suppose he'd lash a poor, but self-reliant wretch, who had presumed to climb to the topmost round of Fame's ladder, without *his* royal permission or assistance, and in despite of his repeated attempts to discourage her? No—no—bless your simple soul; a man never stoops to a meanness. There never was a criticism yet, born of envy, or malice, or repulsed love, or disappointed ambition. No—no. Thank the gods, *I* have a more exalted opinion of masculinity.

FORGETFUL HUSBANDS.

"There is a man out west, so forgetful, that his wife has to put a wafer on the end of her nose, that he may distinguish her from the other ladies; but this does not prevent him from making occasional mistakes."

Take the wafer off your nose, my dear, and put it on your lips! Keep silence and let Mr. Johnson go on "making his mistakes;"—you cannot stop him, if you try; and if he has made up his mind to be near-sighted, all the guide-boards that you can set up, will only drive him home the longest way round!

So trot your babies, smooth your ringlets, digest your dinner, and—agree to differ! Do n't call Mr. Johnson "my dear," or he will have good reason to think you are going to quarrel with him! Look as pretty as a poppet; put on the dress he used to like—and help him to his favorite bit at table, with your accustomed grace; taking care not (?) to touch him, *accidentally*, with your little fat hand, when you are passing it. Ten to one he is on the marrow bones of his soul to you, in less than a week, though tortures could n't wring a confession out of him. Then, if he 's worth the trouble, you are to take advantage of his silent penitence, and go every step of the way to meet him, for he will not approximate to *you*, the width of a straw! If he has not frittered away all your love for him, this is easily done, my dear, and for one whole day after it, he will feel grateful to you for sparing him the humiliation (?) of making an acknowledgment. How many times, my dear "Barkis," you will be "willing" to go through all this, depends upon several little circumstances in your history with which I am unacquainted.

SUMMER FRIENDS.

"If every pain and care we feel
Could burn upon our brow,
How many hearts would move to heal,
That strive to crush us now."

Don't you believe it? They would run from you, as if you had the plague. "Write your brow" with anything else but your "troubles," if you do not wish to be left solus. You have no idea how "good people" will pity you when you tell your doleful ditty! They will "pray for you," give you advice by the bushel, "feel for you"—everywhere but in their pocket-books; and wind up by telling you to "trust in Providence;" to all of which you feel very much like replying as the old lady did when she found herself spinning down hill in a wagon, "I trusted in Providence till the tackling broke!"

Now, listen to me;—just go to work and hew out a path for yourself; get your head above water, and then snap your fingers in their pharisaical faces! Never ask a favor until you are drawing your last breath; and never forget one. "Write your troubles on your brow?" That man was either a knave, or, what is worse, a fool. I suppose he calls himself a poet; if he does, all I have to say is, it's high time the city authorities took away his "license."

HOW THE WIRES ARE PULLED:

OR,

WHAT PRINTER'S INK WILL DO.

"ISN'T it extraordinary, Mr. Stubbs, how Mr. Simpkins can always be dressed in the last tip-top fashion? Don't you and I, and all the world know, that old Allen has a mortgage on his house, and that he never has a dollar by him longer than five minutes at a time. Is n't it extraordinary, Mr. Stubbs?"

"Not at all—not at all—my dear," said Mr. Stubbs, knocking the ashes from his Havana; "to an editor all things are possible;" and he unfolded the damp sheets of the Family Gazette, of which Mr. Simpkins was editor, and commenced reading aloud the following paragraph:

"We yesterday had the gratification of visiting the celebrated establishment of the far-famed Inman & Co., Hatters, No. 172 Wideway. We pronounce their new style of spring hat, for lightness, beauty, and durability, to be unrivaled; it is aptly designated the 'Count D'Orsay hat.' The gentlemanly and enterprising proprietors of the establishment, are unwearied in their endeavors to please the public. There is a *je ne sais quoi* about *their* hats, which can be found nowhere else in the city."

"Well, I don't see," said Mrs. Stubbs, "I—"

"Sh—! sh—! Mrs. Stubbs; don't interrupt the court—here 's another."

"Every one should visit the extensive ware-rooms of Willcut & Co., Tailors, 59 Prince Albert street. There is science wagging in the very tails of Mr. Willcut's coats; in fact, he may be said to be the only tailor in the city, who is a thorough *artist.* His pantaloons are the *knee*-plus-ultra of shear-dom. Mr. Willcut has evidently made the anatomy of masculinity a study—hence the admirable result. The most casual observer, on noticing Mr. Willcut's fine phrenological developments, would at once negative the possibility of his making a *faux pas* on broadcloth."

"Keep quiet, Mrs. Stubbs; listen:"

"The St. Lucifer Hotel is a palatial wonder; whether we consider the number of acres it covers, the splendor of its marble exterior, the sumptuousness of its drawing rooms, or the more than Oriental luxuriousness of its sleeping apartments, the tapestry, mirrors and gilding of which remind one forcibly of the far-famed Tuileries. The host of the St. Lucifer is an Apollo in person, a Chesterfield in manners, and a Lucullus in *taste*; while those white-armed Houris, the female waiters, lap the soul in Elysium."

Mr. Stubbs lifted his spectacles to his forehead, crossed his legs, and nodded knowingly to Mrs. Stubbs.

"That 's the way it 's done, Mrs. Stubbs. That last notice paid his six months' hotel bill at the St. Lucifer, including wine, cigars, and other little editorial perquisites. Do you want to know," said Stubbs, (resuming the paper,)"how he gets his carriages repaired and his horses shod for nothing in the village where his country seat is located? This, now, is a regular stroke of genius. He does it by two words. In an account of his visit to the Sybil's Cave, in which he says, 'MY FRIEND, the blacksmith, and I soon found the spot,' &c., (bah!) Then here is something that will interest you, my dear, on the other page of the Gazette. Mr. Simpkins has used up the dictionary in a half-column announcement of Miss Taffety (the milliner's) 'magnificent opening at —— street.' (Of course she made his wife a present of a new Paris bonnet.")

"Well, I never—" said the simple Mrs. Stubbs. "Goodness knows, if I had known all this before, I would have married an editor myself. Stubbs, why don't *you* set up a newspaper?"

"M-r-s. S-t-u-b-b-s!" said her husband, in an oracular tone, "to conduct a newspaper requires a degree of tact, enterprise and ability to which Jotham Stubbs unfortunately is a stranger. The Family Gazette or its founder is by no means a fair sample of our honorable newspapers, and their upright, intelligent, and respected editors. Great Cæsar!—no!" said Stubbs, rising from his chair, and bringing his hand down emphatically on his corduroys, "no more than you are a fair sample of feminine beauty, Mrs. Stubbs!"

WHO WOULD BE THE LAST MAN?

"Fanny Fern says, 'If there were but one woman in the world, the men would have a terrible time.' Fanny is right; but we would ask her what kind of a time the *women* would have if there were but *one man* in existence?"

What kind of a time would they have? Why, of course no grass would grow under their slippers! The "Wars of the Roses," the battles of Waterloo and Bunker Hill would be a farce to it. Black eyes would be the rage, and both caps and characters would be torn to tatters. I imagine it would not be much of a millennium, either, to the moving cause of the disturbance. He would be as crazy as a fly in a drum, or as dizzy as a bee in a ten-acre lot of honeysuckles, uncertain where to alight. He'd roll his bewildered eyes from one exquisite organization to another, and frantically and diplomatically exclaim — "How happy could I be with either, were t'other dear charmer away!"

"What kind of a time would the women have, were there only one man in the world?"

What kind of a time would they have? What is that to *me?* They might "take their own time," every "Miss Lucy" of them, for all *I* should care; and so might the said man himself; for with me, the limited supply would not increase the value of the article.

"ONLY A COUSIN."

How the rain patters against the windows of your office! How sombre, and gloomy, and cheerless, it looks there! Your little office-boy looks more like an imp of darkness than anything else, as he sits crouched in the corner, with his elbows on his knees and his chin in his hands.

You button your overcoat tight to your chin, (cut possible clients,) and run over to see your cousin Kitty. Ah! that is worth while! A bright, blazing fire; sofa wheeled up to it, and Kitty sitting there, looking so charming in her pretty *neglige.* She looks up sweetly and tranquilly, and says: "Now that's a good Harry; sit down by me, and be agreeable."

Well, you "sit down," (just as close as you like, too!) tell her all the down-town male gossip; consult her confidentially about trimming your whiskers; and desire her candid, unbiased opinion about the propriety and feasibility, with the help of some Macassar, of *coaxing out* a moustache! Then you make a foray into her work-basket, tangling spools most unmercifully, and reading over all the choice bits of poetry that women are so fond of clipping from the newspapers. Then you both go into the china closet, and she gets you a tempting little luncheon; and you grow suddenly merry, and have a contest which shall make the worst pun; you earn for yourself a boxed ear, and are obliged, in self-defence, to imprison the offending hand; your aunt comes in; let her come! are not you and Kitty cousins?

There's a ring at the door, and Mr. Frank ——— is announced. You say, "Unmitigated puppy!" and begin a vehement discussion with your aunt, about anything that comes handy; but that don't prevent you from seeing and hearing all that goes on at the other side of the room. Your aunt is very oblivious, and would n't mind it if you occasionally lost the thread of your discourse. Kitty is the least bit of a coquette! and her conversation is very provocative, racy and sparkling; you privately determine to read her a lecture upon it, as soon as practicable.

It seems as though Mr. Frank —— never would go. Upon his exit, Kitty informs you that she is going to Madame ——'s concert with him. You look serious, and tell her you "should be very sorry to see a cousin of yours enter a concert room with such a brainless fop." Kitty tosses her curls, pats you on the arm, and says, "*Jealous*, hey?" You turn on your heel, and, lighting a cigar, bid her "good-morning," and for a little eternity of a week you never go near her. Meantime, your gentlemen friends tell you how "divine" your little cousin looked at the concert.

You are in a very bad humor; cigars are no sedative — newspapers either. You crowd your beaver down over your eyes and start for your office. On the way you meet Kitty! Hebe! how bright and fresh she looks! and what an unmitigated brute you've been to treat her so! Take care! she knows what you are thinking about! Women are omniscient in such matters! So she peeps archly from beneath those long eyelashes, and says, extending the tip of her little gloved hand—"Want to make up, Harry?"

There's no resisting! That smile leads you, like a will-o' the-wisp, anywhere! So you wait upon her home; nobody comes in, not even your respected aunt; and you never call her "cousin," after that day; but no man living ever won such a darling little wife, as Kitty has promised to be to you, some bright morning.

THE CALM OF DEATH.

> "The moon looks calmly down when man is dying,
> The earth still holds her sway;
> Flowers breathe their perfume, and the wind keeps sighing;
> Naught seems to pause or stay."

Clasp the hands meekly over the still breast — they 've no more work to do; close the weary eyes—they 've no more tears to shed; part the damp locks — there 's no more pain to bear. Closed is the ear alike to Love's kind voice, and Calumny's stinging whisper.

Oh! if in that stilled heart you have ruthlessly planted a thorn; if from that pleading eye you have carelessly turned away; if your loving glance, and kindly word, and clasping hand, have come — *all too late* — then God forgive you! No frown gathers on the marble brow as you gaze — no scorn curls the chiselled lip — no flush of wounded feeling mounts to the blue-veined temples.

God forgive you! for *your* feet, too, must shrink appalled from death's cold river — your faltering tongue ask, "Can this be death?" — your fading eye linger lovingly on the sunny earth — your clammy hand yield its last faint pressure — your sinking pulse give its last feeble flutter.

Oh, rapacious grave; yet another victim for thy voiceless

keeping! What! no word or greeting from all thy household sleepers? No warm welcome from a sister's loving lips? No throb of pleasure from the dear maternal bosom?

Silent all!

Oh, if these broken links were *never* gathered up! If beyond Death's swelling flood there were *no* eternal shore! If for the struggling bark there were no port of peace! If athwart that lowering cloud sprang no bright bow of promise!

Alas for Love, if *this* be all,
And *naught beyond*—oh earth!

"Don't be disagreeable, Smith, I'm just getting inspired!"

MRS. ADOLPHUS SMITH SPORTING THE "BLUE STOCKING."

Well, I think I'll finish that story for the editor of the "Dutchman." Let me see; where did I leave off? The setting sun was just gilding with his last ray—"Ma, I want some bread and molassess"—(yes, dear,) gilding with his last ray the church spire—"Wife, where's my Sunday pants?" (*Under the bed, dear,*) the church spire of Inverness, when a—"There's nothing under the bed, dear, but your lace cap"—(Perhaps they are in the coal hod in the closet,) when a horseman was seen approaching—"Ma'am, the *pertators* is out; not one for dinner"—(Take some turnips,) approaching, covered with dust, and—"Wife! the baby has swallowed a but ton"—(*Reverse him*, dear—take him by the heels,) and waving in his hand a banner, on which was written—"Ma! I've torn my pantaloons"—liberty or death! The inhabitants rushed *en masse*—"Wife! WILL you leave off scribbling? (Don't be disagreeable, Smith, I'm just getting inspired,) to the public square, where De Begnis, who had been secretly—"Butcher wants to see you, ma'am"—secretly informed of the traitors'—"Forgot *which* you said, ma'am, sausages or mutton chop"—movements, gave orders to fire; not less than twenty

——"My gracious! Smith, you have n't been *reversing* that child all this time; he's as black as your coat; and that boy of YOURS has torn up the first sheet of my manuscript. There! it's no use for a married woman to cultivate her intellect. ——Smith, hand me those twins.

CECILE VRAY.

"Died, in ——, Cecile, wife of Mortimer Vray, artist. This lady died in great destitution, among strangers, and was frequently heard to say, 'I wish I were dead!'"

A BRIEF paragraph, to chronicle a broken heart! Poor Cecile! We little thought of this, when conning our French tasks, your long raven ringlets twining lovingly with mine; or, when released from school drudgery, we sauntered through the fragrant woods, weaving rosy dreams of a bright future, which neither you nor I were to see.

I feel again your warm breath upon my cheek — the clasp of your clinging arms about my neck; and the whispered "Don't forget me, Fanny," from that most musical of voices.

Time rolled on, and oceans rolled between: then came a rumor of an "artist lover" — then a "bridal" — now the sad sequel!

Poor Cecile! Those dark eyes restlessly and vainly looking for some familiar face on which to rest, ere they closed forever; that listening ear, tortured by strange footsteps—that fluttering sigh, breathed out on a strange bosom. Poor Cecile!

And *he* (shame to tell) who won that loving heart but to trample it under foot, basks under Italy's sunny skies, bound in flowery fetters, of a foreign syren's weaving

God rest thee, Cecile! Death never chilled a warmer heart; earth never pillowed a lovelier head; Heaven ne'er welcomed a sweeter spirit.

On foreign shores, from broken dreams, a guilty man shall start, as thy last sad, plaintive wail rings in his tortured ear, "*Would I were dead?*"

SAM SMITH'S SOLILOQUY.

By the beard of the Prophet! what a thing it is to be a bachelor! I wonder when this table was dusted last! I wonder how long since that mattress was turned, or that carpet swept, or what was the primeval color of that ewer and wash-basin.

Christopher Columbus! how the frost curtains the windows: how dirge-like the wind moans: how like a great, white pall the snow covers the ground. Five times I've rung that bell for coal, for this rickety old grate, but I might as well thump for admittance at the gate of Paradise.

And speaking of Paradise — Sam Smith, you must be married: you have n't a button to your shirt, nor a shirt to your buttons either.

Wonder if women are such obstinate little monkeys to manage? Wonder if they must be bribed with a new bonnet every day, to keep the peace? Wonder if you bring home a friend unexpectedly to dinner, if they always take to their bed with the sick headache? Wish there was any way of finding out, but by experience. Well, Sam, you are a Napoleonic looking fellow: if *you* can't manage a woman, who can?

How I shall pet the little clipper. I'll marry a blue-eyed

woman: they are the most affectionate. She must not be too tall: a man's wife should n't *look down* upon him. She must not know too much: the Furies take your pert, catamount-y, scribbling women, with a repartee always rolled up under their tongues. She must n't be over seventeen: but how to find that out, Sam, is the question: it is about as easy as to make an editor tell you the truth about his subscription list. She must be handsome — no she must n't either. I should be as jealous as Blue Beard. All the corkscrew, pantalooned, perfumed popinjays would be ogling her. But then, again, there's three hundred and sixty-five days in a year, and three times a day I must sit opposite that connubial face, at the table. What's to be done? Yes; she *must* be handsome: that is as certain as that Louis Napoleon has a Jewish horror of *Ham*.

Wonder if wives are expensive articles? Wonder if their "little hands were ever made to scratch out husbands' eyes?" Wonder if Caudle lectures are "all in your eye," or — occasionally in your ear? Wonder if babies invariably prefer the night-time to cry?

To marry or not to marry, Sam? Whether 't is better to go buttonless, and to shiver, or marry and be always in hot water?

There 's Tom Hillot. Tom 's married. I was his groomsman. I would have given a small fortune to have been in his white satin vest — what with the music, and the roses, and the pretty little bridesmaid! Did n't the bride look bewitching, with the rose-flush on her cheek and the tear on her eyelash? And how provokingly happy Tom looked, when he whirled off with her in the carriage to their new home; and what a pretty little home it was, to be sure. It is just a year to-day since they were married. I dined there yesterday. It strikes me that Tom don't joke as much as he used in his bachelor days; and then he has a way, too, of leaving his sentences unfinished. And I noticed that his wife often touched his foot with her slipper under the table. What do you suppose she did that for? Just as I was buttoning up my coat to come away, I asked Tom if he would go to up Tammany Hall with me. He looked at his wife, and she said, "Oh — *go* by all means, Mr. Hillot;" when Tom immediately declined. I don't understand matrimonial tactics; but it seems to me he ought to have obliged her.

Do you know John Jones and his wife? (peculiar name that,—"Jones!") Well, they are *another* happy couple. It is enough to make bachelor eyes turn green to see them. Mrs. Jones had been four times a widow, when she married John. She knows the value of husbands. She takes precious good care of John. Before he goes to the office in the morning, she pops her head out the window to see if the weathercock indicates a surtout, spencer, cloak, or Tom and Jerry; this point settled, she follows him to the door, and calls him back to close his thorax button "for fear of quinsy." Does a shower come up in the forenoon? She sends him clogs, India-rubbers, an extra flannel shirt, and an oilcloth overall, and prepares two quarts of boiling ginger tea to administer on his arrival, to prevent the damp from "striking in." If he helps himself to a second bit of turkey, she immediately removes it from his plate, and applying a pocket handkerchief to her eyes, asks him "if he has the heart to make her for the fifth time a widow?" You can see, with half an eye, that John must be the happiest dog alive. I'd like to see the miscreant who dares to say he is not!

Certainly — matrimony is an invention of ——. Well, no matter who invented it. I'm going to try it. Where's my blue coat with the bright, brass buttons? The woman has yet to be born who can resist that; and my buff vest and neck-tie, too: may I be shot if I don't offer them both to the little Widow Pardiggle this very night. "Pardiggle!" Phœbus! what a name for such a rose-bud. I'll re-christen her by the euphonious name of Smith. She'll *have* me, of course. She wants a husband—I want a wife: there's one point already in which we perfectly agree. I hate preliminaries. I suppose it is unnecessary for me to begin with the amatory alphabet. With a widow, I suppose you can skip the rudiments. Say what you've got to say in a fraction of a second. Women grow as mischievous as Satan if they think you are afraid of them. Do *I* look as if *I* were afraid? Just examine the growth of my whiskers. The Bearded Lady could n't hold a candle to them, (though I wonder she don't to her own.) *Afraid?* h-m-m! I feel as if I could conquer Asia. What the mischief ails this cravat? It must be the cold that makes my hand tremble so: there—that'll do: that's quite an inspiration. Brummel himself could n't go beyond that. Now for the widow; bless her little round face! I'm immensely obliged to old Pardiggle for giving her a quit claim. I'll make her as happy as a little robin. Do you think I'd bring a tear into her lovely blue eye? Do you think I'd sit after tea, with my back to her, and my feet upon the mantel, staring up chimney for three hours together? Do you think I'd leave her blessed little side, to dangle round oyster-saloons and theatres? Do I *look* like a man to let a woman flatten her pretty little nose against the window-pane night after night, trying to see me reel up street? *No.* Mr. and Mrs. Adam were not more beautified in their nuptial-bower, than I shall be with the Widow Pardiggle.

---

*Re*fused by a widow! Who ever heard of such a thing? Well; there's one comfort: nobody'll ever believe it. She is not so very pretty after all: her eyes are too small, and her hands are rough and red-dy: — not so very *ready* either, confound the gipsy. What amazing pretty shoulders she has! Well, who cares?

> "If she be not fair for me,
> What care I how fair she be?"

Ten to one, she'd have set up that wretch of a Pardiggle for my model. Who wants to be Pardiggle 2nd? I am glad she did n't have me. I mean—I'm glad I did n't have *her!*

LOVE AND DUTY.

The moon looked down upon no fairer sight than Effie May, as she lay sleeping on her little couch, that fair summer night. So thought her mother, as she glided gently in, to give her a silent, good-night blessing. The bright flush of youth, and hope was on her cheek. Her long dark hair lay in masses about her neck and shoulders; a smile played upon the red lips, and the mother bent low to catch the indistinct murmur. She starts, at the whispered name, as if a serpent had stung her; and as the little snowy hand is tossed restlessly upon the coverlid, she sees, glittering in the moonbeams, on that childish finger, the golden signet of betrothal. Sleep sought in vain to woo the eyes of the mother that night. Reproachfully she asked herself, "How could I have been so blind? (but then Effie has seemed to me only a child!) But he! oh, no; the *wine-cup* will be my child's rival; it must not be." Effie was wilful, and Mrs. May knew she must be cautiously dealt with; but she knew, also, that no mother need despair, who possesses the affection of her child.

Effie's violet eyes opened to greet the first ray of the morning sun, as he peeped into her room. She stood at the little mirror, gathering up, with those small hands, the rich tresses so impatient of confinement. How could she fail to know that she was fair?—she read it in every face she met; but there was *one* (and she was hastening to meet him) whose eye had noted, with a lover's pride, every shining ringlet, and azure vein, and flitting blush; his words were soft and low, and skillfully chosen, and sweeter than music to her ear; and so she tied, with a careless grace, the little straw hat under her dimpled chin; and fresh, and sweet, and guileless, as the daisy that bent beneath her foot, she tripped lightly on to the old trysting place by the willows.

Stay! a hand is laid lightly upon her arm, and the pleading voice of a mother arrests that springing step.

"Effie dear, sit down with me on this old garden seat; give up your walk for this morning; I slept but indifferently last night, and morning finds me languid and depressed."

A shadow passed over Effie's face; the little cherry lips pouted, and a rebellious feeling was busy at her heart; but one look in her mother's pale face decided her, and, untying the strings of her hat, she leaned her head caressingly upon her mother's shoulder.

"You are ill, dear mother; you are *troubled;*" and she looked inquiringly up into her face.

"Listen to me, Effie, I have a story to tell you of myself: When I was about your age, I formed an acquaintance with a young man, by the name of Adolph. He had been but a short time in the village, but long enough to win the hearts of half the young girls, from their rustic admirers. Handsome, frank and social, he found himself everywhere a favorite. He would sit by me for hours, reading our favorite authors; and side by side, we rambled through all the lovely paths with which our village abounded. My parents knew nothing to his disadvantage, and were equally charmed as myself with his cultivated refinement of manner, and the indefinable interest with which he invested every topic, grave or gay, which it suited his mood to discuss. Before I knew it, my heart was no longer in my own keeping. One afternoon, he called to accompany me upon a little excursion, we had planned together. As he came up the gravel walk, I noticed that his fine hair was in disorder: a pang, keen as death, shot through my heart, when he approached me, with reeling, unsteady step, and stammering tongue. I could not speak. The chill of death gathered round my heart. I fainted. When I recovered, he was gone, and my mother's face was bending over me, moist with tears. Her woman's heart knew all that was passing in mine. She pressed her lips to my forehead, and only said, 'God strengthen you to choose the right, my child.'

"I could not look upon her sorrowful eyes, or the pleading face of my gray-haired father, and trust myself again to the witchery of that voice and smile. A letter came to me; I dared not read it. (Alas! my heart pleaded too eloquently, even then, for his return.) I returned it unopened; my father and mother devoted themselves to lighten the load that lay upon my heart; but the perfume of a flower, a remembered strain of music, a struggling moonbeam, would bring back old memories, with a crushing bitterness that swept all before it for the moment. But my father's aged hand lingered on my head with a blessing, and my mother's voice had the sweetness of an angel's, as it fell upon my ear!

"Time passed on, and I had conquered myself. Your father saw me, and proposed for my hand; my parents left me free to choose, and Effie dear, *are we not happy?*"

"Oh, mother," said Effie, (then looking sorrowfully in her face,) "did you *never* see Adolph again?"

"Do you remember, my child, the summer evening we sat upon the piazza, when a dusty, travel-stained man came up the steps, and begged for 'a supper?' Do you recollect his bloated, disfigured face? Effie, *that was Adolph!*"

"Not that *wreck* of a *man*, mother?" said Effie, (covering her eyes with her hands, as if to shut him out from her sight.)

"Yes; that was all that remained of that glorious intellect, and that form made after God's own image. I looked around upon my happy home, then upon your noble father — then — upon *him*, and," (taking Effie's little hand and pointing to the *ring* that encircled it,) "in *your* ear, my daughter, I now breathe my mother's prayer for me—'*God help you to choose the right!*'"

The bright head of Effie sank upon her mother's breast, and with a gush of tears she drew the golden circlet from her finger, and placed it in her mother's hand.

"God bless you, my child," said the happy mother, as she led her back to their quiet home.

A FALSE PROVERB.

I WONDER who but the "father of lies," originated this proverb, "Help yourself and then everybody else will help you." Is it not as true as the book of Job that it's just driving the nails into your own coffin, to let anybody know you want help! Is not a "seedy" hat, a threadbare coat, or patched dress, an effectual shower-bath on old friendships? Have not people a mortal horror of a sad face and a pitiful story? Don't they on hearing it, instinctively poke their purses into the farthest, most remote corner of their pockets? Don't they rap their warm garments round their well-fed persons, and advise you, in a saintly tone, "to trust in Providence?" Are they not always "engaged" ever after, when you call to see them? Are they not near-sighted when you meet them in the street?—and don't they turn short corners to get out of your way? "Help yourself,"—of course you will, (if you have any spirit;)—but when sickness comes, or dark days, and your wits and nerves are both exhausted, don't place any dependence on this lying proverb! — or you will find yourself decidedly humbugged. And then, when your heart is so soft that anybody could knock you down with a feather, get into the darkest hole you can find, and cry it out! Then crawl out, bathe your eyes till they shine again, and if you have one nice garment left, out with it, put it on! turn your shawl on the brightest side; put your best and prettiest foot foremost; tie on your go-to-meetin' bonnet, and smile under it, if it half kills you; and see how complaisant the world will be when — you ask nothing of it!

But if (as there are exceptions to all rules,) you should chance to stumble upon a true friend (when you can only render thanks as an equivalent for kindness) "make a note on't," as "Captain Cuttle" says, for it don't happen but once in a life-time!

A MODEL HUSBAND.

"Mrs. Perry, a young Bloomer, has eloped from Monson, Massachusetts, with Levins Clough. When her husband found she was determined to go, he gave her one hundred dollars to start with."

MAGNANIMOUS Perry! Had I been your spouse, I should have handed that "one hundred dollar bill" to Mr. Levins Clough, as a healing plaster for his disappointed affections — encircled your neck with my repentant arms, and returned to your home. Then, I 'd mend every rip in your coat, gloves, vest, pants, and stockings, from that remorseful hour, till the millennial day. I 'd hand you your cigar-case and slippers, put away your cane, hang up your coat and hat, trim your beard and whiskers, and wink at your sherry cobblers, whisky punches, and mint juleps. I 'd help you get a "ten strike" at ninepins. I 'd give you a "night key," and be perfectly oblivious what time in the small hours you tumbled into the front entry. I 'd pet all your stupid relatives, and help your country friends to "beat down" the city shopkeepers. I 'd frown at all offers of "pin money." I 'd let you "smoke" in my face till I was as brown as a herring, and my eyes looked as if they were bound with pink tape; and I 'd invite that pretty widow Delilah Wilkins to dinner, and run out to do some shopping, and stay away till tea-time. Why! there 's nothing I *would n't* do for you — you might have knocked me down with a feather, after such a piece of magnanimity. That "Levins Clough" could stand no more chance than a woodpecker tapping at an iceberg.

HOW IS IT?

"Well, Susan, what do you think of married ladies being happy?" "Why I think there are more AIN'T than IS, than IS that AIN'T."

SUSAN, I shall apply to the Legislature to have your name changed to "Sapphira." You are an unprincipled female.

Just imagine yourself MRS. Snip. It is a little prefix not to be sneezed at. It is only the privileged few, who can secure a pair of corduroys to mend, and trot by the side of; or a pair of coat-flaps alternately to darn, and hang on to, amid the vicissitudes of this patchwork existence.

Think of the high price of fuel, Susan, and the quantity it takes to warm a low-spirited, single woman; and then think of having all that found for you by your husband, and no extra charge for "*gas.*" Think how pleasant to go to the closet and find a great boot-jack on your best bonnet; or "to work your passage" to the looking-glass, every morning, through a sea of dickeys, vests, coats, continuations, and neck-ties; think of your nicely-polished toilette table spotted all over with shaving suds; think of your "Guide to Young Women," used for a razor strap. Think of Mr. Snip's lips being hermetically sealed, day after day, except to ask you "if the coal was out, or if his coat was mended." Think of coming up from the kitchen, in a gasping state of exhaustion, after making a batch of his favorite pies, and finding five or six great dropsical bags disemboweled on your chamber floor, from the contents of which Mr. Snip had selected the "pieces" of your best silk gown, for "rags" to clean his gun with. Think of his taking a watch-guard you made him out of YOUR HAIR, for a dog-collar! Think of your promenading the floor, night after night, with your fretful, ailing baby hushed up to your warm cheek, lest it should disturb your husband's slumbers; and think of his coming home the next day, and telling you, when you were exhausted with your vigils, "that he had just met his old love, Lilly Grey, looking as fresh as a daisy, and that it was unaccountable how much older you looked than she, although you were both the same age.

Think of all that, Susan.

A MORNING RAMBLE.

What a lovely morning! It is a luxury to breathe. How blue the sky; how soft the air; how fragrant the fresh spring grass and budding trees; and with what a gush of melody that little bird eases his joy-burdened heart.

> "This world is very lovely. Oh my God,
> I thank Thee, that I live."

Clouds there are; but, oh, how much of sunshine! Sorrow there is; but, in every cup is mingled a drop of balm. Over our threshold the destroying angel passeth; yet, ere the rush of his dark wing sweepeth past, cometh the Healer.

—Here is a poor, blind man basking in the sunshine, silently appealing, with outstretched palm, to the passer-by. Through his thin, gray locks the wind plays lovingly. A smile beams on his withered face; for, though his eyes are rayless, he can *feel* that chill Winter has gone; and he knows that the flowers are blossoming,—for the sweet West wind cometh, God-commissioned, to waft him their fragrance. Some pedestrians gaze curiously at him: others, like the Levite, "pass by on the other side." A woman approaches. She is plainly clad, and bears a basket on her arm. She has a good, kind, motherly face, as if she were hastening back to some humble home, made brighter and happier by her presence. Life is sweet to her. She catches sight of the poor old man; her eye falls upon the label affixed to his breast: "I am blind!" Oh, what if the brightness and beauty of this glad sunshine were all night, to her vailed lids? What if the dear home faces were for ever shrouded from her yearning sight? What if *she* might never walk the sunny earth, without a guiding hand? She places her basket upon the sidewalk, and wipes away a tear: now she explores her time-worn pocket; finds the hardly-earned coin, and placing it in the palm of the old man, *presses his hand lovingly*, and is gone!

Poor Bartimeus! He may never see the honest face that bent so tenderly over him; but, to his heart's core, he felt that kindly pressure, and the sunshine is all the brighter, and the breeze sweeter and fresher for that friendly grasp, and life is again bright to the poor blind man.

"Oh God! I thank Thee, that I live!"

How swiftly the ferry boat plows through the wave! How gleefully that little child claps its tiny hands, as the snowy foam parts on either side, then dashes away like a thing of life. Here are weary business men, going back to their quiet homes; and pleasure-loving belles, returning from the city. Pacing up and down the deck, is a worn and weary woman, bearing in her arms a child, so emaciated, so attenuated, that but for the restless glance of its dark, sunken eyes, one would think it a little corpse. The mother has left her unhealthy garret in the noisome lane of the teeming city, and paid her last penny to the ferryman, that the health-laden sea breeze may fan the sick child's temples. Tenderly she moves it from one shoulder to another. Now, she lays its little cheek to hers; now, she kisses the little slender fingers; but still the baby moans. The boat touches the pier. All are leaving, but the mother and child; the ferryman tells her to "go too." She says timidly, "I want to return again—I live the other side—I came on board for the baby," (pointing to the dying child.) Poor woman, she did not know that she could not go back without another fee, and she has not a penny. Loathsome as is her distant home, she must go back to it; but how?

One passenger beside herself still lingers listening. Dainty fingers drop a coin into the gruff ferryman's hand,—then a handful into the weary, troubled mother's. The sickly babe looks up and smiles at the chinking coin—the mother smiles, because the baby has smiled again—and then weeps because she knows not how to thank the lovely donor.

"Homeward bound."

Over the blue waters, the golden sunset gleams; tinting the snowy, billowy foam with a thousand iris hues; while at the boat's prow, stands the happy mother, wooing the cool sunset breeze, which kisses soothingly the sick infant's temples.

"This earth is very lovely. Oh my God,
I thank thee that I live!"

HOUR-GLASS THOUGHTS.

The bride stands waiting at the altar; the corpse lies waiting for burial.

Love vainly implores of Death a reprieve; Despair vainly invokes his coming.

The starving wretch, who purloins a crust, trembles in the hall of Justice; liveried sin, unpunished, riots in high places.

Brothers, clad "in purple and fine linen, fare sumptuously every day;" Sisters, in linsey-woolsey, toil in garrets and shrink, trembling, from insults that no fraternal arm avenges.

The Village Squire sows, reaps and garners golden harvests; the Parish Clergyman sighs, as his casting vote cuts down his already meager salary.

The unpaid sempstress be-gems with tears the fairy festal robe; proud beauty floats in it through the ball-room, like a thing of air.

Church spires point, with tapering fingers, to the rich man's heaven; Penitence, in rags, tearful and altarless, meekly stays its timid foot at the threshold.

Sneaking Vice, wrapped in the labeled cloak of Piety, finds "open sesame;" shrinking Conscientiousness, jostled rudely aside, weeps in secret its fancied unworthiness.

The Editor grows plethoric on the applause of the public and mammoth subscription lists; the *unrecognized* journalist, who, behind the scenes, mixes so deftly the newspaperial salad, lives on the smallest possible stipend, and looks like an undertaker's walking advertisement.

The Wife, pure, patient, loving, trustful, sits singing, by the evening fire, repairing, with the busy fingers of economy, the time-worn garment; the Husband, favored by darkness, seeks, with stealthy steps and costly gifts, the syren of the hour, squandering hundreds to win a smile which is ever in the market for the highest bidder.

The polluted libertine, with foul lips, hackneyed heart, but polished manners, finds smiling welcome at the beauteous lips of Virtue; while, from the brow on which that libertine has ineffäceably written "Magdalen," "beauteous Virtue" turns scornfully away.

Wives rant of their "Woman's Rights," in public; Husbands eat bad dinners and tend crying babies, at home.

Mothers toil in kitchens; Daughters lounge in parlors.

Fathers drive the plough; Sons drive tandem.

BOARDING HOUSE EXPERIENCE.

Mr. Ralph Renoux lived by his wits: i. e., he kept a boarding-house; *taking in* any number of ladies and gentlemen, who, in the philanthropic language of his advertisement, "pined for the comforts and elegancies of a home."

Mr. Renoux's house was at the court-end of the city; his drawing-room was unexceptionably furnished, and himself, when "made up," after ten o'clock in the morning, quite *comme il faut*. Mrs. Renoux never appeared; being, in the pathetic words of Mr. Renoux, "in a drooping, invalid state:" nevertheless, she might be seen, by the initiated, haunting the back stairs and entries, and with flying cap-strings, superintending kitchen-cabinet affairs.

Mrs. Renoux was the unhappy mother of three unmarried daughters, with red hair, and tempers to match; who languished over Byron, in elegant *negligées*, of a morning, till after the last masculine had departed; then, in curl-papers and calico long-shorts, performed, for the absentees, the duty of chambermaids; peeping into valises, trunks, bureaus, cigar boxes and coat pockets, and replenishing their perfumed bottles, from the gentlemen's toilet stands, with the most perfect *nonchalance.* At dinner, they emerged from their chrysalis state, into the most butterfly gorgeousness, and exchanged the cracked treble, with which they had been ordering round the over-tasked maid-of-all-work, as they affectionately addressed "Papa."

At the commencement of my story, Renoux was as happy as a kitten with its first mouse — having entrapped, with the bait of his alluring advertisement, a widow lady with one child. "The comforts and elegancies of a home;" — it was just what the lady was seeking: — how very fortunate!

"Certainly, Madam," said Renoux, doubling himself into the form of the letter C. "I will serve your meals in your own room, if you prefer; but, really, Madam, I trust you will sometimes grace the drawing-room with your presence, as we have a very select little family of boarders. Do you choose to breakfast at eight, nine, or ten, Madam? Do you incline to Mocha? or prefer the leaves of the Celestial city? Are you fond of eggs, Madam? Would you prefer to dine at four, or five? Do you wish six courses, or more? There is the bell-rope, Madam. I trust you will use it unsparingly, should any thing be omitted or neglected. I am just on my way down town, and if you will favor me by saying what you would fancy for your dinner to-day, (the market is full of every thing — fish, flesh, fowl and game of all sorts,) you have only to express a wish, Madam, and the thing is here; I should be miserable, indeed, were the request of a *lady* to be disregarded in *my* house, and that lady deprived of her natural protector. Which is it, Madam, fish? flesh? or fowl? Any letters to send to the post-office, Madam? Any commands any where? I shall be *too* happy to be of service"; — and bending to the tips of his patent leather toes, Mr. Renoux, facing the lady, bowed obsequiously and Terpsichore-ally out of the apartment.

The dinner hour came. An Irish servant-girl came with it; and drawing out a table at an Irish angle upon the floor, tossed over it a tumbled table-cloth; placed upon it a castor, minus one leg, some cracked salt-cellars and tumblers; then laid some knives, left-handed, about the table; then, withdrew, to reappear with the result of Mr. Renoux's laborious research "in the market filled with every thing," viz: a consumptive looking mackerel, whose skin clung tenaciously to its back bone, and a Peter Schemel looking chicken, which, in its life-time, must have had a vivid recollection of Noah and the forty days' shower. This was followed by a dessert of stale baker's tarts, compounded of lard and dried apples; and twenty-four purple grapes.

The next morning, Mr. Renoux tip-toed in, smirking and bowing, as if the bill of fare had been the most sumptuous in the world, and expressed the greatest astonishment and indignation, that "the stupid servant had neglected bringing up the other courses which he had provided;" then he inquired "how the lady had rested;" and when she preferred a request for another pillow, (there being only six feathers in the one she had,) he assured her that it should be in her apartment in less than one hour. A fortnight after, he expressed the most intense disgust, that "the rascally upholsterer" had not yet sent *what he had never ordered.* Each morning, Mr. Renoux presented himself, at a certain hour, behind a very stiff dickey, and offered the lady the morning papers. Seating himself on the sofa, he would remark that—it was a very fine day, and that affairs in France appeared to be *in statu quo;* or, that the Czar had ordered his generals to occupy the principalities; that Gorchakoff was preparing to cross the Danube; that the Sultan had dispatched Omar Pasha to the frontiers; that the latter gentleman had presented his card to Gorchakoff, on the point of a yataghan, which courtesy would probably lead to——something else!

During one of these agreeable calls, the lady took occasion slightly to object to Betty's nibbling the tarts, as she brought them up for dinner; whereupon, Mr. Renoux declared, upon the honor of a Frenchman, that "she should be pitched out of the door immediately, if not sooner; and an efficient servant engaged to take her place."

The next day, the "efficient servant" came in, broom in hand, whistling "Oh, Susannna," and passing into the little dressing-room, to "put it to rights," amused herself by trying on the widow's best bonnet, and polishing her teeth and combing her hair with that lady's immaculate and individual head-brush and tooth-brush. You will not be surprised to learn, that their injured and long-suffering owner, took a frantic and "French leave" the following morning, in company with her big and little band-boxes; taking refuge under the sheltering roof of Madame Finfillan.

Madame Finfillan was a California widow; petite, plump and pretty — who bore her cruel bereavement with feminine philosophy, and slid round the world's rough angles with a most eel-like dexterity. In short, she was a Renoux in petticoats. Madame welcomed the widow with great pleasure, because, as she said, she "wished to fill her house only with first-class boarders;" and the widow might be assured that she had the apartments fresh from the diplomatic hands of the Spanish Consul, who would on no account have given them up, had not his failing health demanded a trip to the Continent. Madame also assured the widow, that, (although she said it herself,) every part of her house would bear the closest inspection; that those vulgar horrors, cooking butter, and diluted tea, were never seen on her Epicurean table; that they breakfasted at ten, lunched at two, dined at six, and enjoyed themselves in the *interim;* that her daughter, Miss Clara, was perfectly well qualified to superintend, when business called her mother away. And that nobody knew, (wringing her little white hands,) how *much* business she had to do, what with trotting round to those odious markets, trading for wood and coal, and such like uninteresting things; or what *would* become of her, had she not some of the best friends in the world to look after her, in the absence of Mons. Finfillan.

— Madame then caught up the widow's little boy, and, half smothering him with kisses, declared that there was nothing on earth she loved so well as children; that there were half a dozen of them in the house, who loved her better than their own fathers and mothers, and that their devotion to her was at times quite touching — (and here she drew out an embroidered pocket-handkerchief, and indulged in an interesting little sniffle behind its cambric folds.) Recovering herself, she went on to say, that the manner in which some boarding-house keepers treated children, was perfectly inhuman: that she had a second table for them, to be sure, but it was loaded with delicacies, and that she always put them up a little school lunch herself; on which occasion there was always an amicable little quarrel among them, as to which should receive from her the greatest number of kisses; also, that it was her frequent practice to get up little parties and tableaux, for their amusement. "But here is my daughter, Miss Clara," said she, introducing a fair-haired young damsel, buttoned up in a black velvet jacket, over a flounced skirt.

"Just sixteen yesterday," said Madame: "naughty little blossom, budding out so fast, and pushing her poor mamma off the stage;" (and here Madame paused for a compliment, and looking in the opposite mirror, smoothed her jetty ringlets complacently.) "Yes, every morning little blossom's mamma looks in the glass, expecting to find a horror of a gray hair. But what makes my little pet so pensive to-day? — thinking of her little lover, hey? Has the naughty little thing a thought she does not share with mamma? But, dear me!" — and

Madame drew out a little dwarf watch; "I had quite forgotten it is the hour Mons. Guigen gives me my guitar lesson. Adieu, dinner at six, remember;"—and Madame tripped, coquettishly, out of the room.

"Yes; "dinner at six." Gold salt-cellars, black waiters, and finger-bowls; satin chairs in the parlor, and pastilles burn ing on the side-table; but the sheets on the beds all torn to ribbons; the boarders allowed but one towel a week; every bell-rope divorced from its bell; the locks all out of order on the chamber doors; the "dear children's" bill of fare at the "second table"—sour bread, watery soup, and cold buckwheat cakes;—and "dinner at six," only an invention of the enemy, to save the expense of one meal a day—the good, cozy, old-fashioned tea.

Well, the boarders were all "trusteed" by Madame's butcher, baker and milkman; Miss Clara eloped with the widow's diamond ring and Mons. Peneke; and Madame, who had heard that Mons. Finfillan was "among the things that *were*," was just about running off with Mons. Guigen, when her liege lord suddenly returned from California, with damaged constitution and morals, a dilapidated wardrobe and empty coffers.

Moral. Beware of boarding-houses: in the words of Shakspeare,

Let those keep house who ne'er kept house before
And those who have kept house, keep house the more.

A GRUMBLE FROM THE (H)ALTAR.

This is the second day I 've come home to dinner, without that yard of pink ribbon for Mrs. Pendennis. Now, we shall have a *broil*, not down in the bill of fare. Julius Cæsar; if she only knew how much I have to do; but it would make no difference if she did. I used to think a fool was easily managed. Mrs. Pendennis has convinced me that *that* was a mistake. If I try to reason with her, she talks round and round in a circle, like a kitten chasing its tail. If I set my arms a-kimbo, and look threatening, she settles into a fit of the sulks, to which a November drizzle of a fortnight's duration is a millenium. If I try to get round her by petting, she is as impudent as the ——. Yes, just about. Jerusalem! what a thing it is to be married! And yet, if an inscrutable Providence should bereave me of Mrs. Pendennis, I am not at all sure —— good gracious, here she comes! Do you know I 'd rather face one of Colt's revolvers this minute, than that four feet of womanhood? Is n't it astonishing, the way they do it?

A WICK-ED PARAGRAPH.

CONNUBIAL.—Mr. Albert Wicks, of Coventry, under date of December 28th, advertised his wife as having left his bed and board; and now, under date of March 26th, he appends to his former notice, the following:

"Mrs. Wicks, if you ever intend to come back and live with me any more, you must come now or not at all.

"I love you as I do my life, and if you will come now, I will forgive you for all you have done and threatened to do, which I can prove by three good witnesses: and if not, I shall attend to your case without delay, and soon, too."

THERE, now, Mrs. Wicks, what is to be done? "Three good witnesses!" think of *that!* What the mischief have you been about? Whatever it is, Mr. Wicks is ready to "love you like his life." Consistent Mr. Wicks!

Now take a a little advice, my dear innocent, and don't allow yourself to be badgered or frightened into anything. None but a coward ever threatens a woman. Put that in your memorandum book. It 's all bluster and braggadocio. Thread your darning-needle, and tell him you are ready for him — ready for anything except his "loving you like his life;" that you could not possibly survive that infliction, without having your "wick" snuffed entirely out.

Sew away, just as if there were not a domestic earthquake brewing under your connubial feet. If it sends you up in the air, it sends him, too — there 's a pair of you! Put *that* in his Wick-ed ear! Of course he will sputter away, as if he had swallowed a "Roman candle," and you can take a nap till he gets through, and then offer him your smelling-bottle to quiet his nerves.

That 's the way to quench him!

MISTAKEN PHILANTHROPY.

"Don't moralize to a man who is on his back. Help him up, set him firmly on his feet, and then give him advice and means."

There's an old-fashioned, verdant piece of wisdom, altogether unsuited for the enlightened age we live in! Fished up, prob ably, from some musty old newspaper, edited by some eccentric man troubled with that inconvenient appendage, called a heart! Don't pay any attention to it. If a poor wretch (male or female) comes to you for charity, whether allied to you by your own mother, or mother Eve, put on the most stoical, "get thee behind me" expression you can muster. Listen to him with the air of a man who "thanks God he is not as other men are." If the story carry conviction with it, and truth and sorrow go hand in hand, button your coat up tighter over your pocket-book, and give him a piece of — good advice! If you know anything about him, try to rake up some imprudence or mistake he may have made in the course of his life, and bring that up as a reason why you can't give him anything more substantial, and tell him that his present condition is probably a salutary discipline for those same peccadilloes! Ask him more questions than there are in the Assembly's Catechism, about his private history, and when you've pumped him high and dry, try to teach him (on an empty stomach,) the "duty of submission." If the tear of wounded sensibility begin to flood the eye, and a hopeless look of discouragement settle down upon the façe, "wish him well," and turn your back upon him as quick as possible.

Should you at any time be seized with an unexpected spasm of generosity, and make up your mind to bestow some worn out, old garment that will hardly hold together till the recipi ent gets it home, you've bought him, body and soul; of course you are entitled to the gratitude of a life-time! If he ever presumes to think differently from you after that, he 's an "ungrateful wretch," and "ought to suffer." As to the "golden rule," that was made in old times; everything is changed now; 't aint suited to our meridian.

People should n't get poor; if they do, you don 't want to be bothered with it. It 's disagreeable; it hinders your digestion. You 'd rather see Dives than Lazarus; and it 's my opin ion your taste will be gratified in that particular, (in the other world, if it is not in this!)

INSIGNIFCANT LOVE.

"You, young, loving creature, who dream of your lover by night and by day—you fancy that he does the same of you? One hour, perhaps, your presence has captivated him, subdued him even to weakness; the next, he will be in the world, working his way as a man among men, forgetting, for the time being, your very existence. Possibly, if you saw him, his outer self, so hard and stern, so different from the self you know, would strike you with pain. Or else his inner and diviner self, higher than you dream of, would turn coldly from *your insignificant love.*"

"INSIGNIFICANT love!!" I like that. More especially when out of ten couple you meet, nine of the wives are as far above their husbands, in point of mind, as the stars are above the earth. For the credit of the men I should be sorry to say how many of them would be minus coats, hats, pantaloons, cigars, &c., were it not for their wives' earnings; or how many smart speeches and able sermons have been concocted by their better halves, (while rocking the cradle,) to be delivered to the public at the proper time, parrot fashion, by the lords of creation. Wisdom will die with the men, there 's no gainsaying that!

Catch a smart, talented, energetic woman, and it will puzzle you to find a man that will compare with her for go-aheadativeness. The more obstacles she encounters, the harder she struggles, and the more you try to put her down, the more you won't do it. Children are obliged to write under their crude drawings, "this is a dog," or, "this is a horse." If it were not for coats and pants, we should be obliged to label, "this is a man," in ninety-nine cases out of a hundred!

"Insignificant love!" Why does a man offer himself a dozen times to the same woman? Pity to take so much pains for such a trifle! "Insignificant love!" Who gets you on your feet again, when you fail in business, by advancing the nice little sum settled on herself by her anxious pa? Who cheers you up, when her nerves are all in a double-and-twisted knot, and you come home with your face long as the moral law? Who wears her old bonnet three winters, while you smoke, and drive, and go to the opera? Who sits up till the small hours, to help you find the way up your own staircase? Who darns your old coat, next morning, just as if you were a man, instead of a brute? And who scratches any woman's eyes out, who dares insinuate that her husband is superior to you!

"Insignificant love!" I wish I knew the man who wrote that article! I'd appoint his funeral to-morrow, and it should come off, too!!

A MODEL MARRIED MAN.

Cobbett says that for two years after his marriage, he retained his disposition to flirt with pretty women; but at last his wife—probably having lost all hope of his reforming himself—gently tapped him upon the arm, and remarked—

"Don't do that. I do not like it."

Cobbett says:—"That was quite enough. I had never thought on the subject before; one hair of her head was more dear to me than all other women in the world; and this I knew that she knew; but now I saw that this was not all that she had a right to from me. *I saw that she had the further claim upon me that I should abstain from everything that might induce others to believe that there was any other woman for whom, even if I were at liberty, I had any affection.*"

Now I suppose most women, on reading that, would roll up their eyes and think unutterable things of Mr. Cobbett! But, had *I* borne his musical name, and had that fine speech been addressed to me, I should immediately have dismissed the—house-maid!

It is not in any masculine to get on his knees that way, without a motive! I tell you, that man was a humbug! overshot the mark, entirely; promised ten times as much as a sinful masculine could ever perform. If he'd said about *a quarter part* of that, you might have believed him. His affection for Mrs. Cobbett was skin-deep. He would have flirted with every one of you, the minute her back was turned, to the end of the electrical chapter!

A man who is magnetized as he ought to be, don't waste his precious time making such long-winded, sentimental speeches.

You never need concern yourself, when such a glib tongue makes love to you. Go on with your knitting; *he's convalescent!* getting better of his complaint fast. Now mind what I tell you; that Cobbett was a humbug!

MEDITATIONS OF PAUL PRY, JUN.

Not a blessed bit of gossip have I heard for a whole week! Nobody's run off with anybody's wife; not a *single* case of "Swartwouting;" no minister's been to the theatre; and my friend Tom, editor of the "Sky Rocket," (who never cares whether a rumor be true or false, or where it hits, so that it makes a paragraph,) is quite in despair. He 's really afraid the world is growing virtuous—says it would be a hundred dollars in his pocket, to get hold of a bit of scandal in such a dearth of news; and if the accused party gets obstreperous, he 'd just as lief publish one side as the other! The more fuss the the better; all he 's afraid of is, they won't think it worth noticing!

Ah! we 've some new neighbors in that house; pretty woman there, at the window; glad of that! In the first place, it rests my eyes to look at them; in the next place, where there 's a pretty woman, you may be morally certain there 'll be mischief, sooner or later, i. e. if they don't have somebody like me to look after them; therefore I shall keep my eye on her. That 's her husband in the room, I 'm certain of it, (for all the while she is talking to him, she 's looking out the window!) There he goes down street to his business — a regular humdrum, henpecked, "ledger" looking Lilliputian. Was not cut out for her, that's certain! Well, my lady's wide awake enough! Look at her eye! No use in pursing up that pretty mouth! — that eye tells the story! Nice little plump figure; coquettish turn of the head, and a spring to her step. Well, well, I'll keep my eyes open.

Just as I expected! there's a young man ringing at the door; "patent leather," "kid gloves," white hand, ring on the little finger — hope she won't shut the blinds now. There! she has taken her seat on the sofa at the back part of the room. She don't escape *me* that way, while I own a spy-glass! Jupiter! if he is not twisting her curls round his fingers! Wonder how old "Ledger" would like *that!*

Tuesday.— Boy at the door with a bouquet. Can't ring the bell; I'll just step out and offer to do it for him, and learn who sent it! "Has orders not to tell;" umph! *I've* no orders "not to tell;" so here goes a note to Ledger about it; that little gipsy is stepping RATHER too high.

Wednesday.—Here I am tied up for a month at least; scarcely a whole bone in my body, to say nothing of the way my feelings are hurt. How did I know that young man was "her brother?" Why could n't Ledger correct my mistake in a gentlemanly way, without daguerreotyping it on my back with a horsewhip? It's true I am not always correct in my suspicions, but he ought to have looked at my motives! Suppose it had n't been her brother, now! It's astonishing, the ingratitude of people. It's enough to discourage all my attempts at moral reform!

Well, it 's no use attacking that hornet's nest again ; but I 've no doubt some of the commandments are broken somewhere ; and with the help of some " opodeldoc " I 'll get out and find where it is !

SUNSHINE AND YOUNG MOTHERS.

Folly. For girls to expect to be happy without marriage. Every woman was made for a mother, consequently, babies are as necessary to their "peace of mind," as health. If you wish to look at melancholy and indigestion, look at an old maid. If you would take a peep at sunshine, look in the face of a young mother.

"Young mothers and sunshine"! They are worn to fiddle strings before they are twenty-five! When an old lover turns up, he thinks he sees his grandmother, instead of the dear little Mary who used to make him feel as if he should crawl out of the toes of his boots! Yes! my mind is *quite* made up about *matrimony;* it's a *one-sided* partnership.

"Husband" gets up in the morning, and pays his *devoirs* to the looking-glass; curls his fine head of hair; puts on an immaculate shirt bosom; ties an excruciating cravat; sprinkles his handkerchief with cologne; stows away a French roll, an egg, and a cup of coffee; gets into the omnibus, looks at the pretty girls, and makes love between the pauses of business during the forenoon *generally.* Wife must "hermetically seal" the windows and exclude all the fresh air, (because the baby had "the snuffles" in the night;) and sits gasping down to the table more dead than alive, to finish her breakfast. Tommy turns a cup of hot coffee down his bosom; Juliana has torn off the strings of her school bonnet; James "wants his geography covered;" Eliza can't find her satchel; the butcher wants to know if she 'd like a joint of mutton; the milkman woula like his money; the iceman wants to speak to her "just a minute;" the baby swallows a bean; husband sends the boy home from the store to say *his partner* will dine with him; the cook leaves "all flying," to go to her "sister's dead baby's wake," and husband's thin coat must be ironed before noon.

"*Sunshine and young mothers!*" Where 's my smelling bottle?

UNCLE BEN'S ATTACK OF SPRING FEVER, AND HOW HE GOT CURED.

"It is not possible that you have been insane enough to go to housekeeping in the country, for the summer? Oh, you ought to hear my experience," and Uncle Ben wiped the perspiration from his forehead, at the very thought.

Yes, I tried it once, with city habits and a city wife: got rabid with the dog days, and nothing could cure me but a nibble of green grass. There was Susan, you know, who never was off a brick pavement in her life, and did n't know the difference between a cheese and a grindstone.

Well, we ripped up our carpets, and tore down our curtains, and packed up our crockery, and nailed down our pictures, and eat dust for a week, and then we emigrated to Daisy Ville.

Could I throw up a window or fasten back a blind in that house, without sacrificing my suspenders and waistband button? No, sir! Were not the walls full of Red Rovers? Did n't the doors fly open at every wind gust? Did n't the roof leak like the mischief? Was not the chimney leased to a pack of swallows? Was not the well a half a mile from the house?

Oh, you need n't laugh. Instead of the comfortable naps to which I had been accustomed, I had to sleep with one eye open all night, lest I should n't get into the city in time. I had to be shaving in the morning before a rooster in the barn-yard had stirred a feather; swallowed my coffee and toast by steam, and then, still masticating, made for the front door. There stood Peter with my horse and gig,—for I detest your cars and omnibuses. On the floor of the chaise was a huge basket in which to bring home material for the next day's dinner; on the seat was a dress of my wife's to be left "without fail" at Miss Sewing Silk's, to have the forty-seventh hook moved one-sixth of a degree higher up on the back. Then there was a package of shawls from Tom Fools & Co., to be returned, and a pair of shoes to carry to Lapstone, who was to select another pair for me to bring out at night; and a demijohn to be filled with Sherry. Well, I whipped up Bucephalus, left my sleeping wife and babies, and started for town; cogitating over an intricate business snarl, which bade defiance to any straightening process. I had n't gone half a mile before an old maid (I hate old maids) stopped me to know if I was going into town, and if I was, if I would n't take her in, as the omnibusses made her sick. She said she was niece to Squire Dandelion, and "had a few chores to do a shopping." So I took her in, or rather, she took *me* in, (but she did n't do it but once—for I bought a sulkey next day!) Well, it came night, and I was hungry as a Hottentot, for I never could dine, as your married widowers *pro tem* do, at eating-houses, where one gravy answers for flesh, fish and fowl, and the pudding-sauce is as black as the cook's complexion. So I went round on an empty stomach, hunting up my *expressman parcels*, and wending my way to the stable with arms and pockets running over. When I got home, found my wife in despair, no tacks in the house to nail down carpets, and not one to be had at the store in the village; the cook had deserted because she could n't do without "her *city privileges*," (meaning Jonathan Jones, the "dry dirt" man); and the chambermaid, a buxom country girl with fire red hair, was spinning round the crockery (a la Blitz) because she "could n't eat with the family."

Then Charley was taken with the croup in the night, and in my fright I put my feet into my coat sleeves, and my arms into my pants, and put on one of my wife's ruffles instead of a dicky, and rode three miles in a pelting rain, for some "goose grease" for his throat.

Then we never found out till cherries, and strawberries, and peaches were ripe, how many *friends* (?) we had. There was a horse hitched at every rail in the fence, so long as there was anything left to eat on a tree in the farm; but if my wife went in town shopping, and called on any of them, they were "out, or engaged;" — or if at home, had "just done dinner, and were going to ride."

Then there was no school in the neighborhood for the children, and they were out in the barn-yard feeding the pigs with lump sugar, and chasing the hens off the nest to see what was the prospect for eggs, and making little boats of their shoes, and sailing them in the pond, and milking the cow in the middle of the day, &c.

Then if I dressed in the morning in linen coat, thin pants, and straw hat, I 'd be sure to find the wind " dead east " when I got into the city; or if I put on broadcloth and fixins to match, it would be hotter than Shadrach's furnace, all day — while the dense morning fog would extract the starch from my dicky and shirt-bosom, till they looked very like a collapsed flapjack.

Then our meeting-house was a good two miles distant, and we had to walk, or stay at home; because my factotum (Peter) would n't stay on the farm without he could have the horse Sundays to go to Mill Village to see his affianced Nancy. Then the old farmers leaned on my stone wall, and laughed till the tears came into their eyes, to see "the city gentleman's" experiments in horticulture, as they passed by "to meetin'."

Well, sir, before summer was over, my wife and I looked as jaded as omnibus horses — she with chance "help" and floods of city company, and I with my arduous duties as *express man* for my own family in particular, and the neighbors in general.

And now here we are —" No. 9 Kossuth square." Can reach anything we want, by putting our hands out the front windows. If, as the poet says, "*man made the town*," all I've got to say is — he understood his business!

THE AGED MINISTER VOTED A DISMISSION.

Your minster is "superannuated," is he? Well, call a parish meeting, and vote him a dismission; hint that his usefulness is gone; that ne is given to repetition; that he puts his hearers to sleep. Turn him adrift, like a blind horse, or a lame house dog. Never mind that he has grown gray in your thankless service — that he has smiled upon your infants at the baptismal font, given them lovingly away in marriage to their heart's chosen, and wept with you when Death's shadow darkened your door. Never mind that he has laid aside his pen, and listened many a time, and oft, with courteous grace to your tedious, prosy conversations, when his moments were like gold dust; never mind that he has patiently and uncomplainingly accepted at your hands, the smallest pittance that would sustain life, because "the Master" whispered in his ear, "Tarry here till I come." Never mind that the wife of his youth, whom he won from a home of luxury, is broken down with privation and fatigue, and *your* thousand unnecessary demands upon her strength, patience, and time. Never mind that his children, at an early age, were exiled from the parsonage roof, because there was not "bread enough and to spare," in their father's

"Your minister is getting 'superannuated,' is he? Well, call a parish meeting, and vote him a dismission."

house. Never mind that his library consists only of a Bible, a Concordance, and a Dictionary; and that to the luxury of a religious newspaper, he has been long years a stranger. Never mind that his wardrobe would be spurned by many a mechanic in our cities; never mind that he has "risen early and sat up late," and tilled the ground with weary limbs, for earthly "manna," while his glorious intellect lay in fetters—*for you.* Never mind all *that;* call a parish meeting, and vote him "superannuated." Don't spare him the starting tear of sensibility, or the flush of wounded pride, by delicately offering to settle a colleague, that your aged pastor may rest on his staff in grateful, gray-haired independence. No! *turn the old patriarch out;* give him time to go to the moss-grown church-yard, and say farewell to his unconscious dead, and then give "the right hand of fellowship" to some beardless, pedantic, noisy college boy, who will save your sexton the trouble of pounding the pulpit cushions; and who will tell you and the Almighty, in his prayers, all the political news of the week.

THE FATAL MARRIAGE.

A VERY pretty girl was Lucy Lee. Don't ask me to de scribe her; stars, and gems, and flowers, have long since been exhausted in depicting heroines. Suffice it to say, Lucy was as pretty a little fairy as ever stepped foot in a slipper or twisted a ringlet.

Of course, Lucy knew she was pretty; else why did the gentlemen stare at her so? Why did Harry Graham send her so many bouquets? Why did Mr. Smith and Mr. Jones try to sit each other out in an evening call? Why were picnics and fairs postponed, if she were engaged or ill? Why did so many young men request an introduction? Why did all tne serenaders come beneath her window? Why was a pew or omnibus never full when she appeared at the door? And last, though not least, why did all the women imitate and hate her so?

We will do Miss Lucy the justice to say, that she bore her blushing honors very meekly. She never flaunted her conquest in the faces of less attractive feminines; no, Lucy was the farthest remove from a coquette; but kind words and bright smiles were as natural to her as fragrance to flowers, or music to birds. She never *tried* to win hearts; and between you and me, I think that's the way she did it.

Grave discussions were often held about Lucy's future husband; the old maids scornfully asserting that "beauties generally pick up a crooked stick at last," while the younger ones cared very little *whom* she married, if she only *were* married and out of *their* way. Meanwhile, Lucy smiled at her own happy thoughts, and sat at her little window on pleasant, summer evenings, watching for Harry, (poor Harry,) who, when he came, was at a loss to know if he had ever given her little heart one flutter, so merrily did she laugh and chat with him. Skillful little Lucy, it was very right you should n't let him peep into *your* heart till he had opened a window in *his own.*

Lucy's papa did n't approve of late hours or lovers; moonlight he considered but another name for rheumatism; at nine o'clock, precisely, he rung the bell each evening for family prayers; and when the Bible came in lovers were expected to go out: in case they were obtuse,—chairs set back against the wall, or an extra lamp blown out, or the fire taken apart, were hints sufficiently broad to be understood; and they generally answered the purpose. Miss Lucy's little lamp, glowing immediately after from her bed-room window, gave the *finale* to the "Mede and Persian" order of Mr. Lee's family arrangements.

Still, Lee house was not a hermitage, by any means. More white cravats and black coats passed over "Deacon" Lee's threshold, than into any hotel in Yankeedom. Little Lucy's mother, too, was a modern Samaritan, never weary of experimenting on their dyspeptic and bronchial affections; while Lucy herself (bless her kind heart) knew full well that two-thirds of them had large families, empty purses, and more Judases and Paul Prys than "Aarons and Hurs" in their congregations.

Among the *habitués* of Lee house, none were so acceptable to Lucy's father, as Mr. Ezekiel Clark, a bachelor of fifty, an ex-minister, and now an agent for some "Benevolent Society." Ezekiel had an immensely solemn face; and behind this convenient mask he was enabled to carry out, undetected, various little plans, ostensibly for the "society's" benefit, but privately — for his own personal aggrandizement. When Ezekiel's opinion was asked, he crossed his hands and feet, and fastened his eyes upon the wall, in an attitude of the deepest abstraction, while his questioner stood on one leg, awaiting, with the most intense anxiety, the decision of such an oracular Solomon. Well, not to weary you, the long and short of it was, that Solomon was a stupid fool, who spent his time trying to humbug the religious public in general, and Deacon Lee in particular, into the belief that had *he* been consulted before this world was made, he could have suggested great and manifold improvements. As to Deacon Lee, no cat ever tossed a poor mouse more dexterously than he played with the deacon's free will; all the while very demurely pocketing the spoils in the shape of "donations" to the "society," with which he appeased his washerwoman and tailor, and transported himself across the country, on trips to Newport, Saratoga, &c., &c.

His favorite plan was yet to be carried out; which was no more or less than a modest request for the deacon's pretty daughter, Lucy, in marriage. Mr. Lee rubbed his chin, and said, "Lucy was nothing but a foolish little girl;" but Ezekiel overruled it, by remarking that that was so much the more reason she should have a husband some years her senior, with some knowledge of the world, qualified to check and advise her; to all of which, after an extra pinch of snuff, and another look into Ezekiel's oracular face, Deacon Lee assented.

Poor little Lucy! Ezekiel knew very well that her father's word was law, and when Mr. Lee announced him as her future husband, she knew she was just as much Mrs. Ezekiel Clark, as if the bridal ring had been already slipped on her fairy finger. She sighed heavily, to be sure, and patted her little foot nervously, and when she handed him his tea, thought he looked older than ever; while Ezekiel swallowed one cup after another, till his eyes snapped and glowed like a panther's in ambush. That night poor Lucy pressed her lips to a faded rose, the gift of Harry Graham; then, cried herself to sleep!

Unbounded was the indignation of Lucy's admirers, when the sanctimonious Ezekiel was announced as the expectant bridegroom. Harry Graham took the first steamer for Europe, railing at "woman's fickleness." (Consistent Harry! when never a word of love had passed his moustached lip.)

Shall I tell you how Ezekiel was transformed into the most ridiculous of lovers? how his self-conceit translated Lucy's indifference into maiden coyness? how he looked often in the glass and thought he was not so *very* old after all? how he advised Lucy to tuck away all her bright curls, because they "looked so childish?" how he named to her papa an "early marriage day," — not that he felt nervous about losing his prize—

oh, no (?)—but because "the society's business required his undivided attention."

Well; Lucy, in obedience to her father's orders, stood up in her snow-white robe, and vowed "to love and cherish" a man just her father's age, with whom she had not the slightest congeniality of taste or feeling. But papa had said it was an excellent match, and Lucy never gainsayed papa; still, her long lashes drooped heavily over her blue eyes, and her hand trembled, and her cheek grew deathly pale, as Ezekiel handed her to the carriage that whirled them rapidly away.

Shall I tell you how long months and years dragged wearily on? how Lucy saw through her husband's mask of hypocrisy and self-conceit? how to indifference succeeded disgust? how Harry Graham returned from Europe, with a fair young English bride? how Lucy grew nervous and hysterical? how Ezekiel soon wearied of his sick wife, and left her in one of those *tombs* for the wretched, an insane hospital? and how she wasted, day by day—then *died*, with only a hired nurse to close those weary blue eyes?

In a quiet corner of the old churchyard where Lucy sleeps, a silver-haired old man, each night at dew-fall, paces to and fro, with remorseless tread, as if by that weary vigil he would fain atone to the unconscious sleeper, for turning her sweet young life to bitterness.

FRANCES SARGEANT OSGOOD.

"I 'm passing through the eternal gates,
Ere June's sweet roses blow."

So sang the dying poetess. The "eternal gates" have closed upon her. Those dark, soul-lit eyes beam upon us no more. "June" has come again, with its "sweet roses," its birds, its zephyrs, its flowers and fragrance. It is such a day as her passionate heart would have reveled in — a day of Eden-like freshness and beauty. I will gather some fair, sweet flowers, and visit her grave.

"Show me Mrs. Fanny Osgood's monument, please," said I to the rough gardener, who was spading the turf in Mount Auburn.

"In Orange Avenue, Ma'am," he replied, respectfully indicating, with a wave of the hand, the path I was to pursue.

Tears started to my eyes, as I trod reverently down the quiet path. The little birds she loved so well, were skimming confidingly and joyously along before me, and singing as merrily as if my heart echoed back their gleeful songs.

I approached the enclosure, as the gardener had directed me. There were five graves. *In which* slept the poetess? for there was *not even a headstone!* The flush of indignant feeling mounted to my temples; the warm tears started from my eyes. *She was forgotten!* Sweet, gifted Fanny! *in her own family burial place she was forgotten!* The stranger from a distance, who had worshiped her genius, might in vain make a pilgrimage to do her honor. I, who had personally known and loved her, had not even the poor consolation of decking the bosom of her grave with the flowers I had gathered; I could not kiss the turf beneath which she is reposing; I could not drop a tear on the sod, 'neath which her remains are mouldering back to their native dust. I could not tell, (though I so longed to know,) in which of the little graves — for there were several— slept her "dear May," her "pure Ellen;" the little, timid, household doves, who folded their weary wings when the parent bird was stricken down, by the aim of the unerring Archer.

Though allied by no tie of blood to the gifted creature, who, *somewhere*, lay sleeping there, I felt the flush of shame mount to my temples, to turn away and leave her dust so unhonored. Oh, God! to be so soon forgotten by all the world! — How can even *earth* look so glad, when such a warm, passionate heart lies cold and pulseless? Poor, gifted, forgotten Fanny! She "still lives" in *my* heart; and, Reader, glance your eye over these touching lines, "written during her last illness," and tell me, Shall she not also live in thine?

A MOTHER'S PRAYER IN ILLNESS.

BY MRS. OSGOOD.

Yes! take them first, my Father! Let my doves
Fold their white wings in Heaven safe on thy breast,
Ere I am called away! I dare not leave
Their young hearts here, their innocent, thoughtless hearts!
Ah! how the shadowy train of future ills
Comes sweeping down life's vista, as I gaze?
My May! my careless, ardent-tempered May;
My frank and frolic child! in whose blue eyes
Wild joy and passionate woe alternate rise;
Whose cheek, the morning in her soul illumes;
Whose little, loving heart, a word, a glance,
Can sway to grief or glee; who leaves her play,
And puts up her sweet mouth and dimpled arms
Each moment, for a kiss, and softly asks,
With her clear, flute-like voice, "Do you love me?"
Ah! *let* me stay! ah! let me still be by,
To answer her, and meet her warm caress!
For, I away, how oft, in this rough world,
That earnest question will be asked in vain!
How oft that eager, passionate, petted heart
Will shrink abashed and chilled, to learn, at length,
The hateful, withering lesson of distrust!
Ah! let her nestle still upon this breast,
In which each shade that dims her darling face
Is felt and answered, as the lake reflects
The clouds that cross yon smiling Heaven

And thou,
My modest Ellen! tender, thoughtful, true,
Thy soul attuned to all sweet harmonies;
My pure, proud, noble Ellen! with thy gifts
Of genius, grace and loveliness half-hidden
'Neath the soft vail of innate modesty:

How will the world's wild discord reach thy heart,
To startle and appal! Thy generous scorn
Of all things base and mean — thy quick, keen taste,
Dainty and delicate — thy instinctive fear
Of those unworthy of a soul so pure,
Thy rare, unchildlike dignity of mien,
All — they will all bring pain to thee, my child.

And oh! if ever their grace and goodness meet
Cold looks and careless greetings, how will all
The latent evil yet undisciplined
In their young, timid souls forgiveness find?
Forgiveness and forbearance, and soft chidings,
Which I, their mother, learn'd of love, to give.
Ah! let me stay! albeit my heart is weary,
Weary and worn, *tired of its own sad beat,*
That finds no echo in this busy world
Which cannot pause to answer — tired, alike,
Of joy and sorrow — of the day and night!
Ah! *take them* FIRST, *my Father! and then me;*
And for their sakes — for their sweet sakes, my Father!
Let me find rest beside them, at thy feet.

BEST THINGS.

I HAVE a horror of " best " things, come they in the shape of shoes, garments, bonnets or rooms. In such a harness my soul peers restlessly out, asking " if I be I." I 'm puzzled to find myself. I become stiff and formal and artificial as my surroundings.

But of all the best things, spare me the infliction of a " best room." Out upon a carpet too fine to tread upon, books too dainty to handle, sofas that but mock your weary limbs, and curtains that dare not face a ray of sunlight!

Had I a house, there should be no " best room " in it. No upholsterer should exorcise comfort, or children, from my door-sill. The free, fresh air should be welcome to play through it; the bright, glad sunshine to lighten and warm it; while fresh mantel-flowers should woo us visits from humming-bird and drowsy bee.

For pictures, I 'd look from out my windows, upon a landscape painted by the Great Master—ever fresh, ever varied, and never marred by envious " cross lights; " now, wreathed in morning's silvery mist; now, basking in noon's broad beam; now, flushed with sunset's golden glow; now, sleeping in dreamy moonlight.

For statuary, fill my house with children — rosy, dimpled, laughing children; now, tossing their sunny ringlets from open brows; now, vailing their merry eyes in slumberous dreams, 'neath snow-white lids; now, sweetly grave, on bended knee, with clasped hands, and lisped words of holy prayer.

Did I say I'd have nothing "*best?*" Pardon me. Sunday should be the best day of all the seven — not ushered in with ascetic form, or lengthened face, or stiff and rigid manners. Sweetly upon the still Sabbath air should float the matin hymn of happy childhood; blending with early song of birds, and wafted upward, with flowers' incense, to Him whose very name is LOVE. It should be no day for puzzling the half-developed brain of childhood with gloomy creeds, to shake the simple faith that prompts the innocent lips to say, "Our Father." It should be no day to sit upright on stiff-backed chairs, till the golden sun should set. No; the birds should not be more welcome to warble, the flowers to drink in the air and sunlight, or the trees to toss their lithe limbs, free and fetterless.

"I'm *so sorry* that to-morrow is Sunday!" From whence does this sad lament issue? From under *your* roof, oh mistaken but well-meaning Christian parents — from the lips of *your* child, whom you compel to listen to two or three unintelligible sermons, sandwiched between Sunday schools, and finished off at nightfall by tedious repetitions of creeds and catechisms, till sleep releases your weary victim! No wonder your child *shudders*, when the minister tells him that "Heaven is one eternal Sabbath."

Oh, mistaken parent! relax the over-strained bow —*prevent the fearful rebound*, and make the Sabbath what God designed it, not a weariness, but the "*best*" and happiest day of all the seven.

THE VESTRY MEETING.

THE clock had just struck seven. The sharp-nosed old sexton of the Steeple-Street Church had arranged the lights to his mind, determined the proper latitude and longitude of Bibles and hymn-books, peeped curiously into the little black stove in the corner, and was now admonishing every person who passed in, of the propriety of depositing the "free soil" on his boots upon the entry door-mat.

In they crept, one after another — pale-faced seamstresses, glad of a reprieve; servant girls, who had turned their backs upon unwashed dishes; mothers, whose "crying babies" were astounding the neighbors; old maids, who had nowhere to spend their long evenings; widowers, who felt an especial solici tude lest any of the sisters should be left to return home unpro tected; girls and boys, who came because they were bid, and who had no very clear idea of the performances; and last, though not least, Ma'am Spy, who thought it her duty to see that none of the church-members were missing, and to inquire every Tuesday night, of her friend Miss Prim, if she did n't consider Mrs. Violet a proper subject for church discipline, because she always had money enough to pay her board bills, although her husband had deserted her.

Then there were the four Misses Nipper, who crawled in as if the vestry floor were paved with live kittens, and who had never been known, for four years, to vary one minute in their attendance, or to keep awake from the first prayer to the doxology.

Then, there was Mrs. John Emmons, who sang the loudest, and prayed the longest, and wore the most expensive bonnets, of any female member in the church — whose name was on every committee, who instituted the *select praying circle* for the more *aristocratic* portion of the parish, and whose pertinacious determination to sit next to her husband at the Tuesday night meeting, was regarded by the uninitiated as a beautiful proof of conjugal devotion; but which, after patient investigation, (between you and me, dear reader,) was found to be for the purpose of arresting his coat-flaps when he popped up to make mental shipwreck of himself by making a speech.

Then, there was Mr. Nobbs, whose remarks were a re-hash of the different religious periodicals of the day, diversified with misapplied texts of Scripture, and delivered with an intonation and gesticulation that would have given Demosthenes fits.

Then, there was Zebedee Falstaff, who accomplished more for the amelioration of the human race (according to his own account) than any man of his aldermanic proportions in the nation, and who delivered (on a hearty supper) a sleepy exhortation on the duties of self-denial and charity, much to the edification of one of his needy relatives, to whose tearful story he had that very day turned a deaf ear.

Then, there was Brother Higgins, who was always "just going" to make a speech, "if brother Thomas had n't so exactly anticipated his sentiments a minute before."

Then, there was Mr. Addison Theophilus Shakspeare Milton, full of poetical and religious inspiration, who soared so high in the realms of fancy, that his hearers lost sight of him.

Then, there was little Dr. Pillbox, who gave us every proof in his weekly exhortations of his knowledge of "drugs," not to mention young Smith, who chased an idea round till he lost it, and then took shelter behind a bronchial difficulty which compelled him, "unwillingly (?) to come to a close."

Then, there were some sincere, good-hearted Christians — respectable citizens — worthy heads of families; but whose lips had never been "touched with a live coal from off the altar."

Where was the pastor? Oh, he was there — a slight, fragile, scholar-like looking man, with a fine intellectual face, exquisitely refined tastes and sensibilities, and the meek spirit of "the Master." Had those slender shoulders no cross to bear? When chance sent some fastidious worldling through that vestry door, did it cost him nothing to watch the smile of contempt curl the stranger's lip, as some uneducated, but well-meaning layman, presented with stammering tongue, in ungrammatical phrase, distorted, one-sided, bigoted views of great truths which *his* eloquent tongue might have made as clear as the noon-day, and as cheering and welcome as heaven's own blessed light, to the yearning, dissatisfied spirit? Oh, is there *nothing* in religion, when it can so subdue the pride of intellect as to enable its professor to disregard the stammering tongue, and sit meekly at the feet of the ignorant disciple because he *is* a disciple?

A BROADWAY SHOP REVERIE.

Forty dollars for a pocket-handkerchief! My dear woman! you need a straight-jacket, even though you may be the fortunate owner of a dropsical purse.

I won't allude to the legitimate use of a pocket-handkerchief; I won't speak of the sad hearts *that* "forty dollars," in the hands of some philanthropist, might lighten; I won't speak of the "crows' feet" that will be penciled on your fair face, when your laundress carelessly sticks the point of her remorseless smoothing iron through the flimsy fabric, or the constant espionage you must keep over your treasure, in omnibuses, or when promenading; but I *will* ask you how many of the lords of creation, for whose especial benefit you array yourself, will know whether that cobweb rag fluttering in your hand cost forty dollars, or forty cents?

Pout if you like, and toss your head, and say that you "don't dress to please the gentlemen." I don't hesitate to tell you (at this distance from your finger nails) that is a downright—— mistake! and that the enormous sums most women expend for articles, the cost of which few, save shop-keepers and butterfly feminines, know, is both astounding and ridiculous.

True, you have the sublime gratification of flourishing your forty-dollar handkerchief, of sporting your twenty-dollar "Honiton collar," or of flaunting your thousand-dollar shawl, before the envious and admiring eyes of some weak sister, who has made the possible possession of the article in question a profound and lifetime study; you may pass, too, along the crowded *pavé*, laboring under the hallucination, that every passer-by appreciates your dry-goods value. *Not a bit of it!* Yonder is a group of gentlemen. You pass them in your promenade; they glance carelessly at your *tout-ensemble*, but their eyes rest admiringly on a figure close behind you. It will chagrin you to learn that this locomotive loadstone has on a seventy-five cent hat, of simple straw — a dress of lawn, one shilling per yard — a twenty-five cent collar, and a shawl of the most unpretending price and fabric.

All these items you take in at a glance, as you turn upon her your aristocratic eye of feminine criticism to extract, if possible, the talismanic secret of her magnetism. What is it? Let me tell you. Nature, willful dame, has an aristocracy of her own, and in one of her independent freaks has so daintily fashioned your rival's limbs, that the meanest garb could not *mar* a grace, nor the costliest fabric *add* one. Compassionating her slender purse, nature has also added an artistic eye, which accepts or rejects fabrics and colors with unerring taste; hence her apparel is always well chosen and harmonious, producing the *effect* of a rich toilet at the cost of "a mere song;" and as she sweeps majestically past, one understands why Dr. Johnson pronounced a woman to be "perfectly dressed when one could never remember what she wore."

Now, I grant you, it is very provoking to be eclipsed by a star *without a name* — moving out of the sphere of "upper-ten"-dom — a woman who never wore a "camel's hair shawl," or owned a diamond in her life; after the expense you have incurred, too, and the fees you have paid to Madame Pompadour and Stewart for the first choice of their Parisian fooleries. It is harrowing to the sensibilities. I appreciate the awkwardness of your position; still, my compassion jogs my invention vainly for a remedy — unless, indeed, you consent to crush such democratic presumption, by *labelling* the astounding price of the dry-goods upon your aristocratic back.

H

"THE OLD WOMAN."

Look into yonder window! What do you see? Nothing *new*, surely; nothing but what the angels have looked smilingly down upon since the morning stars first sang together; nothing but a loving mother hushing upon her faithful breast a wailing babe, whose little life hangs by a slender thread. Mortal lips have said, "The boy must die!"

A mother's *hope* never dies. She clasps him closer to her breast, and gazes upward; — food and sleep and rest are forgotten, so that that little flickering taper die not out. Gently upon her soft, warm breast she wooes for it baby slumbers; long, weary nights, up and down the cottage floor she paces, soothing its restless moaning. Suns rise and set — stars pale — seasons come and go; — she heeds them not, so that those languid eyes but beam brightness. Down the meadow — by the brook — on the hill-side — she seeks with him the health-restoring breeze.

God be praised! — health comes at last! What joy to see the rosy flush mantle on the pallid cheek! — what joy to see the shrunken limbs grow round with health! — what joy to see the damp, thin locks grow crisp and glossy!

What matter though the knitting lie neglected, or the spinning-wheel be dumb, so that the soaring kite or bouncing ball but please his boyish fancy, and prompt the gleeful shout? What matter that the coarser fare be *hers*, so that the daintier morsel pass *his* rosy lip? What matter that *her* robe be threadbare, so that *his* graceful limbs be clad in Joseph's rainbow coat? What matter that *her* couch be hard, so that *his* sunny head rest nightly on a downy pillow? What matter that *her* slender purse be empty, so that *his* childish heart may never know denial?

Years roll on. That loving mother's eye grows dim; her glossy locks are silvered; her limbs are sharp and shrunken; her footsteps slow and tottering. And the boy?—the cherished Joseph?—he of the bold, bright eye, and sinewy limb, and bounding step? Surely, from his kind hand shall flowers be strewn on the dim, downward path to the dark valley; surely will her son's strong arm be hers to lean on; his voice of music sweeter to her dull ear than seraphs' singing.

No, no!—the hum of busy life has struck upon his ear, drowning the voice of love. He has become a MAN! refined, fastidious!—and to his forgetful, unfilial heart, (God forgive him,) the mother who bore him is only—"*the old woman!*"

SUNDAY MORNING AT THE DIBDINS.

"JANE," (suddenly exclaims Mrs. Dibdin,) "do you know it is nearly time for your Sabbath School to commence? I hope you have committed your hymns and commandments to memory. Put on your little jet bracelet, and your ruffled pantalettes. Now, say the third commandment, while I fix your curls. It does seem to me as if your hair never curls half as well on Sundays as on week days. Mind, you ask Letty Brown where her mother bought that cunning little straw hat of hers, — not in Sabbath School, of course — that would be very wicked — but after it is over, as you walk along to church.

"Jane, what 's the chief end of man? Don't know? Well, it's the most astonishing thing that that Assembly's Catechism don't stay in your head any better! It seems to go into one ear and out of the other. Now pay particular attention while I tell you what the chief end of man is. The chief end of man is — is —well—I—why don't you hold still? — you are always putting a body out! You had better run up stairs and get your book. Here, stop a minute, and let me tie your sash straight. Pink is very becoming to you, Jane; you inherit your mother's blonde beauty. Come away from that glass, Jane, this minute; don't you know it is wicked to look in the glass on Sunday? See if you can say your 'creed' that your Episcopal teacher wants you to learn. Come; 'I believe'—(In less than one week your toes will be through those drab gaiters, Jane.) Goodness, if there is n't the bell! Why did n't you get your lesson Saturday evening? Oh! I recollect; you were at dancing school. Well—you need n't say anything about that to your teacher; because—because there's 'a time to dance,' and a time to go to meeting, and *now* it is meeting time; so, come here, and let me roll that refractory ringlet over my finger once more, and then, do you walk *solemnly* along to church, as a baptised child should.

"Here! stop a bit!—you may wear this coral bracelet of mine, if you won't lose it. There; now you look *most* as pretty as your mother did, when she was your age. Don't toss your head so, Jane; people will call you vain; and you know I have always told you that it makes very little difference how a little girl *looks*, if she is only a little Christian. There, good-bye;—repeat your catechism, going along; and don't let the wind blow your hair out of curl."

SUNDAY NOON AT THE DIBDINS.

(*Mr. Dibdin reading a pile of business letters, fresh from the post-office; Mrs. Dibdin, in a pearl-colored brocade and lace ruffles, devouring "Bleak House."*)

Mrs. Dibdin.—"Jane, is it possible I see you on the holy Sabbath day, with Mother Goose's Melodies? Put it away, this minute, and get your Bible. There 's the pretty story of Joseph building the ark, and Noah in the lion's den, and Isaac killing his brother Cain, and all that."

Jane. — "Well, but, mamma, you know I can't spell the big words. Won't you read it to me?"

Mrs. Dibdin. — "I am busy reading now, my dear; go and ask your papa."

Jane. — "Please, papa, will you read to me in my little Bible? mamma is busy."

Mr. Dibdin. — "My dear, will you be kind enough to pull that bell for Jane's nursery maid? — she is getting troublesome."

* * * * * * * *

Exit Miss Jane to the nursery, to listen to Katy's and her friend Bridget's account of their successful flirtations with John O'Calligan and Michael O'Donahue.

ITEMS OF TRAVEL.

"All the world and his wife" are travelling; and a nice day it is to commence a journey. How neat and tasteful those ladies look in their drab travelling dresses; how self-satisfied their cavaliers, freshly shaved and shampooed, in their brown linen over-alls. What apoplectic looking carpet-bags; full of newspapers, and oranges, and bon-bons, and novels, and night-caps! Saratoga, Newport, Niagara, White Hills, Mammoth Cave — of these, the ladies chatter.

Well, here come the cars. Band-boxes, trunks, baskets, and bundles are counted, and checks taken; a grave discussion is solemnly held, as to which side of the cars the sun shines on; seats are chosen with due deliberation, and the locomotive does its own "puffing" to the bystanders, and darts off.

It is noon! How intense the heat; how annoying the dust; how crowded the cars; how incessant the cries of that poor tired baby! The ladies' bonnets are getting awry, their fore-heads flushed, and their smooth tresses unbecomingly *frowsed*, (see Fern Dictionary.) Now their little chattering tongues have a reprieve, for Slumber has laid her leaden finger on each drooping eyelid: even Alexander Smith's new poem has slidden from between taper fingers. Dream not lovingly of the author, fair sleeper: poets and butterflies lose their brilliancy when caught.

How intensely ugly men look asleep! doubled up like so many jack-knives — sorry looking "blades" — with their mouths wide open, and their limbs twisted into all sorts of Protean shapes. Stay; there 's one in yonder corner who is an exception. That man knows it is becoming to him to go to sleep. He has laid his head against the window and taken off his hat, that the wind might lift those black curls from his broad white brow; — he knows that his eye-lashes are long and dark, and that his finely chiselled lips need no defect-concealing moustache; — he knows that he can afford to turn towards us his fine profile, with its classical outline; — he knows that his cravat is well tied, and that the hand upon which he supports his cheek is both well-formed and daintily white. Wonder if he knows anything else?

We halt suddenly. "Back! back!" says the conductor. The sleepers start to their feet; the old maid in the corner gives a little hysterical shriek; brakemen, conductor, and engineer jump off, push back their hats, and gaze nervously down the road. "What 's the matter?" echo scores of anxious voices. "What 's the matter?" Oh, nothing; only a mother made childless: only a little form — five minutes ago bounding with happy life — lying a mangled corpse upon the track. The engineer says, with an oath, that "the child was a fool not to get out of the way," and sends one of the hands back to pick up the dismembered limbs and carry them to its mother, who forbade even the winds of heaven to blow too roughly on her boy; then he gives the "iron horse" a fresh impetus, and we dash on; imagination paints a scene in yonder house which many a frantic parent will recognize; and from which (even in thought) we turn shuddering away — while the weary mother in the corner covers her fretful babe with kisses, and thanks God, through her tears, that her loving arms are still its sheltering fold.

NEWSPAPER-DOM.

It is beyond my comprehension how Methusaleh lived nine hundred and sixty-nine years without a newspaper; or, what the mischief Noah did, during that "forty days" shower, when he had exhausted the study of Natural History. It makes me yawn to think of it. Or what later generations did, the famished half-hour before meals; or, when traveling, when the old stage-coach crept up a steep hill, some dusty hot summer noon. Shade of Franklin! how they must have been *ennuyéd!*

How did they ever know when flour had "riz"—or what was the market price of pork, small tooth combs, cotton, wool, and molasses? How did they know whether Queen Victoria had "made her brother an uncle or an aunt?" What christianized gouty old men and snappish old ladies? What kept the old maids from making mince-meat of pretty young girls? What did love-sick damsels do for "sweet bits of poetry" and "touching continued stories?" Where did their papas find a solace when the coffee was muddy, the toast smoked, and the beef-steak raw, or done to leather? What did cab-drivers do, while waiting for a tardy patron? What did draymen do, when there was "a great calm" at the dry-goods store of Go Ahead & Co.? What screen did husbands dodge behind, when their wives asked them for money?

Some people define happiness to be one thing, and some another. I define it to be a room "carpeted and furnished" with "exchanges," with a place cleared in the middle for two arm-chairs — one for a clever editor, and one for yourself. I say it is to take up those papers, one by one, and laugh over the funny things and skip the stupid ones, — to admire the ingenuity of would-be literary lights, who pilfer one half their original (?) ideas, and steal the remainder. I say it is to shudder a thanksgiving that you are not in the marriage list, and to try, for the hundredth time, to solve the riddle: how can each paper that passes through your hands be "the best and cheapest periodical in the known world?"

I say it is to look round an editorial sanctum, inwardly chuckling at the forlorn appearance it makes without feminine fingers to keep it tidy: to see the looking-glass veiled with cobwebs; the dust on the desk thick enough to write your name in; the wash-bowl and towel mulatto color; the soap liquified to a jelly, (editors like soft soap!); the table covered with a heterogeneous mass of manuscripts, and paper folders, and wafers, and stamps, and blotting-paper, and envelopes, and tailors' bills, and letters complimentary, belligerent and pacific.

I say it is to hear the editor complain, with a frown, of the heat and his headache; to conceal a smile, while you suggest the *probability* of relief if a window should be opened; to see him start at your superior profundity; to hear him say, with a groan, how much "proof" he has to read, before he can leave for home; to take off your gloves and help him correct it; — to hear him say, there is a book for review, which he has not time to look over; to take a folder and cut the leaves, and affix guide-boards for notice at all the fine passages; to see him kick over an innocent chair, because he cannot get hold of the right word for an editorial; to feel (while you help him to it) very much like the mouse who gnawed the lion out of the net, and then to take up his paper some days after, and find a paragraph endorsed by him, "deploring the intellectual inferiority of women."

That 's what I call happiness!

HAVE WE ANY MEN AMONG US?

WALKING along the street the other day, my eye fell upon this placard, —

MEN WANTED.

Well; they have been "wanted" for some time; but the article is not in the market, although there are plenty of spurious imitations. Time was, when a lady could decline writing for a newspaper without subjecting herself to paragraphic attacks from the editor, invading the sanctity of her private life. Time was, when she could decline writing without the editor's revenging himself, by asserting falsely that "he had often refused her offered contributions?" Time was, when if an editor heard a vague rumor affecting a lady's reputation, he did not endorse it by republication, and then meanly screen himself from responsibility by adding, "we presume, however, that this is only an *on dit!*" Time was, when a lady could be a successful authoress, without being obliged to give an account to the dear public of the manner in which she appropriated the proceeds of her honest labors. Time was, when whiskered braggadocios in railroad cars and steamboats did not assert, (in blissful ignorance that they were looking the lady authoress straight in the face!) that they were "on the most intimate terms of friendship with her!" Time was, when *milk-and-water husbands and relatives* did not force a defamed woman to unsex herself in the manner stated in the following paragraph:

"MAN SHOT BY A YOUNG WOMAN.— One day last week, a young lady of good character, daughter of Col. ——, having been calumniated by a young man, called upon him, armed with a revolver. The slanderer could not, or did not deny his allegations; whereupon she fired, inflicting a dangerous if not a fatal wound in his throat."

Yes; it is very true that there are "MEN wanted." Wonder how many 1854 will furnish?

HOW TO CURE THE BLUES.

And so you have "the blues," hey! Well, I pity you! No I don't either; there 's no need of it. If one friend proves a Judas, never mind! plenty of warm, generous, nice hearts left for the winning. If you are poor, and have to sell your free agency for a sixpence a week to some penurious relative, or be everlastingly thankful for the gift of an old garment that won't hang together till you get it home! go to work like ten thousand evil spirits, and make yourself *independent!* and see with what a different pair of spectacles you 'll get looked at! Nothing like it! You can have everything on earth you want, when you don't *need* anything.

Don't the Bible say, "To him that hath shall be given?" No mistake, you see. When the wheel turns round with you on the top, (saints and angels!) you can do anything you like—play any sort of a prank — pout or smile, be grave or gay, saucy or courteous, it will pass muster! You never need trouble yourself, — can't do anything wrong if you try. At the most, it will only be an "eccentricity!" But you never need be such a fool as to expect that anybody will find out you are a *diamond* till you get a *showy setting!* You 'll get knocked and cuffed around, and roughly handled, with paste and tinsel, and rubbish, till that auspicious moment arrives. Then! won't all the sheaves bow down to your sheaf? — not one rebellious straggler left in the field! But stay a little.

In your adversity, found you one faithful heart that stood firmly by your side and shared your tears, when skies were dark, and your pathway thorny and steep, and summer friends fell off like autumn leaves? By all that 's noble in a woman's heart, give that one the first place in it now. Let the world see *one* heart proof against the sunshine of prosperity. You can't repay such a friend — all the mines of Golconda could n't do it. But in a thousand delicate ways, prompted by a woman's unerring tact, let your heart come forth gratefully, generously, lovingly. Pray heaven he be on the shady side of fortune — that your heart and hand may have a wider field for gratitude to show itself. Extract every thorn from his pathway, chase away every cloud of sorrow, brighten his lonely hours, smooth the pillow of sickness, and press lovingly his hand in death.

RAIN IN THE CITY.

Patter, patter, patter! down comes the city shower, on dusty and heated pavements; gleefully the willow trees shake out their long green tresses, and make their toilettes in the little mirror pools beneath. The little child runs out, with outspread palm, to catch the cool and pearly drops. The weary laborer, drawing a long, grateful breath, bares the flushed brow of toil; boyhood, with bare and adventurous foot, wades through gutter rivers, forgetful of birch, and bread and butter. Ladies skutter tiptoe, with uplifted skirts, to the shelter of some friendly omnibus; gentlemen, in the independent consciousness of corduroys, take their time and umbrellas, while the poor jaded horses shake their sleek sides, but do not say *neigh* to their impromptu shower-bath.

The little sparrows twitter their thanks from the dripping eaves, circling the piazza, then laving their speckled breasts at the little lakelets in the spout. Old Towser lies with his nose to the door-mat, sniffing " the cool," with the philosophy of Diogenes. Petrarch sits in the parlor with his Laura, too happy when some vivid lightning flash gives him an excuse for closer quarters. Grandpapa puts on his spectacles, walks to the win dow, and taking a look at the surrounding clouds, says, " How this rain will make the corn grow." The old maid opposite sets out a single geranium, scraggy as herself, invoking some double blossoms. Forlorn experimenter! even a spinster's affections must centre somewhere.

See that little pinafore mariner stealing out, with one eye on the nursery window, to navigate his pasteboard boat in the street pools. There 's a flash of sunshine! What a glorious rainbow! The little fellow tosses his arms aloft, and gazes at it. Ten to one, the little Yankee, instead of admiring its gorgeous splendor, is wishing he could invert it for a swing, and seizing it at both ends, sweep through the stars with it. Well, it is nothing new for a child to like "the *milky way*."

Fair weather again! piles of heavy clouds are drifting by, leaving the clear blue sky as serene as when "the morning stars first sang together." Nature's gems sparkle lavishly on glossy leaf and swaying branch, on bursting bud and flower; while the bow of peace melts gently and imperceptibly away, like the dying saint into the light of Heaven.

Oh, earth *is* gloriously fair! Alas! that the trail of the serpent should be over it all!

MRS. WEASEL'S HUSBAND.

"A woman, a dog, and a walnut tree,
The more they are beaten the better they be."

"ANY man who believes that, had better step into my shoes," said little Mr. Weasel. "I suppose I 'm what you call 'the head of the family,' but I should n't know it if somebody did n't tell me of it. Heigho! who 'd have thought it five and twenty years ago? Did n't I stifle a tremendous strong penchant for Diana Dix, (never smoked, I remember, for four hours after it,) because I had my private suspicions she 'd hold the reins in spite of my teeth, and so I offered myself to little Susey Snow, (mistake in her name, by the way.) You might have spanned her round the waist, or lifted her with one hand. She never looked anybody in the face when they spoke to her, and her voice was as soft as —— my brains! I declare, it 's unaccountable how deceitful female nature is! Never was so taken in in my life; she 's a regular Vesuvius crater! Her will? (don't mention it!) Try to pry up the Alps with a cambric needle! If she 'd only fly into a passion, I think I could venture to pluck up a little spirit; but that cool, determined, never-say-die look! would turn Cayenne pepper to oil. It wilts *me* right down, like a cabbage leaf. I 'd as lief face a loaded cannon! I wish I could go out evenings; but she won't let me. Tom Jones asked me yesterday why I was n't at Faneuil Hall the night before. I told him I had the bronchitis. He saw through it! Sent me a pair of reins the next day,—'said to be a certain cure!' Ah! it's very well for *him* to laugh, but it's no joke to me. I suppose it's time to feed that baby; Mrs. Weasel will be home pretty soon, from the 'Woman's Rights Convention.' No, I won't, either; I'll give it some paregoric, and run up garret and smoke one cigar. I feel as though I *could n't look a humming-bird in the eye!* Nice cigar!—*very* nice! What a fool I am to be ordered round by a little blue-eyed woman, three feet high! I'm a very good looking fellow, and I won't stand it! Is n't that little Weasel as much her baby as it is mine? Certainly."

"M-r. W-e-a-s-e-l!"

"Hem,—my—dear—(oh! that eye of hers!)—you see, my dear, (there, I won't do it again, Mrs. Weasel.) How's 'the Convention,' dear? Carried the day, I hope?—made one of your smart speeches, hey? 'Tis n't every man owns such a chain-lightning wife;—look out for your rights, dear; (deuce knows *I* dare not!")

COUNTRY SUNDAY vs. CITY SUNDAY.

'Tis Sunday in the city.

The sun glares murkily down, through the smoky and stench-laden atmosphere, upon the dirty pavements; newsboys, with clamorous cries, are vending their wares; milkmen rattle over the pavements, and startle drowsy sleepers by their shrill whoopings; housemaids are polishing door knobs, washing sidewalks, and receiving suspicious looking baskets and parcels from contiguous groceries and bakeshops.

The sun rolls on his course; purifying the air and benignly smiling upon all the dwellers in the city, as though he would gently win them from unholy purposes to heavenly meditations and pursuits.

— And now the streets are filled with a motley show of silks, satins, velvets, feathers and jewels — while carriages and vehicles of every description roll past, freighted with counter-freed youths and their Dulcineas, bent upon a holiday. Hundreds of "drinking saloons" belch forth their pestiferous breath, upon which is borne, to the ear of the passer-by, (perhaps a lady or tender child,) the profane curse and obscene gibe; and from their portals reel intoxicated brutes, who once were men. Military companies march to and fro; now, at slow and solemn pace, to the mournful strains of a dead-march; now, (having rid themselves of the corpse of their dead comrade,) they gaily "step out," blithe and merry, to the cheering strains of an enlivening quickstep, based on an Ethiopian melody; the frivolous tones blending discordantly with the chimes of the Sabbath bells. And stable-keepers, oyster and ice-cream venders, liquor sellers, *et id omne genus*, are reaping a golden harvest, upon which the "Lord of the Sabbath" shall, sooner or later, send "a blight and a mildew."

'Tis Sunday in the country.

Serene and majestic, in the distance, lie the blue, cloud-capped hills; while, at their base, the silver stream winds gracefully, sparkling in the glad sunlight. Now the fragrant branches stir with feathered life; and one clear, thrilling carol lifts the finger from the dumb lip of Nature, heralding a full orchestra of untaught choristers, which plume their wings, and soaring, seem to say, Praise Him! praise Him!

Obedient to the sweet summons, the silver-haired old man and rosy child, along grassy, winding paths, hie to the little village church. On the gentle maiden's kindly arm leans the bending form of "four score years and ten," gazing, with dimmed but grateful eye, on leafy stem, and bursting bud, and full-blown flower; or, listening to the wind dallying with the tall tree-tops, or kissing the fields of golden grain, which wave their graceful recognition, as it sweeps by on its fragrant path.

And now, slowly the Sabbath sun sinks beneath the western hills in gold and purple glory. Gently the dew of peace descends on closed eyes and flowers; while holy stars creep softly out, to keep their tireless watch o'er happy hearts and Sabbath-loving homes.

SOBER HUSBANDS.

"**If your husband looks grave, let him alone; don't disturb or annoy him.**"

Oh, pshaw! were I married, the soberer my husband looked, the more fun I'd rattle about his ears. *Do n't disturb him!* I guess so! I'd salt his coffee — and pepper his tea — and sugar his beef-steak — and tread on his toes — and hide his newspaper — and sew up his pockets — and put pins in his slippers — and dip his cigars in water,— and I would n't stop for the great Mogul, till I had shortened his long face to my liking. Certainly, he'd "get vexed;" there would n't be any fun in teasing him if he did n't; and that would give his melancholy blood a good, healthful start; and his eyes would snap and sparkle, and he'd say, "Fanny, WILL you be quiet or not?" and I should laugh, and pull his whiskers, and say decidedly, "*Not!*" and then I should tell him he had n't the slightest idea how handsome he looked when he was vexed, and then he would pretend not to hear the compliment — but would pull up his dickey, and take a sly peep in the glass (for all that!) and then he'd begin to grow amiable, and get off his stilts, and be just as agreeable all the rest of the evening *as if he was n't my husband;* and all because I did n't follow that stupid bit of advice "to let him alone." Just as if *I* did n't know! Just imagine ME, Fanny, sitting down on a cricket in the corner, with my forefinger in my mouth, looking out the sides of my eyes, and waiting till that man got ready to speak to me! You can see at once it would be — be —. Well, the amount of it is, *I should n't do it!*

OUR STREET.

Sing away, little bird! only you, the trees, and myself, are stirring, but you have an appreciative audience. Your sweet carol and the graceful waving of yonder tree, as the soft wind turns up its silver-lined leaves in the sunlight, fill my heart with a quiet gladness.

Whom have we here? with ragged skirt, bare mud-begrimm'd feet and ankles, tattered shawl, and tangled masses of hair fluttering round a face ploughed deep with time and trouble. See — she stoops, and, stretching her skeleton fingers towards the gutter, grasps some refuse rags and paper, and thrusts them greedily into the dirty sack she bears upon her shoulders. Good heavens! that dirty mass of rags a *woman?* How wearily she leans against yonder tree, gazing upward into its branches! Perhaps that little bird's matin song has swept some chord for long years untouched in that callous heart; telling her of the shelter of a happy home, where Plenty sat at the board and Love kept guard at the threshold. Oh! who can tell? One more song, my little bird, ere she goes; not so *mockingly* joyous, but sweet, and soft, and low — a requiem for blighted youth and blasted hopes; for know that the blue sky to whose arch you soar, bends over misery enough to make the bright seraphs weep.

OUR STREET.

Bless me! what yell is that? "Yeei — ho — oe — yeei — ho." It is only a milkman, and that horrid cry simply means, "Milk for sale." What a picture of laziness is the vender! Jump off your cart, man, thump on the kitchen door with your milk-dipper, and rouse that sleepy cook who is keeping you waiting her pleasure; that's the way to do business: pshaw! your manliness must have been diluted with your milk. One by one they emerge, the dead-and-alive looking housemaids, dragging their brooms after them lazily and helplessly, and bandy words with the vexed milkman, and gossip with each other, as they rest their chins on their broom-handles, on "kitchen cabinet" affairs.

Here comes an Italian, balancing a shelf-load of plaster Cupids and Venuses, and dove-circled vases. How mournfully his dark eyes look out from beneath his tasseled cap, as he lifts his burden from his head for a momentary reprieve. They tell of weary feet, a heavy heart, and a light purse. They tell, with a silent reproach, that our hearts are as cold as our clime. Oh! not *all*, good Pietro! For your sake, I'll make myself mistress of that sleeping child; though, truth to say, the sculptor who moulded it has most wofully libelled Nature. Would I could see the sunny skies upon which your dark eyes first opened, and all the glorious forms that beauty wears in your vine-clad home beyond the seas.

How the pedestrians hurry along! — merchants to their cares and their counting-rooms, and shop-girls and seamstresses to their prisons. Here comes a group of pale-faced city children, on their way to school. God bless the little unfortunates!

Their little feet should be crushing the strawberries, ripe and sweet, on some sunny hill-slope, where breath of new-mown hay and clover blossoms would give roses to their cheeks and strength and grace to their cramped and half-developed limbs. Poor little creatures! they never saw a patch of blue sky bigger than their satchels, or a blade of grass that dared to grow without permission from the mayor, aldermen and common council. Poor little skeletons! tricked out like the fashion-prints, and fed on diluted skim-milk and big dictionaries. I pity you.

A hand-organ! ground by a modern Peter Schemmel, and accompanied by a woman whose periphery it would be vain to compute by inches, singing,

"I'd be a butterfly."

Ye gods and graces! if ye heed her prayer, grant that she alight not on my *two-lips!* Now she is warbling,

"Home! sweet home,"

as if she was n't making it for me, this minute, a perfect place of torment! Avaunt! thou libel upon feminity! — creep into corduroys and apply for the office of town crier.

A funeral! That is nothing uncommon in a densely popu lated city; so, nobody turns to look, as it winds along, slowly, as will the sad future to that young husband — that father of an hour. Sad legacy to him, those piles of tiny robes, and dainty little garments, whose elaborate and delicate embroidery was purchased at such a fearful price. Nature will have her revenge for a reckless disregard of her laws: so, there she lies, the young mother, with the long-looked-for babe upon her girlish breast. Sad comment upon a foolish vanity.

What have we here? — A carriage at the door? Ah! I recollect; there was a wedding at that house last night—lights flashing, music swelling — white arms gleaming through tissue textures, and merry voices breaking in upon my slumbers late in the small hours.

Ah yes — and this is the bride's leave-taking. How proud and important that young husband looks, as he stands on the steps, with the bride's traveling shawl upon his arm, giving his orders to the coachman! Now he casts an impatient glance back through the open door into the hall, half jealous of the tear sparkling in the young wife's eye, as the mother presses her tenderly to her breast, as the father lays the hand of blessing on her sunny head, and brothers and sisters, half glad, half sad, offer their lips for a good-bye kiss.

Hurry her not away! Not even the heart she has singled out from all the world to lean upon, can love so fondly, so truly, as those she leaves behind. Dark days may come, when love's sunshine shall be o'erclouded by cares and sickness, from which young manhood, impatient, shrinks. *Let her linger:* so shall your faith in her young wifely love be strengthened by such strong filial yearning for these, her cradle watchers. Let her linger: silver hairs mingle in the mother's tresses; the father's dark eye grows dim with age, and insatiate Death heeds nor prayer, nor tear, nor lifted eye of supplication. Let her linger.

New-York! New-York! who but thyself would have tolerated for twelve mortal hours, with the thermometer at 90 degrees, that barrel of refuse fish and potatoes, sour bread and damaged meat, questionable vegetables and antique puddings, steaming on that sunny sidewalk, in the forlorn hope that some pig's patron might be tempted, by the odoriferous hash, to venture on its transportation. Know, then, O pestiferous Gotham, that half a score of these gentry, after having sounded it with a long pole to the bottom, for the benefit of my olfactories, have voted it a nuisance to which even a pig might make a *gutter*-al remonstrance. Oh! Marshal Tukey, if California yet holds you, in the name of the Asiatic cholera, and *my* "American constitution," recross the Isthmus and exorcise that barrel!

Look on yonder door-step. See that poor, worn creature seated there, with a puling infant at her breast, from whence it draws no sustenance: on either side are two little creatures, apparently asleep, with their heads in her lap. Their faces are very pallid, and their little limbs have nothing of childhood's rounded symmetry and beauty. "Perhaps she is an impostor," says Prudence, seizing my purse-strings, "getting up that tableau for just such impressible dupes as yourself." "Perhaps she is *not*," says Feeling; "perhaps at this moment despair whispers in her tempted ear 'curse God and die!' Oh! then, how sad to have 'passed her by, on the other side!'" Let *me* be "duped," rather than that wan face should come between my soul and Heaven.

WHEN YOU ARE ANGRY.

"When you are angry, take three breaths before you speak."

I COULD N'T do it, said Mrs. Penlimmon. Long before that time I should be as placid as an oyster. "Three breaths!" I could double Cape Horn in that time. I 'm telegraphic,—if I had to stop to reflect, I should never be saucy. I can't hold anger any more than an April sky can retain showers; the first thing I know, the sun is shining. You may laugh, but that 's better than one of your foggy dispositions, drizzling drops of discomfort a month on a stretch; no computing whether you 'll have anything but gray clouds overhead the rest of your life. No: a good heavy clap of thunder for me — a lightning flash; then a bright blue sky and a clear atmosphere, and I am ready for the first flower that springs up in my path.

"Three breaths!" how absurd! as if people, when they get excited, ever *have* any breath, or if they have, are conscious of it. I should like to see the Solomon who got off that sage maxim. I should like better still to give him an opportunity to test his own theory! It 's very refreshing to see how good people can be, when they have no temptation to sin; how they can sit down and make a code of laws for the world in general and sinners in particular.

"Three breaths!" I would n't give a three-cent piece for anybody who is that long about anything. The days of stage coaches have gone by. Nothing passes muster now but comets, locomotives and telegraph wires. Our forefathers and foremothers would have to hold the hair on their heads if they should wake up in 1854. They 'd be as crazy as a cat in a shower-bath, at all our whizzing and rushing. Nice old snails! It 's a question with me whether I should have crept on at their pace, had I been a cotemporary. Christopher Columbus would have discovered the New World much quicker than he did, had I been at his elbow.

LITTLE BESSIE;

OR, MISS PRIM'S MODEL SCHOOL.

School is out! What stretching of limbs; what unfettering of tongues and heels; what tossing-up of pinafores and primers; what visions of marbles, and hoops, and dolls, and apples, and candy, and gingerbread! How welcome the fresh air; how bright the sunshine; how tempting the grassy play-ground! Ah, there's a drop of rain — there's another; there's a thunder clap! "Just as school is out—how provoking!" echo a score of voices; and the pouting little prisoners huddle together in the school-house porch, and console themselves by swapping jack-knives and humming tops, and telling marvellous stories of gypsies and giants; while Miss Prim, the dyspeptic teacher, shakes her head and the ferule, and declares that the former will "fly into fifty pieces;" upon which some of the boys steal out of doors and amuse themselves by sounding the puddles with their shoes, while others slyly whittle the desks, or draw caricatures on their slates, of Miss Prim's long nose.

Drip, drip — spatter, spatter! How the rain comes down, as if it could n't help it; no prospect of "holding up."

Here come messengers from anxious mothers, with India

rubbers, extra tippets, and umbrellas; and there 's a chaise at the door, for Squire Lenox's little rosy daughter; and a wagon for the two Prince girls; and a stout Irish girl, with a blanket shawl, to carry home little lame Minnie May, who is as fragile as a lily, and just as sweet. And there 's a servant man for Master Simpkins, the fat dunce with the embroidered jacket, whose father owns "the big Hotel, and wishes his son to have a seat all by himself."

And now they are all gone; — all save little Bessie Bell, the new scholar,— a little four-year-older, who is doing penance over in the corner for "a misdemeanor."

Bessie's mother is a widow. She has known such bright, sunny days, in the shelter of a happy home, with a dear arm to lean upon! Now, her sweet face is sad and care-worn, and when she speaks, her voice has a heart-quiver in it: but, somehow, when she talks to you, you do not notice that her dress is faded, or her bonnet shabby and rusty. You instinctively touch your hat to her, and treat her very courteously, as if she were a fine lady.

As I said before, this is little Bessie's first day at school; for, she is light and warmth and sunshine to her broken-hearted mother. But, little Bessie must have bread to eat. A shop woman offered her mother a small pittance to come and help her a part of every day; but she is not to bring her child; so, Bessie must go to school, to be out of harm's way, and her mother tells Miss Prim, as she seats her on the hard bench, that "she is very timid and tender-hearted;" and then she kisses Bessie's little quivering lip, and leaves her with a heavy heart.

Bessie dare not look up for a few minutes; — it is all very odd and strange, and if she were not so frightened she would cry aloud. By-and-by she gains a little courage, and peeps out from beneath her drooping eye-lashes. Her little pinafore neighbor gives her a sweet smile—it makes her little heart so happy, that she throws her little dimpled arms about her neck and says, (out loud) "I love you!"

Poor, affectionate little Bessie! she did n't know that that was a "misdemeanor;" nor had she ever seen that bug-bear, a "School Committe." Miss Prim had; — and Miss Prim never wasted her lungs talking; so, she leisurely untied her black silk apron from her virgin waist, and proceeded to make an African of little Bessie, by pinning it tightly over her face and head — an invention which herself and "the Committee" considered the *ne plus ultra* of discipline. Bessie struggled, and said she "never would kiss anybody again — never — never;" but Miss Prim was inexorable, and, as her victim continued to utter smothered cries, Miss Prim told her "that she would keep her after the other children had gone home."

One class after another recited; Bessie's sobs became less loud and frequent, and Miss Prim flattered herself, now that they had ceased altogether, that she was quite subdued, and congratulated herself complacently upon her extraordinary talent for "breaking in new beginners."

And now, school being done, the children gone, her bonnet and India rubbers being put on, and all her spinster "fixings" settled to her mind, visions of hot tea and buttered toast began to float temptingly through her brain, and suggest the propriety of Bessie's release.

"Bessie!"— no answer. "Bessie!"— no reply. Miss Prim laid the ferule across the little fat shoulders. Bessie did n't wince. Miss Prim unpinned the apron to confront the face that was bold enough to defy her and "the Committee." Little Bessie was *dead!*

Well; there was a pauper funeral, and a report about that a child had been "frightened to death at school;" but Bessie's mother was a poor woman, consequently the righteous Committee "did n't feel called upon to interfere with such idle reports."

THE DELIGHTS OF VISITING.

What is it to go away on a visit? Well, it is to take leave of the little velvet rocking-chair, which adjusts itself so nicely to your shoulders and spinal column; to cram, jam, squeeze, and otherwise compress your personal effects into an infinitessimal compass; to be shook, jolted, and tossed, by turns, in carriage, railroad and steamboat; to be deafened with the stentorian lungs of cab-drivers, draymen and porters; to clutch your baggage as if every face you saw was a highwayman; (or to find yourself transported with rage, at finding *it* transported by steam to Greenland or Cape Horn.) It is to reach your friend's house, travel-stained, cold and weary, with an unbecoming crook in your bonnet; to be utterly unable to get the frost out of your tongue, or "*the beam into your eye*," and to have the felicity of hearing some strange guest remark to your friend, as you say an early good-night, "Is it possible THAT is your friend, Miss Grey?"

It is to be ushered into the "best chamber," (always a *north* one) of a cold January night; to unhook your dress with stiffened digits; to find every thing in your trunk *but* your nightcap; to creep between polished *linen* sheets, on a congealed *mattress*, and listen to the chattering of your own teeth until daylight.

It is to talk at a mark twelve hours on the stretch; to eat and drink all sorts of things which disagree with you; to get up sham fits of enthusiasm at trifles; to learn to yawn circumspectly behind your finger-tips; to avoid all allusion to topics unsuited to your pro tem. latitude; to have somebody forever at your nervous elbow, *trying to make you* "*enjoy yourself;*" to laugh when you want to cry; to be loquacious when you had rather be taciturn; to have mind and body in unyielding harness, for lingering, consecutive weeks; and then to invite your friends, with a hypocritical smile, to play the same farce over with you, "whenever business or pleasure calls them" to Frogtown!

HELEN HAVEN'S "HAPPY NEW YEAR."

"I'M miserable; there's no denying it," said Helen. "There's nothing in this endless fashionable routine of dressing, dancing and visiting, that can satisfy me. Hearts enough are laid at my feet, but I owe them all to the accidents of wealth and position. The world seems all emptiness to me. There *must* be something beyond this, else why this ceaseless reaching of the soul for some unseen good? Why do the silent voices of nature so thrill me? Why do the holy stars with their burning eyes utter such silent reproaches? Have I nothing to do but amuse myself with toys like a child? Shall I live only for *myself?* Does not the sun that rises upon my luxury, shine also upon the tear-stained face of sorrow? Are there not slender feet stumbling wearily in rugged, lonely paths? Why is *mine* flower-bestrewn? How am I better? Whose sorrowful heart have I lightened? What word of comfort has fallen from my lips on the ear of the grief-stricken? What am I here for? What is my mission?"

"And you have only this wretched place to nurse that sick child in?" said Helen; "and five lesser ones to care for? Will you trust that sick child with me?"

"She is not long for this world, my lady; and I love her as well as though I had but one. Sometimes I've thought the more care I have for her, the closer my heart clings to her. She is very patient and sweet."

"Yes, I know," said Helen; "but I have it in my power to make her so much more comfortable. It may preserve, at least lengthen her life."

When little Mary opened her eyes the next morning, she half believed herself in fairy-land. Soft fleecy curtains were looped about her head, her little emaciated hand rested upon a silken coverlid, a gilded table stood by her bed-side, the little cup from which her lips were moistened was of bright silver, and a sweet face was bending over her, shaded by a cloud of golden hair, that fell like a glory about her head.

"Where am I?" said the child, crossing her little hand across her bewildered brain.

Helen smiled. "You are *my* little bird now, dear. How do you like your cage?"

"It is very, *very* pretty," said Mary, with childish delight; "but won't you get tired of waiting upon a poor little sick girl? Mamma was used to it. *You* don't look as if you could work."

"Don't I?" said Helen, with a slight blush; "for all that, you'll see how nicely I can take care of you, little one. I'll sing to you; I'll read to you; I'll tell you pretty stories; and when you are weary of your couch, I'll fold you in my arms, and rock you so gently to sleep. And when you get better and stronger, you shall have so many nice toys to play with, and I'll crown your little bright head with pretty flowers, and make you nice little dresses; and now I'm going to read to you. Betty has been out, and bought you a little fairy story about a wonderful puss; and here's 'Little Timothy Pip;' which will you have?"

"Mamma used to read to me out of the Bible," said little Mary, as her long lashes swept her cheek.

Helen started; a bright crimson flush passed over her face, and bending low, she kissed the child's forehead reverentially.

"About the crucifixion, please," said Mary, as Helen seated herself by her side.

That Holy Book! Helen felt as if her hands were "unclean." She began to read; perhaps the print might not have been clear; but she stopped often, and drew her small hand across her eyes. Her voice grew tremulous. Years of worldliness had come between her and that sad, touching story. It came upon her now with startling force and freshness. Earth, with its puerile cares and pleasures, dwindled to a point. Oh, what "cross" had her shoulders borne? What "crown of thorns" had pierced her brows? How had her careless feet turned aside from the footsteps of Calvary's meek sufferer!

"Thank you," said little Mary, rousing Helen from her reverie; "mamma used to pray to God to make me patient, and take me to Heaven."

"Tears started to Helen's eyes. How could she tell that sinless little one she *knew not how to pray?* Ah! *she* was the pupil, Mary the teacher! Laying her cheek to hers, she said in a soft whisper, "Pray for *us both*, dear Mary."

With sweet, touching, simple eloquence that little silvery voice floated on the air! The little emaciated hand upon which Helen's face was pressed, was wet with tears — *happy* tears! Oh, this was what that restless soul had craved! Here at "the cross," that world-fettered spirit should plume itself for an angel's ceaseless flight. Aye, and a little *child had led "her" there!*

Adolph Grey wandered listlessly through that brilliant ball-room. There were sweet voices, and sweeter faces, and graceful, floating forms; but his eye rested on none of them.

"Pray, where is Lady Helen?" said he, wandering up to his gay hostess, with a slight shade of embarrassment.

"Ah, you may well ask that! I'm *so* vexed at her! Every man in the room is as savage as a New Zealander. She has turned Methodist, that's all. Just imagine; our peerless Helen thumbing greasy hymn-books at vestry meetings, listening to whining preachers, and hunting up poor dirty beggar children! I declare, I thought she had too much good sense. Well, there it is; and you may as well hang *your* harp on the willows. She'll have nothing to say to you *now;* for you know you are a sinner, Grey."

"Very true," said Grey, as he went into the ante-room to cloak himself for a call upon Helen; "I *am* a sinner; but if any woman can make a saint of me, it is Lady Helen. I have looked upon women only as toys to pass away the time; but under that gay exterior of Helen's there was always something to which my better nature bowed in reverence. 'A Methodist,' is she? Well, be it so. She has a soul above yonder frivolity, and I respect her for it."

If in after years the great moral questions of the day had more interest for Adolph Grey than the pleasures of the turf, the billiard room, or the wine party, who shall say that Lady Helen's influence was not a blessed one?

Oh, if woman's beauty, and power, and witchery were oftener used for a high and holy purpose, how many who now bend a careless knee at her shrine, would hush the light laugh and irreverent jest, and almost feel, as she passed, *that an angel's wing had rustled by!*

DOLLARS AND DIMES.

"Dollars and dimes, dollars and dimes,
An empty pocket is the worst of crimes.

YES; and don't you presume to show yourself anywhere, until you get it filled. "Not among good people?" No, my dear Simplicity, not among "good people." They will receive you with a galvanic ghost of a smile, scared up by an indistinct recollection of the "ten commandments," but it will be as short-lived as their stay with you. You are not welcome — that 's the amount of it. They are all in a perspiration lest you should be delivered of a request for their assistance, before they can get rid of you. They are "very busy," and what 's more, they always will be busy when you call, until you get to the top of fortune's ladder.

Climb, man! climb! Get to the top of the ladder, though adverse circumstances and false friends break every round in it! and see what a glorious and extensive prospect of human nature you'll get when you arrive at the summit! Your gloves will be worn out shaking hands with the very people who did n't recognize your existence two months ago. "You must come and make me a long visit;" "you must stop in at any time;" "*you'll* always be welcome;" it is such a *long* time since they had the pleasure of a visit from you, that they begin to fear you never intended to come; and they 'll cap the climax by inquiring with an injured air, "if you are nearsighted, or why you have so often passed them in the street without speaking."

Of course, you will feel very much like laughing in their faces, and so you can. You can't do anything wrong, now that your "pocket is full." At the most, it will only be "an eccentricity." You can use anybody's neck for a footstool, bridle anybody's mouth with a silver bit, and have as many "golden opinions" as you like. You won't see a frown again between this and your tombstone!

OUR NELLY.

"Who is she?" "Why, that is our Nelly, to be sure. Nobody ever passed Nelly without asking, 'Who is she?' One can't forget the glance of that blue eye; nor the waving of those golden locks; nor the breezy grace of that lithe figure; nor those scarlet lips; nor the bright, glad sparkle of the whole face; and then, she is not a bit proud, although she steps so like a queen; she would shake hands just as quick with a horny palm as with a kid glove. The world can't spoil 'our Nelly;' her heart is in the right place.

"You should have seen her thank an old farmer, the other day, for clearing the road that she might pass. He shaded his eyes with his hand when she swept by, as if he had been dazzled by a sudden flash of sunlight, and muttered to himself, as he looked after her — 'Won't she make somebody's heart ache?' Well, she has; but it is because from among all her lovers she could marry but one, and (God save us!) that her choice should have fallen upon Walter May. If he don't quench out the love-light in those blue eyes, my name is not John Morrison. I've seen his eyes flash when things did n't suit him; I've seen him nurse his wrath to keep it warm till the smouldering embers were ready for a conflagration. He's as vindictive as an

Indian. I'd as soon mate a dove with a tiger, as give him 'our Nelly.' There's a dozen noble fellows, this hour, ready to lay down their lives for her, and yet out of the whole crowd she must choose Walter May! Oh, I have no patience to think of it. Well-a-day! mark my words, he will break her heart before a twelvemonth! He's a pocket edition of Napoleon."

A year had passed by, and amid the hurry of business and the din of the great city, I had quite forgotten Glenburn and its fairy queen. It was a time to recall her to mind, that lovely June morning — with its soft fleecy clouds, its glad sunlight, its song of birds, and its breath of roses; and so I threw the reins on Romeo's neck, that he might choose his own pace down the sweet-briar path, to John Morrison's cottage. And there sat John, in the doorway, smoking his pipe, with Towser crouched at his feet, in the same old spot, just as if the sun had never gone down behind the hills since I parted with him.

"And 'our Nelly?'" said I, taking up the thread of his year-old narrative as though it had never been broken — "and 'our Nelly?'"

"Under the sod," said the old man, with a dark frown; "under the sod. He broke her heart, just as I told you he would. Such a bridal as it was! I'd as lief have gone to a funeral. And then Walter carried her off to the city, where she was as much out of her element as a humming-bird in a meeting-house;

and tried to make a fine lady of her, with stiff, city airs, and stiff, city manners. It was like trying to fetter the soft west wind, which comes and goes at its own sweet will; and Nelly — who was only another name for *Nature* — pined and drooped like a bird in a darkened cage.

" One by one her old friends dropped off, wearied with repeated and rude repulses from her moody husband, till he was left, as he desired, master of the field. It was astonishing the ascendency he gained over his sweet wife, contemptible as he was. She made no objection to his most absurd requirements; but her step lost its spring, her eye its sparkle; and one might listen long for her merry-ringing laugh. Slowly, sadly to Nelly came that terrible conviction from which a wife has no appeal.

Ah! there is no law to protect woman from negative abuse! — no mention made in the statute book (which *men frame for themselves*), of the constant dropping of daily discomforts which wear the loving heart away — no allusion to looks or words that are like poisoned arrows to the sinking spirit. No! if she can show no mark of brutal fingers on her delicate flesh, he has fulfilled his legal promise to the letter — to love, honor and cherish her. *Out* on such a mockery of justice!

" Well, sir; Nelly fluttered back to Glenburn, with the broken wing of hope, to die! So wasted! so lovely! The lips that blessed *her*, could not choose but curse *him*. She leaned on a broken reed," said her old gray-haired father, as he closed her blue eyes forever. " 'May God forgive him, for I never can,' said an old lover, whose heart was buried in her grave.

"'NELLY MAY, *aged* 18.'

"You'll read it in the village churchyard, Sir. Eighteen! Brief years, Sir, to drain all of happiness Life's cup could offer!"

J

"STUDY MEN, NOT BOOKS."

Oh, but books are such safe company! They keep your secrets well; *they* never boast that they made your eyes glisten, or your cheek flush, or your heart throb. You may take up your favorite author, and love him at a distance just as warmly as you like, for all the sweet fancies and glowing thoughts that have winged your lonely hours so fleetly and so sweetly. Then you may close the book, and lean your cheek against the cover, as if it were the face of a dear friend; shut your eyes and soliloquise to your heart's content, without fear of misconstruction, even though you should exclaim in the fullness of your enthusiasm, "What an *adorable soul that man has!*" You may put the volume under your pillow, and let your eye and the first ray of morning light fall on it together, and no Argus eyes shall rob you of that delicious pleasure, no carping old maid, or strait-laced Pharisee shall cry out, "*it is n't proper!*" You may have a thousand petty, provoking, irritating annoyances through the day, and you shall come back again to your dear old book, and forget them all in *dream land.* It shall be a friend that shall be always at hand; that shall never try you by caprice, or pain you by forgetfulness, or wound you by distrust.

Study *men!*"

Well, try it! I don't believe there 's any *neutral territory* where that interesting study can be pursued as it should be. Before you get to the end of the first chapter, they 'll be making love to you from the mere force of habit — and because silks, and calicoes, and delaines, naturally suggest it. It 's just as natural to them as it is to sneeze when a ray of sunshine flashes suddenly in their faces. "Study men!" That 's a game, my dear, that *two* can play at. Do you suppose they are going to sit quietly down and let you dissect their hearts, without returning the compliment? No, indeed! that 's *where they differ slightly from "books!"— they always expect an equivalent.*

Men are a curious study! Sometimes it pays to read to "the end of the volume," and then again, it don't — mostly the latter!

"MURDER OF THE INNOCENTS;"

OR, HOME THE PLACE FOR MARRIED FOLKS

HAPPY Mrs. Emily! Freed from the thraldom of housekeeping, and duly installed mistress of a fine suite of rooms at —— Hotel. No more refractory servants to oversee, no more silver or porcelain to guard, no more cupboards, or closets, or canisters to explore; no more pickles or preserves to make; no more bills of fare to invent, — and over and above all, mistress of a bell-wire which was not "tabooed" on washing and ironing days.

Time to lounge on the sofa, and devour "yellow-covered literature;" time to embroider caps, and collars, and chemisettes; time to contemplate the pretty face where housekeeping *might* have planted "crows feet," had she not fortunately foreseen the symptoms, and turned her back on dull Care and all his croaking crew.

Happy Mrs. Emily! No bird let loose from a cage was ever more joyous; not even her own little children — for she had two of them, and pretty creatures they were too, with their cherry lips, and dimpled limbs, and flaxen ringlets; and very weary they grew, of their gloomy nursery, with its one window, commanding a view of a dingy shed and a tall spectral-looking distilhouse chimney, emitting clouds of smoke and suffocating vapor. Nannie, the nurse, did n't fancy it, either, so she spent her time in the lobbies and entries, challenging compliments from white-jacketed waiters, while the children peeped curiously into the half-open doors, taking drafts of cold air on their bare necks and shoulders. Sometimes they balanced themselves alarmingly on the spiral ballustrade, gazing down into the dizzy Babel below, inhaling clouds of cigar smoke, and listening, with round-eyed wonder, to strange conversations, which memory's cud should chew, for riper years to digest.

"No children allowed at the *table d'hôte* "—so the "hotel regulations" pompously set forth—the landlord's tablecloths, gentlemen's broadcloth, and ladies' silk dresses being sworn foes to *little Paul Pry fingers.* Poor little exiles! they took their sorrowful meals in the servants' hall, with their respective nurses, the bill of fare consisting of a rehash of yesterday's French dishes, (spiced for the digestion of an ostrich.) This was followed by a dessert of stale pastry and ancient raisins, each nurse *at the outset* propitiating her infant charge with a huge bunch, that she might regale herself with the substantials!—mamma, meanwhile, blissfully ignoring the whole affair, absorbed in the sublime occupation of making German worsted dogs.

Papa, too, had *his* male millennium. No more marketing to do; no more coal, or wood, or kindling to buy; no cistern, or pump, or gaspipe to keep in repair. Such a luxury as it was to have a free pass to the "smoking room," (alias *bar-room,*) where the atmosphere was so dense that he could n't tell the latitude of his nose, and surrounded by "hale fellows well met." His eldest boy accompanied him, listening, on his knee, to questionable jokes, which he repeated at bed-time to pert Nannie, the nurse, who understood their significance much better than his innocent little lordship.

Papa, to be sure, had *some* drawbacks, but they were VERY trifling; — for instance, his shirts were quite buttonless, his dickeys stringless, and his stockings had ventilator toes; — but then, how could mamma be seen patching and mending in such an aristocratic atmosphere? — she might lose caste; and as to Nannie, *her* hands were full, what with babies and billet-doux.

You should have seen Mrs. Emily in the evening; with sparkling eyes and bracelets, flounced robe and daintily-shod feet, twisting her Chinese fan, listening to moustached idlers. and recollecting, with a shudder, the long Caudle evenings, *formerly* divided between *her* husband, *his* newspaper, and *her* darning-needle.

Then the *petite soupers* at ten o'clock in the evening, where the ladies were enchanting, the gentlemen *quite entirely* irresistible; where wit and champagne corks flew with equal celerity; and headaches, and dyspepsia, and nightmare, lay *perdu* amid fried oysters, venison steaks, chicken salad, and *India-rubber, anti-temperance jellies.*

Then followed the midnight reünion in the drawing-room, where promiscuous polkaing and waltzing, (seen through champagne fumes,) seemed not only proper, but delightful.

It was midnight. There was hurrying to and fro in the entry halls and lobbies; a quick, sharp cry for medical help; the sobs and tears of an agonized mother, and the low moan of a dying child; for nature had rebelled at last, at impure air, unwholesome food, and alternate heats and chills.

"No hope," the doctor said; "no hope," papa mechanically repeated; "*no hope!*" echoed inexorable Death, as he laid his icy finger on the quivering little lips.

It was a dearly bought lesson. The Lady Emily never for got it. Over her remaining bud of promise she tearfully bends, finding her quiet happiness in the healthful, sacred and safe retreat of the *home fireside.*

AMERICAN LADIES.

"The American ladies, when promenading, cross their arms in front, and look like trussed turkeys."

Well, you ought to pity us, for we have no such escape-valves for our awkwardness as you have — no dickeys to pull up — no vests to pull down — no breast pockets, side pockets, flap pockets to explore — no cigars between our teeth — no switch canes in our hands — no beavers to twitch, when we meet an acquaintance. Don't you yourselves oblige us to reef in our rigging, and hold it down tight with our little paws over our belts, under penalty of being dragged half a mile by one of your buttons, when you tear past us like so many comets.

Is it any joke to us to stand *vis-a-vis*, with a strange man, before a crowd of grinning spectators, while you are disentangling the "Gordian knot," instead of whipping out your penknife and sacrificing your offending button, as you ought to do?

Is it any joke to see papa scowl, when we ask him for the "needful," to restore the lace or fringe you tore off our shawl or mantilla?

Do you suppose we can stop to walk *gracefully*, when our minds have to be in a prepared state to have our pretty little toes crushed, or our bonnets knocked off, or our skirts torn from our belts, or ourselves and our gaiter boots jostled into a mud-puddle?

Do you *ever* "keep to the right, as the law directs?" Don't you always go with your heads hindside before, and then fetch up against us as if we were made of cast-iron? Don't you put your great lazy hands in your pockets, and tramp along with a cane half a mile long sticking out from under your armpits, to the imminent danger of our optics? "*Trussed turkeys*," indeed! No wonder, when we are run a-*fowl* of every other minute.

THE STRAY SHEEP.

"He 's going the wrong way — straying from the true fold; going off the track," said old Deacon Green, shaking his head ominously, as he saw young Neff enter a church to hear an infidel preacher. "Can't understand it; he was taught his catechism and ten commandments as soon as he could speak; he knows the right way as well as our parson; I can't un derstand it."

Harry Neff had never seen a day pass since his earliest childhood, that was not ushered in and closed with a family prayer. He had not partaken of a repast upon which the divine blessing was not invoked; the whole atmosphere of the old homestead was decidedly orthodox. Novels, plays and Byronic poetry were all vetoed. Operas, theatres and the like most decidedly frowned upon; and no lighter literature was allowed upon the table, than missionary reports and theological treatises.

Most of his father's guests being clergymen, Harry was early made acquainted with every crook and turn of orthodoxy. He had laid up many a clerical conversation, and pondered it in his heart, when they imagined his thoughts on anything but the subject in debate. At his father's request, they had each and all taken him by the button, for the purpose of long, private conversations — the old gentleman generally prefacing his request by the remark that "his heart was as hard as a flint."

Harry listened to them all with respectful attention, manifesting no sign of impatience, no nervous shrinking from the probing process, and they left him, impressed with a sense of his mental superiority, but totally unable to affect his feelings in the remotest degree.

Such a pity! they all said, that he should be so impenetrable; such wonderful argumentative powers as he had; such felicity of expression; such an engaging exterior. Such a pity! that on all these brilliant natural gifts should not have been written, "Holiness to the Lord."

Yes, dear reader, it *was* a pity. Pity, when our pulpits are so often filled with those, whose only recommendation for their office is a good heart and a black coat. It was a pity that graceful gesticulation, that rare felicity of expression, that keen perception of the beautiful, that ready tact and adaptation to circumstances and individuals, should not have been effective weapons in the *gospel armory*. Pity, that voice of music should not have been employed, to chain the worldling's fastidious ear to listen to Calvary's story.

Yet it was a pity that glorious intellect had been laid at an unholy shrine; pity "he had strayed from the true fold." How was it?

Ah! the solution is simple. "Line upon line, precept upon precept," is well — but *practice is better!* Religion *must not be all lip-service;* the "fruits of love, meekness, gentleness, forbearance, long-suffering" must follow. Harry was a keen observer. He had often heard the harsh and angry word from lips upon which the Saviour's name had just lingered. He had felt the unjust, quick, passionate blow from the hand which a moment before had been raised in supplication to Heaven. He had seen the purse-strings relax at the bidding of worldliness, and tighten at the call of charity. He had seen principle sacrificed to policy, and duty to interest. He had himself been misappreciated. The shrinking sensitiveness which drew a vail over his most sacred feelings, had been harshly construed into hard-heartedness and indifference. Every duty to which his attention was called, was prefaced with the supposition that he was averse to its performance. He was cut off from the gay pleasures which buoyant spirits and fresh young life so eloquently plead for; and in their stead no innocent enjoyment was substituted. He saw Heaven's gate shut most unceremoniously, upon all who did not subscribe to the parental creed, outraging both his own good sense and the teachings of the Bible; and so religion, (which should have been rendered so lovely,) put on to him an ascetic form. Oh, what marvel that the flowers in the broad road were so passing fair to see? that the forbidden fruit of the "tree of knowledge" was so tempting to the youthful touch?

Oh, Christian parent! be consistent, be judicious, be *cheerful.* If, as historians inform us, "no smile ever played" on the lips of Jesus of Nazareth, surely *no frown marred the beauty of that holy brow.*

Dear reader, *true* religion is *not* gloomy. "Her ways *are* ways of pleasantness, her paths *are* peace." No man, no woman, has chart or compass, or guiding star, without it.

Religion is not a *fable*. Else why, when our household gods are shivered, do our tearful eyes seek only Heaven?

Why, when disease lays its iron grasp on bounding life, does the startled soul so earnestly, *so* tearfully, *so* imploringly, call on its forgotten Saviour?

Ah! the house "built upon the sand" may do for sunny weather; but when the billows roll, and tempests blow, and lightnings flash, and thunders roar, *we need the "Rock of Ages."*

THE FASHIONABLE PREACHER.

Do you call *this* a church? Well, I heard a prima-donna here a few nights ago: and bright eyes sparkled, and waving ringlets kept time to moving fans; and opera glasses and ogling, and fashion and folly reigned for the nonce triumphant. *I* can't forget it; I can't get up any devotion *here*, under these latticed balconies, with their fashionable freight. If it were a good old country church, with a cracked bell and unhewn rafters, a pine pulpit, with the honest sun staring in through the windows, a pitch-pipe in the gallery, and a few hob-nailed rustics scattered round in the uncushioned seats, I should feel all right; but my soul is in fetters here; it won't soar — its wings are earth-clipped. Things are all too fine! Nobody can come in at that door, whose hat and coat and bonnet are not fashionably cut. The poor man (minus a Sunday suit) might lean on his staff, in the porch, a long while, before he 'd dare venture in, to pick up *his* crumb of the Bread of Life. But, thank God, the unspoken prayer of penitence may wing its way to the Eternal Throne, though our mocking church spires point only with *aristocratic fingers* to the *rich man's heaven.*

— That hymn was beautifully read; there 's poetry in the preacher's soul. Now he takes his seat by the reading-desk;

now he crosses the platform, and offers his hymn-book to a female who has just entered. What right has *he* to know there is a woman in the house? 'Tis n't clerical! Let the bonnets find their own hymns.

Well, I take a listening attitude, and try to believe I am in church. I hear a great many original, a great many *startling* things said. I see the gauntlet thrown at the dear old orthodox sentiments which I nursed in with my mother's milk, and which (please God) I 'll cling to till I die. I see the polished blade of satire glittering in the air, followed by curious, eager, youthful eyes, which gladly see the searching "Sword of the Spirit" parried. Meaning glances, smothered smiles and approving nods follow the witty clerical sally. The orator pauses to mark the effect, and his face says, That stroke *tells!* and so it did, for "the Athenians" are not all dead, who "love to see and hear some new thing." But he has another arrow in his quiver. Now his features soften — his voice is low and thrilling, his imagery beautiful and touching. He speaks of human love; he touches skilfully a chord to which every heart vibrates; and stern manhood is struggling with his tears, ere his smiles are chased away.

Oh, there 's intellect there — there 's poetry there — there 's genius there; but I remember Gethsemane — I forget not Calvary! I know the "rocks were rent," and the "heavens darkened," and "the stone rolled away;" and a cold chill strikes to my heart when I hear "Jesus of Nazareth" lightly mentioned.

Oh, what are intellect, and poetry, and genius, when with Jewish voice they cry, "*Away with* HIM!"

With "Mary," let me "bathe his feet with my tears, and wipe them with the hairs of my head."

And so, I "went away sorrowful," that this human preacher, with such great intellectual possessions, should yet "lack the *one thing needful.*"

"CASH."*

Don't think I'm going to perpetrate a monetary article. No fancy that way! I ignore anything approaching to a *stock!* I refer now to that omnipresent, omniscient, ubiquitous, express-train little victim, so baptized in the dry-goods stores, who hears nothing but the everlasting word cash dinned in his juvenile ears from matin to vespers; whose dangerous duty it is to rush through a crowd of expectant and impatient feminines, without suffering his jacket-buttons to become too intimately acquainted with the fringes of their shawls, or the laces of their mantillas! and to dodge so dexterously as not to knock down, crush under foot, or otherwise damage the string of juveniles that said women are bound to place as obstructions in said "Cash's" way!

See him double, and turn, and twist, like a rabbit in a wood, while that word of command flies from one clerk's lip to another. Poor, demented little Cash! Where *is* your anxious maternal? Who finds you in patience and shoe leather? Does your pillow ever suggest anything to your weary brain but pillarless quarters, and crossed sixpences, and faded bank bills? When do you find time, you poor little victim, to comb your hair, digest your victuals, and say your catechise?

* The boy employed in stores to fetch and carry change.

Do you ever look back with a sigh to the days of peppermints, peanuts and pinafores? Or forward, in the dim distance, to a vision of a long-tailed coat, a high-standing dickey, and no more "*Cash*," save in your pantaloons' pocket? Don't you ever catch yourself wishing that a certain rib of Adam's had never been subtracted from his paradisiacal side?

Poor, miserable little Cash! you have my everlasting sympathy! I should go shopping twenty times, where I now go once, did 'nt it harrow up my feelings to see you driven on so, like a locomotive! "Here 's hoping" you may soon be made sensible of more than *one* meaning to the word CHANGE!

ONLY A CHILD.

"Who is to be buried here?" said I to the sexton. "Only a child, ma'am."

Only a child! Oh! had you ever been a mother — had you nightly pillowed that little golden head — had you slept the sweeter for that little velvet hand upon your breast — had you waited for the first intelligent glance from those blue eyes —had you watched its cradle slumbers, tracing the features of him who stole your girlish heart away—had you wept a widow's tears over its unconscious head — had your desolate, timid heart gained courage from that little piping voice, to wrestle with the jostling crowd for daily bread — had its loving smiles and prattling words been sweet recompense for such sad exposure — had the lonely future been brightened by the hope of that young arm to lean upon, that bright eye for your guiding star — had you never framed a plan, or known a hope or fear, of which that child was not a part; — if there was naught else on earth left for you to love — if disease came, and its eye grew dim; and food, and rest, and sleep were forgotten in your anxious fears—if you paced the floor, hour by hour, with that fragile burden, when your very touch seemed to give comfort and healing to that little quivering frame—had the star of hope set at last—had you hung over its dying pillow, when the strong breast you should have wept on was in the grave, where your child was hastening — had you caught *alone* its last faint cry for the "*help*" you could not give — had its last fluttering sigh been breathed out on *your* breast — Oh! could you have said — "'Tis *only* a child?"

MR. PIPKIN'S IDEAS OF FAMILY RETRENCHMENT.

MRS. PIPKIN, I am under the disagreeable necessity of informing you, that our family expenses are getting to be enormous. I see that carpet woman charged you a dollar for one day's work. Why, that is positively a man's wages; — such presumption is intolerable. Pity you did not make it yourself, Mrs. Pipkin; wives ought to lift their end of the yoke; that 's my creed.

Little Tom Pipkin. — Papa, may I have this bit of paper on the floor? it is your tailor's bill — says, "$400 for your last year's clothes."

Mr. Pipkin. — Tom, go to bed, and learn never to interrupt your father when he is talking. Yes, as I was saying, Mrs. Pipkin, wives should hold up their end of the yoke; and it is high time there was a little retrenchment here; superfluities must be dispensed with.

Bridget. — Please, sir, there are three baskets of champagne just come for you, and four boxes of cigars.

Mr. Pipkin. — Will you please lock that door, Mrs. Pipkin, till I can get a chance to say what I have to say to you on this subject. I was thinking to-day, that you might dispense with your nursery maid, and take care of baby yourself.

He don't cry much, except nights; and since I 've slept alone up stairs, I don't hear the little tempest at all. It is really quite a relief—that child's voice is a perfect ear-splitter.

I think I shall get you, too, to take charge of the marketing and providing, (on a stipulated allowance from me, of course,) it will give me so much more time to —— attend to *business*, Mrs. Pipkin. I shall take my own dinners down town at the —— House. I hear Stevens is an excellent "caterer;" (though that 's nothing to me, of course, as my only object in going is to meet business acquaintances from different parts of the Union, to drive a bargain, &c., &c.)

Well—it will cost you and the children little or nothing for your dinners. There 's nothing so disgusting to a man of refinement, like myself, as to see a *woman* fond of eating; and as to children, any fool knows they ought not to be allowed to stuff their skins, like little anacondas. Yes, our family expenses are enormous. My partner sighed like a pair of bellows at that last baby you had, Mrs. Pipkin; oh, it 's quite ruinous—but I can't stop to talk now, I 'm going to try a splendid horse which is offered me at a bargain—(too frisky for you to ride, my dear, but just the thing for me.)

You had better dismiss your nursery girl this afternoon; that will begin to look like retrenchment. Good-bye; if I am not home till late, don't sit up for me, as I have ordered a supper at ——— House for my old friend, Tom Hillar, of New Orleans. We 'll drink this toast, my dear: "Here 's hoping the last little Pipkin may never have his nose put out of joint."

A CHAPTER FOR NICE OLD FARMERS.

Can anybody tell why country people so universally and pertinaciously persist in living in the *rear of the house?* Can anybody tell why the front door and windows are never opened, save on Fourth of July and at Thanksgiving time? Why Zedekiah, and Timothy, and Jonathan, and the old farmer himself, must go *round* the house in order to get *into* it? Why the whole family (oblivious of six empty rooms,) take their "vapor bath," and their meals, simultaneously, in the vicinity of a red hot cooking range, in the dog-days? Why the village artist need paint the roof, and spout, and window frames bright crimson, and the doors the color of a mermaid's tresses? Why the detestable sunflower (which I can never forgive "Tom Moore" for noticing) must always flaunt in the garden? Why the ungraceful prim poplar, fit emblem of a stiff old bachelor, is preferred to the swaying elm, or drooping willow, or majestic horse-chestnut.

I should like to pull down the green paper window-curtains, and hang up some of snowy muslin. I should like to throw wide open the hall door, and let the south wind play through. I should like to go out into the woods, and collect fresh, sweet wild-flowers to arrange in a vase, in place of those defunct dried grasses, and old-maid "everlastings." I should like to show Zedekiah how to nail together some bits of board, for an embryo lounge; I should like to stuff it with cotton, and cover it with a neat "patch." I should like to cushion the chairs after the same fashion. Then I should like, when the white-haired old farmer came panting up the road at twelve o'clock, with his scythe hanging over his arm, to usher him into that cool, comfortable room, set his bowl of bread and milk before him, and after he had discussed it, coax him (instead of tilting back on the hind legs of a hard chair,) to take a ten-minutes nap on my "model" sofa, while I kept my eye on the clouds, to see that no thunder shower played the mischief with his hay.

I should like to place a few common-sense, practical books on the table, with some of our fine daily and weekly papers. You may smile; but these inducements, and the comfortable and pleasant air of the apartment, would bring the family oftener together after the day's toil, and by degrees they would lift the covers of the books, and turn over the newspapers. Constant interchange of thought, feeling and opinion, with discussions of the important and engrossing questions of the day, would of course necessarily follow.

The village tavern-keeper would probably frown upon it; but I will venture to predict for the inmates of the farm-house a growing love for "home," and an added air of intelligence and refinement, of which they themselves might possibly be unconscious.

MADAME ROUILLON'S "MOURNING SALOON."

"You need n't make that dress 'deep mourning,' Hetty; the lady who ordered it said it was only her sister for whom she was to 'mourn.' A three-quarter's length vail will answer; and I should introduce a few jet bugles round the bonnet trimmings. And, by the way, Hetty, Mrs. La Fague's husband has been dead now nearly two months, so that new dress of hers will admit of a little alleviation in the style of trimming — a few knots of love-ribbon on the boddice will have a softening effect; and you must hem a thin net vail for her bonnet; — it 's almost time for her to be 'out of mourning.'

— "And, Hetty, run down to Stewart's, right away, and see if he has any more of those grief-bordered pocket-handkerchiefs. Mr. Grey's servant said the border must be full an inch deep, as his master wished it for his wife's funeral, and it is the eighth time within eight years that the poor afflicted man has suffered a similar calamity. Remember, Hetty,— an inch deep, with a tomb-stone and a weeping-willow embroidered on the corner, with this motto: 'Hope never dies;'— and, Hetty, be sure you ask him what is the latest style for '*half*-mourning' for grandmothers, mothers-in-law, country cousins, and poor relations. *Dépèchezvous*, Hetty, for you have six 'weepers' (weeds) to take off the six Mr. Smiths' hats. Yes, I know you 'only put them on last week;' but they are going to Philadelphia, where nobody knows them, and, of course, it is n't necessary to 'mourn' for their mother there.

—"What are you staring at, child? You are as primitive as your fore-mother Eve. This 'mourning' is probably an invention of Satan to divert people's minds from solemn subjects, but that 's nothing to me, you know; so long as it fills my pocket, I 'm in league with his Majesty."

FASHION IN FUNERALS.

"It has become *unfashionable* in New-York for ladies to attend funerals to the grave. *Even the mother may not accompany the little lifeless form of her beloved child beyond the threshold without violating the dread laws of Fashion.*"

Are there such mothers? Lives there one who, at Fashion's bidding, stands back, nor presses her lips to the little marble form that once lay warm and quivering beneath her heart-strings? — who with undimmed eye recalls the trusting clasp of that tiny hand, the loving glance of that vailed eye, the music of that merry laugh — its low, pained moan, or its last fluttering heart-quiver? — who would not (rather than strange hands should touch the babe,) *herself* robe its dainty limbs for burial? — who shrinks not, starts not, when the careless, business hand would remove the little darling from its cradle-bed, where loving eyes so oft have watched its rosy slumbers, to its last, cold, dreamless pillow? — who lingers not, *when all have gone*, and vainly strives, with straining eye, to pierce *below* that little fresh laid mound? — who, when a merry group go dancing by, stops not, with sudden thrill, to touch some sunny head, or gaze into some soft blue eye, that has oped afresh the fount of her tears, and sent to the troubled lips the murmuring heart-plaint, "Would to God I had died for thee, my child — my child?" — who, when the wintry blast comes eddying by, sleeps not, because she cannot fold to her warm breast the little lonely sleeper in the cold churchyard? And oh! is there one, who, with such "treasure laid up in Heaven," clings not the less to earth, strives not the more to keep her spirit undefiled, fears not the less the dim, dark valley, cheered by a cherub voice, inaudible save to the dying *mother?* Oh, stony-eyed, stony-hearted, relentless Fashion! turn for us day into night, if thou wilt; deform our women; half clothe, with flimsy fabric, our victim children; wring the last penny from the sighing, overtasked, toiling husband; *banish to the backwoods thy country cousin*, Comfort; reign supreme in the banquet hall; revel undisputed at the dance;—but when that grim guest, whom none invite—whom none dare deny—strides, with defiant front, across our threshold, stand back, thou heartless harlequin, and leave us alone with our dead: so shall we list the lessons those voiceless lips should teach us—

"All is vanity."

HOUSEHOLD TYRANTS.

"A HUSBAND may kill a wife gradually, and be no more questioned than the grand seignor who drowns a slave at midnight."—*Thackeray, on Household Tyrants.*

OH! Mr. Thackeray! I ought to have known from experience, that beauty and brains never travel in company — but I *was* disenchanted when I first saw your nose, and I *did* say that you were too stout to look intellectual. But I forgive you in consideration of the above paragraph, which, for truth and candor, ought to be appended to the four Gospels.

I'm on the marrow bones of my soul to you, Mr. Thackeray. I honor you for "turning State's evidence" against your own culprit-sex. If there's any little favor I can do for you, such as getting you naturalized, (for you are a sight too cute and clever for an Englishman,) I'll fly round and get the documents made out for you to-morrow.

I tell you, Mr. Thackeray, the laws over here allow husbands to break their wives' *hearts* as much as they like, so long as they don't break their *heads.* So the only way we can get along, is to allow them to scratch our faces, and then run to the police court, and shew "his Honor" that Mr. Caudle can "*make his mark.*"

Why — if we were not *cunning,* we should get circumvented all the time by these domestic Napoleons. Yes, indeed; we sleep with one eye open, and "get up early in the morning," and keep our arms a-kimbo.

— By-the-way, Mr. Thackeray, what do you think of us, *as a people?* — taking us "by and large," as our honest farmers say. P-r-e-t-t-y tall nation for a *growing* one; don't you think so? Smart men — smarter women — good broad streets — no smoking or spitting allowed in 'em — houses all built with an eye to architectural beauty — newspapers don't tell how many buttons you wear on your waistcoat — Jonathan never stares at you, as if you were an imported hyena, or stirs you up with the long pole of criticism, to see your size and hear your roar. Our politicians never whip each other on the floor of Congress, and grow black in the face because their *choler* chokes them! No mushroom aristocracy over here — no "coats of arms" or liveried servants: nothing of that sham sort, in our "great and glorious country," as you have probably noticed. If you are "round takin' notes," I'll jog your English elbow now and then. Ferns have eyes — and they are not green, either.

WOMEN AND MONEY.

"A wife should n't ask her husband for money at meal-times."—*Exchange.*

By no manner of means; *nor at any other time;* because, it is to be hoped, he will be gentlemanly enough to spare her that humiliating necessity. Let him hand her his porte-monnaie every morning, with *carte-blanche* to help herself. The consequence would be, she would lose all desire for the contents, and hand it back, half the time without abstracting a single *sou.*

It 's astonishing men have no more diplomacy about such matters. *I* should like to be a husband! There *are* wives whom I verily believe might be trusted to make way with a ten dollar bill without risk to the connubial donor! I 'm not speaking of those doll-baby libels upon womanhood, whose chief ambition is to be walking advertisements for the dressmaker; but a rational, refined, sensible woman, who knows how to look like a lady upon small means; who would both love and respect a man less for requiring an account of every copper; but who, at the same time, would willingly wear a hat or garment that is "out of date," rather than involve a noble, generous-hearted husband in unnecessary expenditures.

I repeat it—"It *is n't every man who has a call to be a husband.*" Half the married men should have their "licenses" taken away, and the same number of judicious bachelors put in their places. I think the attention of the representatives should be called to this. They can't expect to come down to town and peep under all the ladies' bonnets the way they do, and have all the newspapers free gratis, and two dollars a day besides, without "paying their way!

It 's none of *my* business, but I question whether their wives, whom they left at home, stringing dried apples, know how spruce they look in their new hats and coats, or how facetious they grow with their landlady's daughter; or how many of them pass themselves off for bachelors, to verdant spinsters. Nothing truer than that little couplet of *Shakspeare's*—

"When the cat's away
The mice *will* play."

THE SICK BACHELOR.

Here I am, a doomed man — booked for a fever, in this gloomy room, up four flights of stairs; nothing to look at but one table, two chairs, and a cobweb; pulse racing like a locomotive; head throbbing as if it were hooped with iron; mouth as parched as Ishmael's in the desert; not a bell-rope within reach; sun pouring in through those uncurtained windows, hot enough to singe off my eye-lashes; all my confidential letters lying loose on the table, and I could n't get up to them if you held one of Colt's revolvers to my head. All my masculine friends (?) are parading Broadway, I suppose; peeping under the pretty girls' bonnets, or drinking "sherry cobblers." A sherry cobbler! Bacchus! what a luxury! I believe Satan suggested the thought to me.

Heigh-ho! I suppose the Doctor (whom they have sent for) will come before long; some great, pompous Æsculapius, with an owl phiz, a gold-headed cane, an oracular voice, and callous heart and hands; who will first manipulate my wrist, and then take the latitude and longitude of my tongue; then, he will punch me in my ribs, and torment me with more questions than there are in the Assembly's Catechism; then, he 'll bother me for writing materials, to scratch off a hieroglyphic humbug prescription, ordering five times as much medicine as I need; then, I shall have to pay for it; then, ten to one, the apothecary's boy will put up poison, by mistake! Cæsar! how my head spins round; Hippodrome racing is nothing to it.

Hist! there 's the Doctor. No! it is that little unregenerate cub, my landlady's pet boy, with a bran new drum (as I 'm a sinner), upon which he is beating a crucifying tattoo. If I only had a boot-jack to throw at him. No! that won't do: his mother would n't make my gruel. I 'll bribe him with a sixpence, to keep the peace. The little embryo Jew! he says *he won't do it under a quarter!* Twitted by a little pinafore! *I*, Tom Haliday, six feet in my stockings! I shall go frantic.

"Doctor is coming!" Well, let him come. I 'm as savage as if I 'd just dined off a cold missionary. I 'll pretend to be asleep, and let old Pill-box experiment.

How gently he treads: how soft his hand is: how cool and delicious his touch! How tenderly he parts my hair over my throbbing temples! His magnetic touch thrills every drop of blood in my veins: it is marvellous how soothing it is. I feel as happy as a humming-bird in a lily cup, drowsy with honey-dew. Now he 's moved away. I hear him writing a prescription. I 'll just take a peep and see what he looks like. Cæsar Aggripina! if it is n't a *Female Physician!* dainty as a Peri —*and my beard three days old!* What a bust! (Wonder how my hair looks?) What a foot and ankle! What shoulders; what a little round waist. Fever? I 've got *twenty* fevers, and the heart-complaint besides. What the mischief sent that little witch here? She will either kill or cure me, pretty quick.

Wonder if she has any more *masculine* patients? Wonder if they are handsome? Wonder if she lays that little dimpled hand on *their* foreheads, as she did on mine? Now she has done writing, I 'll shut my eyes and groan, and then, may be, she will *pet* me some more; bless her little soul!

She says, "poor fellow!" as she holds my wrist, "his pulse is too quick." In the name of Cupid, what does she *expect?* She says, as she pats my forehead with her little plump fingers, "'Sh—'sh! Keep cool." Lava and brimstone! does she take me for an iceberg?

Oh, Cupid! of all your devices, this feminine doctoring for a bachelor, is the *ne plus ultra* of witchcraft. If I don't have a prolonged "run of fever," my name is n't Tom Haliday!

She 's gone! and — I 'm gone, too!

A MOTHER'S INFLUENCE.

"AND so you sail to-morrow, Will? I shall miss you."

"Yes; I'm bound to see the world. I've been beating my wings in desperation against the wires of my cage these three years. I know every stick, and stone, and stump in this odious village by heart, as well as I do those stereotyped sermons of Parson Grey's. They say he calls me 'a scapegrace'—pity I should have the name without the game," said he, bitterly. "I have n't room here to run the length of my chain. I'll show him what I can do in a wider field of action."

"But how did you bring your father over?"

"Oh, he's very glad to be rid of me; quite disgusted because I've no fancy for seeing corn and oats grow. The truth is, every father knows at once too much and too little about his own son; the old gentleman never understood me; he soured my temper, which is originally none of the best, roused all the worst feelings in my nature, and is constantly driving me *from* instead of *to* the point he would have me reach."

"And your mother?"

"Well, there you have me; that's the only humanized portion of my heart—the only soft spot in it. She came to my bed-side last night, after she thought I was asleep, gently kissed my forehead, and then knelt by my bed-side. Harry, I've been wandering round the fields all the morning, to try to get rid of that prayer. Old Parson Grey might preach at me till the millennium, and he would n't move me any more than that stone. It makes all the difference in the world when you know a person *feels* what they are praying about. I'm wild and reckless and wicked, I suppose; but I shall never be an infidel while I can remember my mother. You should see the way she bears my father's impetuous temper; that's *grace*, not *nature*, Harry; but don't let us talk about it — I only wish my parting with her was well over. Good-bye; God bless you, Harry; you'll hear from me, if the fishes don't make a supper of me;" and Will left his friend and entered the cottage.

Will's mother was moving nervously and restlessly about, tying up all sorts of mysterious little parcels that only mothers think of, "in case he should be sick," or in case he should be this, that, or the other, interrupted occasionally by exclamations like this from the old farmer: "Fudge — stuff — great overgrown baby — making a fool of him — never be out of leading strings;" and then turning short about and facing Will as he entered, he said,

"Well, sir, look in your sea-chest, and you'll find gingerbread and physic, darning-needles and tracts, 'bitters' and Bibles, peppermint and old linen rags, and opodeldoc. Pshaw! I was more of a man than you are when I was nine years old. Your mother always made a fool of you, and that was entirely unnecessary, too, for you were always short of what is called *common sense*. You need n't tell the captain you went to sea because you did n't know enough to be a landsman; or that you never did any thing right in your life, except by accident. You are as like that *ne'er do well* Jack Halpine, as two peas. If there *is* anything in you, I hope the salt water will fetch it out. Come, your mother has your supper ready, I see."

Mrs. Low's hand trembled as she passed her boy's cup. It was his last meal under that roof for many a long day. She did not trust herself to speak — her heart was too full. She heard all his father so injudiciously said to him, and she knew too well from former experience the effect it would have upon his impetuous, fiery spirit. She had only to oppose to it a mother's prayers, and tears, and all-enduring love. She never condemned in *Will's hearing*, any of his father's philippics; always excusing him with the general remark that he did n't understand him. *Alone*, she mourned over it; and when with her husband, tried to place matters on a better footing for both parties.

Will noted his mother's swollen eyelids; he saw his favorite little tea-cakes that she had busied herself in preparing for him, and he ate and drank what she gave him, without tasting a morsel he swallowed, listening for the hundredth time to his father's account of "what *he* did when he was a young man."

"Just half an hour, Will," said his father, "before you start; run up and see if you have forgotten any of your duds."

It was the little room he had always called his own. How many nights he had lain there listening to the rain pattering on the low roof; how many mornings awakened by the chirp of the robin in the apple-tree under the window. There was the little bed with its snowy covering, and the thousand and one little comforts prepared by his mother's hand. He turned his head — she was at his side, her arms about his neck. "God keep my boy!" was all she could utter. He knelt at her feet as in the days of childhood, and from those wayward lips came this tearful prayer, "Oh God, spare my mother, that I may look upon her face again in this world!"

Oh, in after days, when that voice had died out from under the parental roof, how sacred was that spot to her who gave him birth! *There was hope for the boy! he had recognized his mother's God.* By that invisible silken cord she still held the wanderer, though broad seas roll between.

Letters came to Moss Glen — at stated intervals, then more irregularly, picturing only the bright spots in his sailor life (for Will was proud, and they were to be scanned by his father's eye.) The usual temptations of a sailor's life when in port were not unknown to him. Of every cup the syren Pleasure held to his lips, he drank to the dregs; but there were moments in his maddest revels, when that angel whisper, "God keep my boy," palsied his daring hand, and arrested the half-uttered oath. Disgusted with himself, he would turn aside for an instant, but only to drown again more recklessly "that still small torturing voice."

"You 're a stranger in these parts," said a rough farmer to a sun-burnt traveller. "Look as though you 'd been in foreign parts."

"Do I?" said Will, slouching his hat over his eyes. "Who lives in that little cottage under the hill?"

"Old Farmer Low — and a tough customer he is, too; it 's a word and a blow with him. The old lady has had a hard time of it, good as she is, to put up with all his kinks and quirks. She bore it very well till the lad went away; and then she began to droop like a willow in a storm, and lose all heart, like. Doctor's stuff did n't do any good, as long as she got no news of the boy. She 's to be buried this afternoon, sir."

Poor Will staid to hear no more, but tottered in the direction of the cottage. He asked no leave to enter, but passed over the threshold into the little "best parlor," and found himself alone with the dead. It was too true! Dumb were the lips that should have welcomed him; and the arms that should have enfolded him were crossed peacefully over the heart that beat true to him till the last.

Conscience did its office. Long years of mad folly passed in swift review before him; and over that insensible form a vow was made, and registered in Heaven.

"Your mother should have lived to see this day, Will," said a gray-haired old man, as he leaned on the arm of the clergyman, and passed into the village church.

"Bless God, my dear father, there is '*joy in Heaven* over one sinner that repenteth;' and of all the angel band, there is one seraph hand that sweeps *more rapturously* its harp to-day for 'the lost that is found.'"

MR. PUNCH MISTAKEN.

"A man will own that he is in the wrong — a woman, never; she is only *mistaken*." — *Punch.*

Mr. Punch, did you ever see an enraged American female? She is the expressed essence of wild-cats. Perhaps you did n't know it, when you penned that incendiary paragraph; or, perhaps you thought that in crossing the "big pond," salt water might neutralize it; or, perhaps you flattered yourself we should not see it, over here; but here it is, in my clutches, in good strong English: I am not even "*mistaken.*"

Now, if you will bring me a live specimen of the genus homo, who was ever known "to own that he was in the wrong," I will draw in my horns and claws, and sneak ingloriously back into my American shell. But you can't do it, Mr. Punch! You never saw that curiosity, either in John Bull's skin or Brother Jonathan's. 'Tis an animal which has never yet been discovered, much less captured.

A man own he was in the wrong! I guess so! You might tear him in pieces with red-hot pincers, and he would keep on singing out "I did n't do it; I did n't do it." No, Mr. Punch, a man never "owns up" when he is in the wrong; especially if the matter in question be one which he considers of no im portance; for instance, the non-delivery of a letter, which may have been entombed in his pocket for six weeks.

No sir; he just settles himself down behind his dickey, folds his belligerent hands across his stubborn diaphragm, plants his antagonistic feet down on terra-firma as if there were a stratum of loadstone beneath him, and thunders out,

"Come one, come all; this rock shall fly
From its firm base, as soon as I."

FERN MUSINGS.

I NEVER was on an august school committee, but, if I *was*, I 'd make a *sine-qua-non* that no school-marm should be inaugu rated who had not been a married mother; I do n't believe in old maids; they all know very well that they have n't fulfilled their female destiny, and I would n't have them wreaking their bilious vengeance on *my* urchins, (if I had any.) No woman gets the acid effectually out of her temper, till she has taken matrimony "the natural way."

No; I don't believe in spinster educational teaching any more than I do in putting dried up old bachelors on the school committee. What bowels of mercies have either, I 'd like to know, for the poor little restless victims of narrow benches and short recesses? The children are to "hold up their hands" (are they?) if they have a request to make? What good does that do, if the teacher won't take any notice of the Free Mason sign? "They are not to enter complaints." So some poor timid little girl must be pinched black and blue by a little Napoleon in jacket and trowsers, till she is forced to shriek out with pain, when *she* is punished by being kept half an hour after school for "making a disturbance!" They are "not to eat in school," are they? Perhaps they have made an indifferent breakfast; (perhaps they are poor, and have had none at all, and A, B, C, D, does n't digest well on an empty stomach;) but the spinster teacher can hear them recite with a tempting bunch of grapes in her hand, which she leisurely devours before their longing eyes.

They "must not smile in school," must they? Not when "Tom Hood" in a pinafore, cuts up some sly prank that brings "down the house;" yes — and the ferule too, on everybody's hand but his own; (for he has a way of drawing on his "deacon face," to order.)

They may go out in recess, but they must speak in a whisper out doors, as if they all had the bronchitis! No matter if Queen Victoria should ride by, no little brimless hat must go up in the air till "the committee had set on it!"

Oh fudge! I should like to keep school myself. I 'd make "rag babies" for the little girls, and "soldier caps" for the boys; and I *do n't think* I would make a rule that they should not sneeze till school was dismissed; and when their little cheeks began to flush, and their little heads droop wearily on their plump shoulders, I 'd hop up and play, "hunt the slipper;" or, if we were in the country, we 'd race over the meadow, and catch butterflies, or frogs, or toads, or *snakes*, or anything on earth except a "school committee."

THE TIME TO CHOOSE.

"The best time to choose a wife is early in the morning. If a young lady is at all inclined to sulks and slatternness, it is just before breakfast. As a general thing, a woman don't get on her temper, till after 10 A. M."—*Young Man's Guide.*

MEN never look slovenly before breakfast; no, indeed. They never run round in their stocking feet, vestless, with dressing-gown inside out; soiled handkerchief hanging out of the pocket by one corner. Minus dicky—minus neck-tie; pantaloon straps flying; suspenders streaming from their waisthand; chin shaved on one side, and lathered on the other; hair like porcupine quills; face all in a snarl of wrinkles because the fire wont kindle, and because it snows, and because the office boy do n't come for the keys, and because the newspaper has n't arrived, and because they lost a bet the night before, and because there's an omelet instead of a broiled chicken, for breakfast, and because they are out of sorts and shaving soap, out of cigars and credit, and because they can't "get their temper on" till they get some money and a mint julep.

Any time "before ten o'clock," is the time to choose a husband——*perhaps!*

SPRING IS COMING.

Tiny blades of grass are struggling between the city's pavements. Fathers, and husbands, sighing, look at the tempting shop windows, dolefully counting the cost of a "spring outfit." Muffs, and boas, and tippets, are among the things that *were;* and shawls, and "Talmas," and mantles, and "*little loves of bonnets*," reign supreme, though maiden aunts, and sage mammas, still mutter —"East winds, east winds," and choose the sunnier sidewalk.

Housekeepers are making a horrible but necessary Babel, stripping up carpets, and disembowelling old closets, chests, and cupboards. Advertisements already appear in the newspapers, setting forth the superior advantages of this or that dog-day retreat. Mrs. Jones drives *Mr.* Jones distracted, at a regular hour every evening, hammering about "change of scene, and air," and the "health of the dear children;" which, translated, means a quantity of new bonnets and dresses, and a trip to Saratoga, for herself and intimate friend, Miss Hob-Nob; while Jones takes his meals at a restaurant — sleeps in the deserted house, sews on his missing buttons and dickey strings, and spends his leisure time where *Mrs.* Jones don't visit.

Spring is coming!

Handsome carriages roll past, freighted with lovely women,

(residents of other cities, for an afternoon ride.) Dash on, ladies! You will scarcely find the environs of Boston surpassed, where-ever you may drive. A thousand pleasant surprises await you; lovely winding paths and pretty cottages, and more ambitious houses with groups of statuary hidden amid the foliage. But forget not to visit our sweet Mount Auburn. Hush the light laugh and merry jest as the gray-haired porter throws wide the gate for your prancing horses to tread the hallowed ground. The dark old pines throw out their protecting arms above you, and in their dense shade sleep eyes as bright, forms as lovely, as your own — while "the mourners go about the streets." Rifle not, with sacrilegious hand, the flowers which bloom at the headstone — tread lightly over the beloved dust! Each tenanted grave entombs bleeding, *living* hearts; each has its history, which eternity alone shall reveal.

Spring is coming!

The city belle looks fresh as a new-blown rose — tossing he bright curls in triumph, at her faultless costume and beautiful face. Her lover's name is Legion — for she hath also *golden charms!* Poor little butterfly! bright, but ephemeral! You were made for something better. Shake the dust from your earth-stained wings and — *soar!*

Spring is coming!

From the noisome lanes and alleys of the teeming city, swarm little children, creeping forth like insects to bask in God's sunshine — so *free to all.* Squalid, forsaken, neglected; they are yet of those to whom the Sinless said, "Suffer little children to come unto me." The disputed crust, th savage curse, the brutal blow, their only patrimony! One's heart *aches* to call THIS *childhood!* No "spring!" no summer, to them! Noisome sights, noisome sounds, noisome odors! and the leprosy of sin following them like a curse! One longs to fold to the warm heart those little forsaken ones; to smooth those matted ringlets; to throw between them and sin the shield of virtue — to teach their little lisping lips to say "*Our Father!*"

Spring is coming!

Yes, its blue skies are over us — its soft breezes shall fan us — the fragrance of its myriad flowers be wafted to us. Its mossy carpet shall be spread for our careless feet — our languid limbs shall be laved at its cool fountains. Its luscious fruits shall send health through our leaping veins — while from mountain top, and wooded hill, and flower-wreathed valley, shall float one glad anthem of praise from tiniest feathered throats!

Dear reader! From that human heart of thine shall no burst of grateful thanks arise to Him who *giveth all?* While nature adores — shall *man be dumb?* God forbid!

STEAMBOAT SIGHTS AND REFLECTIONS.

I AM looking, from the steamer's deck, upon as fair a sunrise as ever poet sang or painter sketched, or the earth ever saw. Oh, this broad, blue, rushing river! sentineled by these grand old hills, amid which the silvery mist wreaths playfully; half shrouding the little eyrie homes, where love wings the uncounted hours; while looming up in the hazy distance, is the Babel city, with glittering spires and burnished panes — one vast illumination. My greedy eye with miserly eagerness devours it all, and hangs it up in Memory's cabinet, a fadeless picture; upon which dame Fortune (the jilt) shall never have a mortgage.

Do you see yonder figure leaning over the railing of the boat, gazing on all this outspread wealth of beauty? One longs to hear his lips give utterance to the burning thoughts which cause his eye to kindle and his face to glow. A wiry sister, (whose name should be "Martha," so careful, so troubled looks her spinstership,) breaks the charmed spell by asking him, in a cracked treble, "if *them* porters on the pier can be safely trusted with her bandbox and umberil." My stranger eyes meet his, and we both laugh involuntarily — (pardon us, oh ye prim ones) — *without an introduction!*

I.

Close at my elbow sits a rough countryman, with so much "free soil" adhering to his brogans they might have been used for beet-beds, and a beard rivaled only by Nebuchadnezzar's when he experimented on a grass diet. He has only one word to express his overpowering emotions at the glowing panorama before us, and that is "*pooty*,"—houses, trees, sky, rafts, railroad cars and river, all are "*pooty;*" and when, in the fulness of a soul craving sympathy, he turned to his dairy-fed Eve to endorse it, that matter-of-fact feminine shower-bath-ed his enthusiasm, by snarling out "pooty enough, I 'spose, but *where 's my breakfast?*"

Ah! here we are at the pier, at last. And now they emerge, our night-travelers, from state-room and cabin into the fresh cool air of the morning. Venus and Apollo! what a crew. Solemn as a hearse, surly as an Englishman, blue as an indigo-bag! There 's a poor shivering babe, twitched from a warm bed by an ignorant young mother, to encounter the chill air of morning, with only a flimsy covering of lace and embroidery; — there 's a languid southern belle, creeping out, *à la tortoise*, and turning up her little aristocratic nose as if she sniffed a pestilence; — there 's an Irish bride (green as Erin) in a pearl-colored silk dress surmounted by a coarse blanket shawl; — there 's a locomotive hour-glass, (alias a dandy,) a blue-eyed, cravat-choked, pantaloon be-striped, vest-garnished, disgusting "institution!" (give him and his quizzing glass plenty of sea-room); — and there 's a clergyman, God bless his care-worn face, with a valise full of salted-down sermons and the long-coveted "leave of absence;" — there 's an editor, kicking a newsboy for bringing "coals to Newcastle" in the shape of "extras;" — and there 's a good-natured, sunshiny "family man," carrying the baby, and the carpet-bag, and the traveling shawl, lest his pretty little wife should get weary; — and there 's a poor bonnetless emigrant, stunned by the Babel sounds, inquiring, despairingly, the name of some person whom nobody knows or cares for; — and last, but not least, there 's the wiry old maid "Martha," asking "*thim* porters on the pier," with tears in her faded green eyes, to be "keerful of her bandbox and umberil."

On they go. Oh, how much of joy — how much of sorrow, in each heart's unwritten history.

A GOTHAM REVERIE.

Babel, what a place! — what a dust — what a racket — what a whiz-buzz! What a throng of human beings. "Jew and Gentile, bond and free;" every nation the sun ever shone upon, here represented. What pampered luxury—what squalid misery, on the same *pavé*. What unwritten histories these myriad hearts might unfold. How much of joy, how much of sorrow, how much of crime. Now, queenly beauty sweeps past, in sin's gay livery. Cursed he who first sent her forth, to walk the earth, with her woman's brow shame-branded. Fair mother — pure wife — frown scornfully at her if you can; *my* heart aches for her. I see one who once slept, sweet and fair, on a mother's loving breast. I see one whose bitterest tear may never wash her stain away. I see one on whom mercy's gate is forever shut, by her own unrelenting, unforgiving sex. I see one who was young, beautiful, poor and friendless. They who make long prayers, and wrap themselves up in self-righteousness, as with a garment, turned a deaf ear, as she plead for the bread of honest toil. Earth looked cold, and dark, and dreary; feeble feet stumbled wearily on life's rugged, thorny road. Oh, judge her not harshly, pure but frigid censor; who shall say that with her desolation — her temptation—your name too might not have been written "Magdalen."

SICKNESS COMES TO YOU IN THE CITY.

How unmercifully the heavy cart wheels rattle over the stony pavements; how unceasing the tramp of busy, restless feet; how loud and shrill the cries of mirth and traffic. You turn heavily to your heated pillow, murmuring, "Would God it were night!" The pulse of the great city is stilled at last; and balmy sleep, so coveted, seems about to bless you — when hark! a watchman's rattle is sprung beneath your window, evoking a score of stentorian voices, followed by a clanging bell, and a rushing engine, announcing a conflagration. Again you turn to your sleepless pillow; your quivering nerves and throbbing temples sending to your pale lips this prayer, "Would to God it were morning!"

Death comes, and releases you. You are scarcely missed. Your next-door neighbor, who has lived within three feet of you for three years, may possibly recollect having seen the doctor's chaise before your door, for some weeks past; then, that the front blinds were closed; then, that a coffin was carried in; and he remarks to his wife, as he takes up the evening paper, over a comfortable dish of tea, that "he should n't wonder if neighbor Grey were dead," and then they read your name and age in the bill of mortality, and wonder "what disease you died of;" and then the servant removes the tea-tray, and they play a game of whist, and never think of you again, till they see the auctioneer's flag floating before your door.

The house is sold; and your neighbor sees your widow and little ones pass out over the threshold in tears and sables (grim poverty keeping them silent company); but what of that? The world is *full* of widows and orphans; one can't always be thinking of a charnel-house; and so he returns to his stocks and dividends, and counting-room, and ledger, in a philosophical state of serenity.

Some time after, he is walking with a friend; and meets a lady in rusty mourning, carrying a huge bundle, from which "slop work," is seen protruding, (a little child accompanies her, with its feet out at the toes.) She has a look of hopeless misery on her fine but sad features. She is a *lady still* (spite of her dilapidated wardrobe and her bundle.) Your neighbor's companion touches his arm, and says, "Good God! is n't that Grey's widow?" He glances at her carelessly, and answers, "Should n't wonder;" and invites him home to dine on trout, cooked in claret, and hot-house peaches, at half a dollar a-piece.

SICKNESS COMES TO YOU IN THE COUNTRY.

On the fragrant breeze, through your latticed window, come the twitter of the happy swallow, the chirp of the robin, and the drowsy hum of the bee. From your pillow you can watch the shadows come and go, over the clover meadow, as the clouds go drifting by. Rustic neighbors lean on their spades at sunset at your door, and with sympathising voices "hope you are better." The impatient hoof of the prancing horse is checked by the hand of pity; and the merry shout of the sunburnt child (musical though it be,) dies on the cherry lip, at the uplifted finger of compassion. A shower of rose-leaves drifts in over your pillow, on the soft sunset zephyr. Oh, earth *is* passing fair; but *Heaven is fairer!*

Its portals unclose to you! Kind, neighborly hands wipe the death-damp from your brow; speak words of comfort to your weeping wife, caress your unconscious children. Your fading eye takes it all in, but your tongue is powerless to speak its thanks. They close your drooping lids, they straighten your manly limbs, they lay your weary head on its grassy pillow, they bedew it with sympathetic tears; they pray God, that night, in their cottage homes, to send His kind angel down, to whisper words of peace to the broken hearts you have left behind.

They do something besides pray. From unknown hands, the widow's "cruse of oil," and "barrel of meal," are oft replenished. On your little orphans' heads, many a rough palm is laid, with tearful blessing. Many a dainty peach, or pear, or apple is tossed them, on their way to school. Many a ride they get "to mill," or "hay-field," or "village," while their mother shades her moistened eyes in the door-way, quite unable to speak. The old farmer sees it; and knowing better how to bestow a kindness than to bear such expressive thanks, cuts Dobbin in the flanks, then starting tragically at the *premeditated rear*, asks her, with an hysterical laugh, "*if she ever saw such an uneasy beast!*"

Wide open fly their cottage doors and hearts, at "Christmas" and "Thanksgiving," for your stricken household. There may be little city etiquette at the feast, there may be ungrammatical words and infelicitous expressions,— but, thank God, unchilled by selfishness, unshrivelled by avarice, human hearts throb warmly there — *loving* — *pitiful* — *Christ-like!*

HUNGRY HUSBANDS.

"The hand that can make a pie is a continual feast to the husband that marries its owner."

Well, it is a humiliating reflection, that the straightest road to a man's heart is through his palate. He is never so amiable as when he has discussed a roast turkey. Then 's your time, "Esther," for "half his kingdom," in the shape of a new bonnet, cap, shawl, or dress. He 's too complacent to dispute the matter. Strike while the iron is hot; petition for a trip to Niagara, Saratoga, the Mammoth Cave, the White Mountains, or to London, Rome, or Paris. Should he demur about it, the next day cook him another turkey, and pack your trunk while he is eating it.

There 's nothing on earth so savage — except a bear robbed of her cubs — as a hungry husband. It is as much as your life is worth to sneeze, till dinner is on the table, and his knife and fork are in vigorous play. Tommy will get his ears boxed, the ottoman will be kicked into the corner, your work-box be turned bottom upwards, and the poker and tongs will beat a tattoo on that grate that will be a caution to dilatory cooks.

After the first six mouthfuls you may venture to say your soul is your own; his eyes will lose their ferocity, his brow its furrows, and he will very likely recollect to help you to a cold potato! Never mind — *eat it.* You might have to swallow a worse pill — for instance, should he offer to kiss you!

Well, learn a lesson from it — keep him well fed and languid — live yourself on a low diet, and cultivate your thinking powers; and you 'll be as spry as a cricket, and hop over all the objections and remonstances that his dead-and-alive energies can muster. Yes, feed him well, and he will stay contentedly in his cage, like a gorged anaconda. If he were my husband, would n't I make him heaps of *pison* things! Bless me! I've made a mistake in the spelling; it should have been *pies and things!*

LIGHT AND SHADOW;

OR, WHO IS RESPONSIBLE?

It was a simple dress of snowy muslin, innocent of the magic touch of a French *modiste*. There was not an inch of lace upon it, nor a rosette, nor a flower; it was pure, and simple, and unpretending as its destined wearer. A pair of white kid gloves, of fairy-like proportions, lay beside it, also a tiny pair of satin slippers. There was no bridal *trousseau;* no — Meta had no rich uncles, or aunts, or cousins, — no *consistent* god-parents who, promising at her baptism that she should "renounce the pomp and vanities of the world," redeemed their promise by showering at her bridal feet, diamonds enough to brighten many a starving fellow-creature's pathway to the tomb.

Did I say there was no bridal *trousseau?* There was *one* gift, a little clasp Bible, with "Meta Grey" written on the fly-leaf, in the bridegroom's bold, handsome hand. Perchance some gay beauty, who reads this, may curl her rosy lip scornfully; but well Meta knew how to value such a gift. Through long dreary years of orphanage "God's Word" had been to her what the star in the East was to Bethlehem's watching shepherds. Her lonely days of toil were over now. There was a true heart, whose every pulsation was love for her — a brave arm to defend her helplessness, and a quiet, sunny home where Peace, like a brooding dove, should fold his wings, while the happy hours flew uncounted by.

Yes; Meta was looked for, every hour. She was to leave the group of laughing hoidens, (before whom she had forbidden her lover to claim her,) and thereafter confine her teachings to one pupil, whose "reward of merit" should be the love-light in her soft, dark eyes. Still, it was weary waiting for her; her last letter was taken, for the hundredth time, from its hiding-place, and read and refolded, and read again, although he could say it all, with his eyes shut, in the darkest corner in Christendom. But you know all about it, dear reader, if you own a heart, and if you don't, the sooner you drop my story the better.

Well; he paced the room up and down, looked out the window, and down the street: then he sat down in the little rocking-chair he had provided for her, and tried to imagine it was tenanted by *two;* then, delicious tears sprang to his eyes, that such a sweet fount of happiness was opened to him — that the golden morn, and busy noon, and hushed and starry night, should find them *ever* side by side. Care? — he did n't know it! Trouble? — what trouble could *he* have, when all his heart craved on earth was bounded by his clasping arms? And then, Meta was an orphan — he was scarcely sorry — there would be none for her heart to go out to now but himself; he must be brother, sister, father, mother — *all* to her; and his heart gave a full and joyful response to each and every claim.

—But what a little loiterer! He was half vexed; he paced the room in his impatience, handled the little slippers affectionately, and caressed the little gloves as if they were filled by the plump hand of Meta, instead of his imagination. Why *did n't* she fly to him? Such an angel should have wings — he was sure of that.

— Wings? God help you, widowed bridegroom! Who shall have the heart to read you this sad paragraph?

"One of the Norwalk Victims.— The body of a young lady, endowed with extraordinary personal beauty, remains yet unrecognized. On her countenance reposes an expression of pleasure, in striking and painful contrast to the terrible scene amid which she breathed her last. She was evidently about twenty years old, doubtless the glory of some circle of admiring friends, who little dream where she is, and of her shocking condition."

A MATRIMONIAL REVERIE.

"The love of a spirited woman is better worth having than that of any other female individual you can start."

I wish I had known that before! I'd have plucked up a little spirit, and not gone trembling through creation, like a plucked chicken, afraid of every animal I ran *a-fowl* of. I have not dared to say my soul was my own since the day I was married, and every time Mr. Jones comes into the entry and sets down that great cane of his, with a thump, you might hear my teeth chatter, down cellar! I always keep one eye on him, in company, to see if I am saying the right thing; and the middle of a sentence is the place for me to stop, (I can tell you,) if his black eyes snap! It 's so aggravating to find out my mistake at this time o' day. I ought to have carried a stiff upper lip, long ago. Wonder if little women can look dignified? Wonder how it would do to turn straight about now? I 'll try it!

Harry will come home presently and thunder out, as usual, "Mary, why the deuce is n't dinner ready?" I 'll just set my teeth together, put my arms akimbo, and look him right straight ——— oh, mercy! I can't! I should dissolve! Bless your soul, he 's a six-footer; such whiskers — none of your sham settlements! Such eyes! and such a nice mouth. Come to think of it, I really believe I love him! Guess I 'll go along the old way!

WHAT LOVE WILL ACCOMPLISH.

"This will never do," said little Mrs. Kitty; "how I came to be such a simpleton as to get married before I knew how to keep house, is more and more of an astonisher to me. I *can* learn, and I *will!* There's Bridget told me yesterday there was n't time to make a pudding before dinner. I had my private suspicions she was imposing upon me, though I did n't know enough about it to contradict her. The truth is, I'm no more mistress of this house than I am of the Grand Seraglio. Bridget knows it, too; and, there's Harry (how hot it makes my cheeks to think of it!) could n't find an eatable thing on the dinner table yesterday. He loves me too well to say anything, but he had such an ugly frown on his face when he lit his cigar and went off to his office. Oh, I see how it is:

"'One must eat in matrimony,
And love is neither bread nor honey,
And so, you understand.'"

"What on earth sent yon over here in this dismal rain?" said Kitty's neighbor, Mrs. Green. "Just look at your gaiters."

"Oh, never mind gaiters," said Kitty, untying her "rigolette," and throwing herself on the sofa. "I don't know any more about cooking than a six-weeks' kitten; Bridget walks over my head with the most perfect Irish *nonchalance;* Harry looks as solemn as an ordained bishop; the days grow short, the bills grow long, and I'm the most miserable little Kitty that ever mewed. Do have pity on me, and initiate me into the mysteries of broiling, baking, and roasting; take me into your kitchen now, and let me go into it while the fit is on me. I feel as if I could roast Chanticleer and all his hen-harem!"

"You don't expect to take your degree in one forenoon?" said Mrs. Green, laughing immoderately.

"Not a bit of it! I intend to come every morning, if the earth don't whirl off its axle. I've locked up my guitar and my French and Italian books, and that irresistible 'Festus,' and nerved myself like a female martyr, to look a gridiron in the face without flinching. Come, put down that embroidery, there's a good Samaritan, and descend with me into the lower regions, before my enthusiasm gets a shower-bath," and she rolled up her sleeves from her round white arms, took off her rings, and tucked her curls behind her ears.

Very patiently did Mrs. Kitty keep her resolution; each day added a little to her store of culinary wisdom. What if she did flavor her first custards with peppermint instead of lemon? What if she did "baste" a turkey with saleratus instead of salt? What if she did season the stuffing with ground cinnamon instead of pepper? Rome was n't built in a day; — cooks can't be manufactured in a minute.

Kitty's husband had been gone just a month. He was expected home that very day. All the morning the little wife had been getting up a congratulatory dinner, in honor of the occasion. What with satifaction and the kitchen fire, her cheeks glowed like a milkmaid's. How her eyes sparkled, and what a pretty little triumphant toss she gave her head, when that big trunk was dumped down in the entry ! It is n't a bad thing, sometimes, to have a secret even from one's own husband.

"On my word, Kitty," said Harry, holding her off at arm's length, "you look most provokingly 'well-to-do' for a widow 'pro tem.' I don't believe you have mourned for me the breath of a sigh. What have you been about ? who has been here ? and what mine of fun is to be prophesied from the merry twinkle in the corner of your eye ? Anybody hid in the closet or cupboard ? Have you drawn a prize in the lottery ?"

"Not since I married you," said Mrs. Kitty ; "and you are quite welcome to that sugar-plum to sweeten your dinner."

"How Bridget has improved," said Harry, as he plied his knife and fork industriously ; "I never saw these woodcock outdone, even at our bachelor club-rooms at ——— House. She shall have a present of a pewter cross, as sure as her name is McFlanigan, besides absolution for all the detestable messes she used to concoct with her Catholic fingers."

"Let me out ! let me out !" said a stifled voice from the closet ; "you can't expect a woman to keep a secret forever."

"What on earth do you mean, Mrs. Green ?" said Harry, gaily shaking her hand.

" Why, you see, 'Bridget has improved;' i. e. to say, little Mrs. Kitty there received from my hands yesterday a diploma, certifying her Mistress of Arts, Hearts and Drumsticks, having spent every morning of your absence in perfecting herself as a housekeeper. There now, don't drop on your knees to her till I have gone. I know very well when three is a crowd, or, to speak more fashionably, when I am '*de trop*,' and I'm only going to stop long enough to remind you that there are some *wives* left in the world, and that Kitty is one of 'em."

And now, dear reader, if you doubt whether Mrs. Kitty was rewarded for all her trouble, you'd better take a peep into that parlor, and while you are looking, let me whisper a secret in your ear confidentially. You may be as beautiful as Venus, and as talented as Madame de Stael, but you never 'll reign supreme in your liege lord's affections, till you can roast a turkey.

MRS. GRUMBLE'S SOLILOQUY.

"THERE 's no calculating the difference between men and women boarders. Here 's Mr. Jones, been in my house these six months, and no more trouble to me than my gray kitten. If his bed is shook up once a week, and his coats, cravats, love-letters, cigars and patent-leather boots left undisturbed in the middle of the floor, he is as contented as a pedagogue in vacation time.

"Take a woman to board, and (if it is perfectly convenient) she would like drapery instead of drop-curtains; she 'd like the windows altered to open at the top, and a wardrobe for her flounced dresses, and a few more nails and another shelf in her closet, and a cricket to put her feet on, and a little rocking-chair, and a big looking-glass, and a pea-green shade for her gas-burner.

"She would like breakfast about ten minutes later than your usual hour; tea ten minutes earlier, and the gong, which shocks her nerves *so*, altogether dispensed with.

"She can't drink coffee, because it is exhilarating; broma is too insipid, and chocolate too heavy. She don't fancy cocoa. 'English breakfast tea' is the only beverage which agrees with her delicate spinster organization.

"She can't digest a roast or a fried dish; she might *possibly* peck at an egg, if it were boiled with one eye on the watch. Pastry she never eats, unless she knows from what dairy the butter came, which enters into its composition. Every article of food prepared with butter, salt, pepper, mustard, vinegar or oil; or bread that is made with yeast, soda, milk or saleratus, she decidedly rejects.

"She is constantly washing out little duds of laces, collars, handkerchiefs, chemisettes and stockings, which she festoons up to the front windows, to dry; giving passers-by the impression that your house is occupied by a *blanchesseuse;* — then jerks the bell-wire for an hour or more, for relays of hot smoothing irons, to put the finishing stroke to her operations.

"She is often afflicted with interesting little colds and influenzas, requiring the immediate consolation of a dose of hot lemonade or ginger tea; choosing her time for these complaints when the kitchen fire has gone out and the servants are on a furlough. Oh! nobody knows, but those who've tried, how immensely troublesome women are! I'd rather have a whole regiment of men boarders. All you have to do is, to wind them up in the morning with a powerful cup of coffee, give them *carte-blanche* to smoke, and a night-key, and your work is done."

HENRY WARD BEECHER.

WHAT a warm Sunday! and what a large church! I wonder if it will be half-filled! Empty pews are a sorry welcome to a pastor. Ah! no fear; here comes the congregation in troops and families; now the capacious galleries are filled; every pew is crowded, and seats are being placed in the aisles.

The preacher rises. What a young "David!" Still, the "stone and sling" will do their execution. How simple, how child-like that prayer; and yet how eloquent, how fervent. How eagerly, as he names the text, the eye of each is riveted upon the preacher, as if to secure his individual portion of the heavenly manna.

Let us look around, upon the audience. Do you see yonder gray-haired business man? Six days in the week, for many years, he has been Mammon's most devoted worshipper. According to time-honored custom, he has slept comfortably in his own pew each Sunday, lulled by the soft voice of the shepherd who "prophesieth smooth things." One pleasant Sabbath, chance, (I would rather say an overruling Providence,) led him here. He settles himself in his accustomed Sunday attitude, but sleep comes not at his bidding. He looks disturbed. The preacher is dwelling upon the permitted but fraudulent tricks of business men, and exposing plainly their turpitude in the sight of that God who holds "evenly the scales of justice." As he proceeds, Conscience whispers to this aged listener, "Thou art the man!" He moves uneasily on his seat; an angry flush mounts to his temples: What right has that boy-preacher to question the integrity of men of such unblemished mercantile standing in the community as himself? He is not accustomed to such a spiritual probing knife. *His* spiritual physician has always "healed the hurt of his people slightly." He don't like such plain talking, and sits the service out only from compulsion. But when he passes the church porch, he does not leave the sermon there, as usual. No. He goes home perplexed and thoughtful. Conscience sides with the preacher; self-interest tries to stifle its voice with the sneering whisper of "priest-craft." Monday comes, and again he plunges into the maelstrom of business, and tries to tell the permitted lie with his usual *nonchalance* to some ignorant customer, but his tongue falters and performs its duty but awkwardly; a slight blush is perceptible upon his countenance; and the remainder of the week chronicles similar and repeated failures.

Again it is Sunday. He is not a church-member: he can stay at home, therefore, without fear of a canonical committee of Paul Prys to investigate the matter: he can look over his debt and credit list if he likes, without excommunication: he certainly will not put himself again in the way of that plain-spoken, stripling priest. The bell peals out, in musical tones, seemingly this summons: "Come up with us, and we will do you good." By an irresistible impulse, he finds himself again a listener. "Not that he *believes* what that boy says:" Oh no: but, somehow, he likes to listen to him, even though he attack that impregnable pride in which he has wrapped himself up as in a garment.

Now, why is this? Why is this church filled with such wayside listeners?

Why, but that all men — even the most worldly and unscrupulous — pay involuntary homage to earnestness, sincerity, independence and Christian boldness, in the "man of God?"

Why? Because they see that he stands in that sacred desk, not that his lips may be tamed and held in, with a silver bit and silken bridle: not because preaching is his "trade," and his hearers must receive their *quid pro quo* once a week — no, they all see and feel that his *heart* is in the work — that he *loves* it — that he comes to them fresh from his closet, his face shining with the light of "the Mount," as did Moses'.

The preacher is remarkable for fertility of imagination, for rare felicity of expression, for his keen perception of the complicated and mysterious workings of the human heart, and for the uncompromising boldness with which he utters his convictions. His earnestness of manner, vehemence of gesture and rapidity of utterance, are, at times, electrifying; impressing his hearers with the idea that language is too poor and meager a medium for the rushing tide of his thoughts.

Upon the lavish beauty of earth, sea, and sky, he has evidently gazed with the poet's eye of rapture. He walks the green earth in no monk's cowl or cassock. The tiniest blade of grass with its "drap o' dew," has thrilled him with strange delight. "God is love," is written for him in brilliant letters, on the arch of the rainbow. Beneath that black coat, his heart leaps like a happy child's to the song of the birds and the tripping of the silver-footed stream, and goes up, in the dim old woods, with the fragrance of their myriad flowers, in grateful incense of praise, to Heaven.

God be thanked, that upon all these rich and rare natural gifts, "Holiness to the Lord" has been written. Would that the number of such gospel soldiers was "legion," and that they might stand in the forefront of the hottest battle, wielding thus skillfully and unflinchingly the "Sword of the Spirit."

AN OLD MAID'S DECISION.

"I can bear misfortune and poverty, and all the other ills of life, but to be an *old maid*—to droop and wither, and wilt and die, like a single pink—I can't *endure* it; and *what's more, I won't!*"

Now there 's an appeal that ought to touch some bachelor's heart. There she is, a poor, lone spinster, in a nicely furnished room — sofa big enough for *two; two* arm chairs, *two* bureaus, *two* looking-glasses — everything hunting in couples except herself! I don't wonder she 's frantic! She read in her childhood that "matches were made in Heaven," and although she 's well aware there are some *Lucifer matches*, yet she has never had a chance to try either sort. She has heard that there "never was a soul created, but its twin was made somewhere," and she 's a melancholy proof that 't is a mocking lie. She gets tired sewing — she can't knit forever on that eternal stocking — (besides, *that* has a *fellow* to it, and is only an aggravation to her feelings.) She has read till her eyes are half blind, — there 's nobody to agree with her if she likes the book, or argue the point with her if she don't. If she goes out to walk, every woman she meets has her husband's arm. To be sure, they are half of them ready to scratch each other's eyes out; but that 's a little business matter between themselves. Suppose she feels devotional, and goes to evening lectures, some ruffianly coward is sure to scare her to death on the way. If she takes a journey, she gets hustled and boxed round among cab-drivers, and porters, and baggage-masters; her bandbox gets knocked in, her trunk gets knocked off, and she 's landed at the wrong stopping place. If she wants a load of wood, she has to pay twice as much as a man would, and then she gets cheated by the man that saws and splits it. She has to put her own money into the bank and get it out, hire her own pew, and wait upon herself into it. People tell her "husbands are often great plagues," but she knows there are times when they are indispensable. She is very good looking, black hair and eyes, fine figure, sings and plays beautifully, but she "can't be an old maid, and *what 's more* — SHE WON'T."

A PUNCH AT "PUNCH."

"What is the height of a woman's ambition? Diamonds."—[*Punch.*

SAGACIOUS Punch! Do you know the reason? It is because the more "diamonds" a woman owns, the more *precious* she becomes in the eyes of your discriminating sex. What pair of male eyes ever saw a "crow's foot," grey hair, or wrinkle, in company with a *genuine diamond?* Don't you go down on your marrow-bones, and vow that the owner is a Venus, a Hebe, a Juno, a sylph, a fairy, an angel? Would you stop to look (*connubially*) at the most bewitching woman on earth, whose only diamonds were "*in her eye?*" Well, it is no great marvel, Mr. Punch. The race of *men* is about extinct. Now and then you will meet with a specimen; but I'm sorry to inform you that the most of them are nothing but coat tails, walking behind a moustache, destitute of sufficient energy to earn their own cigars and "Macassar," preferring to dangle at the heels of a *diamond* wife, and meekly receive their allowance, as her mamma's prudence and her own inclinations may suggest.

FATHER TAYLOR, THE SAILOR'S PREACHER.

YOU have never heard FATHER TAYLOR, the Boston Seaman's preacher? Well — you should go down to his church some Sunday. It is not at the court-end of the town. The urchins in the neighborhood are guiltless of shoes or bonnets. You will see quite a sprinkling of "Police" at the corners. Green Erin, too, is well represented: with a dash of Africa — checked off with "dough faces."

Let us go into the church: there are no stained-glass windows — no richly draperied pulpit — no luxurious seats to suggest a nap to your sleepy conscience. No odor of patchouli, or *nonpareil*, or *bouqet de violet* will be wafted across your patrician nose. Your satin and broadcloth will fail to procure you the highest seat in the synagogue,— they being properly reserved for the "old salts."

Here they come! one after another, with horny palms and bronzed faces. It stirs my blood, like the sound of a trumpet, to see them. The seas they have crossed! the surging billows they have breasted! the lonely, dismal, weary nights they have kept watch! — the harpies in port who have assailed their generous sympathies! the sullen plash of the sheeted dead, in its vast ocean sepulchre! — what stirring thoughts and emotions do their weather-beaten faces call into play! God bless the sailor! — Here they come; sure of a welcome — conscious that they are no intruders on aristocratic landsmen's soil — sure that each added face will send a thrill of pleasure to the heart of the good old man, who folds them all, as one family, to his patriarchal bosom.

There he is! How reverently he drops on his knee, and utters that silent prayer. Now he is on his feet. With a quick motion he adjusts his spectacles, and says to the tardy tar doubtful of a berth, "Room here, brother!" pointing to a seat *in the pulpit.* Jack don't know about *that!* He can climb the rigging when Boreas whistles his fiercest blast; he can swing into the long boat with a stout heart, when creaking timbers are parting beneath him: but to mount the *pulpit!* — Jack doubts his qualifications, and blushes through his mask of bronze. "Room enough, brother!" again reässures him; and, with a litle extra fumbling at his tarpaulin, and hitching at his waistband, he is soon as much at home as though he were on his vessel's deck.

The hymn is read with a *heart-tone.* There is no mistaking either the poet's meaning or the reader's devotion. And now, if you have a "scientific musical ear," (which, thank heaven, I have not,) you may criticise the singing, while I am not ashamed of the tears that steal down my face, as I mark the effect of good *Old Hundred* (minus trills and flourishes) on Neptune's honest, hearty, whole-souled sons.

— The text is announced. There follows no arrangement of dickys, or bracelets, or eye-glasses. You forget your ledger and the fashions, the last prima donna, and that your neighbor is not one of the "upper ten," as you fix your eye on that good old man, and are swept away from worldly moorings by the flowing tide of his simple, earnest eloquence. You marvel that these uttered truths of his, never struck your thoughtless mind before. My pen fails to convey to you the play of expression on that earnest face — those emphatic gestures — the starting tear or the thrilling voice; — but they all *tell* on "Jack."

And now an infant is presented for baptism. The pastor takes it on one arm. O, surely he is himself a father, else it would not be poised so gently. Now he holds it up, that all may view its dimpled beauty, and says: "Is there one here who doubts, should this child die to-day, its right among the blessed?" One murmured, spontaneous *No!* bursts from Jacks' lips, as the baptismal drops lave its sinless temples. Lovingly the little lamb is folded, with a kiss and a blessing, to the heart of the earthly shepherd, ere the maternal arms receive it.

Jack looks on and weeps! And how can he help weeping? *He* was once as pure as that blessed innocent! His *mother*— the sod now covers her — often invoked heaven's blessing on *her* son; and well he remembers the touch of her gentle hand and the sound of her loving voice, as she murmured the imploring prayer for him: and how has her sailor boy redeemed his youthful promise? He dashes away his scalding tears, with his horny palm; but, please God, that Sabbath — that scene — shall be a talisman upon which memory shall ineffaceably inscribe,

"Go, and sin no more."

SIGNS OF THE TIMES.

E-Q-U-I — equi, D-O-M-E — dome, "Equidome." Betty, hand me my dictionary.

Well, now, who would have believed that I, Fanny Fern, would have tripped over a "stable?" That all comes of being "raised" where people persist in calling things by their right names. I'm very certain that it is useless for me to try to circumnavigate the globe on stilts. There 's the "Hippodrome!" I had but just digested that humbug: my tongue kinked all up trying to pronounce it; and then I could n't find out the meaning of it; for Webster did n't inform me that it was a place where vicious horses broke the necks of vicious young girls for the amusement of vicious spectators.

— "Jim Brown!" What a relief. I can understand that. I never saw Jim, but I 'm positively certain that he 's a monosyllable on legs — crisp as a cucumber. Ah! here are some more suggestive signs.

"Robert Link — Bird Fancier." I suggest that it be changed to Bob-o' Link; in which opinion I shall probably be backed up by all musical people.

Here we are in Broadway junior, alias the "Bowery." I don't see but the silks, and satins, and dry goods generally, are quite equal to those in Broadway; but, of course, Fashion turns her back upon them, for they are only half the price.

What have we here, in this shop window? What are all those silks, and delaines, and calicoes, ticketed up that way for?—"Superb," "Tasty," "Beautiful," "Desirable," "Cheap for 1*s*.," "Modest," "Unique," "Genteel," "Grand," "Gay!" It is very evident that Mr. Yardstick takes all women for fools, or else he has had a narrow escape from being one himself.

There 's a poor, distracted gentleman in a milliner's shop, trying to select a bonnet for his spouse. What a *non compos!* See him poise the airy nothings on his great clumsy hands! He is about as good a judge of bonnets as I am of patent ploughs. See him turn, in despairing bewilderment, from blue to pink, from pink to green, from green to crimson, from crimson to yellow. The little witch of a milliner sees his indecision, and resolves to make a *coup d'état;* so, perching one of the bonnets (blue as her eyes) on her rosy little face, she walks up sufficiently near to give him a magnetic shiver, and holding the strings coquettishly under her pretty little chin, says:

"Now, I 'm sure, you can't say *that* is n't pretty!"

Of course he can't!

So, the bonnet is bought and band-boxed, and Jonathan (who is sold with the bonnet) takes it home to his wife, whose black face looks in it like an overcharged thunder-cloud set in a silver lining.

Saturday evening is a busy time in the Bowery. So many little things wanted at the close of the week. A pair of new shoes for Robert, a tippet for Sally, a pair of gloves for Johnny, and a stick of candy to bribe the baby to keep the peace while mamma goes to "meetin" on Sunday. What a heap of people! What a job it must be to take the census in New York. Servant girls and their beaux, country folks and city folks, big boys and little boys, ladies and women, puppies and men! There 's a poor laboring man with his market basket on one arm, and his wife on the other. He knows that he can get his Sunday dinner cheaper by purchasing it late on Saturday night, when the butchers are not quite sure that their stock will "keep" till Monday. And then it is quite a treat for his wife, when little Johnny is asleep, to get out to catch a bit of fresh air, and a sight of the pretty things in the shop windows, even if she cannot have them; but the little feminine diplomatist knows that husbands always feel clever of a Saturday night, and that then 's the time "*just to stop and look*" at a new ribbon or collar.

See that party of country folks, going to the "National" to see "Uncle Tom." Those pests, the bouquet sellers, are offering them their stereotyped, cabbage-looking bunches of flowers with,

"Please buy one for your lady, sir."

Jonathan don't understand dodging such appeals; beside, he would scorn to begrudge a "quarter" for *his lady!* So he buys the nuisance, and scraping out his hind foot, presents it, with a bow, to Araminta, who "walks on thrones" the remainder of the evening.

There 's a hand organ, and a poor, tired little girl, sleepily playing the tambourine. All the little ragged urchins in the neighborhood are grouped on that door step, listening. The connoisseur might criticise the performance, but no Cathedral *Te Deum* could be grander to that unsophisticated little audience. There is one little girl, who spite of her rags, is beautiful enough for a seraph. *Poor and beautiful!* God help her.

WHOM DOES IT CONCERN?

"Stitch—stitch—stitch! Will this *never* end?" said a young girl, leaning her head wearily against the casement, and dropping her small hands hopelessly in her lap. "Stitch—stitch—stitch! from dawn till dark, and yet I scarce keep soul and body together;" and she drew her thin shawl more closely over her shivering shoulders.

Her eye fell upon the great house opposite. There was comfort there, and luxury, too; for the rich, satin curtains were looped gracefully away from the large windows; a black servant opens the hall door: see, there are statues and vases and pictures there: now, two young girls trip lightly out upon the pavement, their lustrous silks, and nodding plumes, and jeweled bracelets glistening, and quivering, and sparkling in the bright sunlight. Now poising their silver-netted purses upon their daintily gloved fingers, they leap lightly into the carriage in waiting, and are whirled rapidly away.

That little seamstress is as fair as they: her eyes are as soft and blue; her limbs as lithe and graceful; her rich, brown hair folds as softly away over as fair a brow; her heart leaps, like theirs, to all that is bright and joyous; it craves love and sympathy, and companionship as much, and yet she must stitch

"Tut, tut, young woman! don't quarrel with your bread and butter!"

—stitch—stitch—and droop under summer's heat, and shiver under winter's cold, and walk the earth with the skeleton starvation ever at her side, that costly pictures, and velvet carpets, and massive chandeliers, and gay tapestry, and gold and silver vessels may fill the house of her employer—that *his* flaunting equipage may roll admired along the highway, and India's fairest fabrics deck his purse-proud wife and daughters.

It was a busy scene, the ware-room of Simon Skinflint & Co. Garments of every hue, size and pattern, were there exposed for sale. Piles of coarse clothing lay upon the counter, ready to be given out to the destitute, brow-beaten applicant who would make them for the smallest possible remuneration; piles of garments lay there, which such victims had already toiled into the long night to finish, ticketed to bring enormous profits into the pocket of their employer: groups of dapper clerks stood behind the counter, discussing, in a whisper, the pedestals of the last new *danseuse*—ogling the half-starved young girls who were crowding in for employment, and raising a blush on the cheek of humble innocence by the coarse joke and free, libidinous gaze; while their master, Mr. Simon Skinflint, sat, rosy and rotund, before a bright Lehigh fire, rubbing his fat hands, building imaginary houses, and felicitating himself generally, on his far-reaching financial foresight.

"If you could but allow me a trifle more for my labor," murmured a low voice at his side; "I have toiled hard all the week, and yet—"

"Young woman," said Mr. Skinflint, pushing his chair several feet back, elevating his spectacles to his forehead, and drawing his satin vest down over his aldermanic proportions—"young woman, do you observe that crowd of persons besieging my door for employment? Perhaps you are not aware that we turn away scores of them every day; perhaps you do n't know that the farmers' daughters, who are at a loss what to do long winter evenings, and want to earn a little dowry, will do our work for less than we pay you? But you feminine operatives do n't seem to have the least idea of trade. Competition is the soul of business, you see," said Mr. Skin flint, rubbing his hands in a congratulatory manner. "Tut—tut—young woman! do n't quarrel with your bread and butter; however, it is a thing that do n't concern me at all; if you *won't* work, there are plenty who *will*,"—and Mr. Skinflint drew out his gold repeater, and glanced at the door.

A look of hopeless misery settled over the young girl's face, as she turned slowly away in the direction of home. *Home* did I say? The word was a bitter mockery to poor Mary. She had a home once, where she and the little birds sang the live-long day: where flowers blossomed, and tall trees waved, and merry voices floated out on the fragrant air, and the golden sun went gorgeously down behind the far-off hills; where a mother's loving breast was her pillow, and a father's good-night blessing wooed her rosy slumbers. It was past now. They were all gone—father, mother, brother, sister. Some with the blue sea for a shifting monument; some sleeping dreamlessly in the little church-yard, where her infant footsteps strayed. Rank grass had o'ergrown the cottage gravel walks; weeds choked the flowers which dust-crumbled hands had planted; the brown moss had thatched over the cottage eaves, and still the little birds sang on as blithely as if Mary's household gods had not been shivered.

Poor Mary! The world was dark and weary to her: the very stars, with their serene beauty, seemed to mock her misery. She reached her little room. Its narrow walls seemed to close about her like a tomb. She leaned her head wearily against the little window, and looked again at the great house opposite. How brightly, how cheerfully the lights glanced from the windows! How like fairies glided the young girls over the softly carpeted floors! How swiftly the carriages whirled to the door, with their gay visitors? Life was such a rosy dream to *them*—such a brooding nightmare to *her!* Despair laid its icy hand on her heart. Must she *always* drink, unmixed, the cup of sorrow? Must she weep and sigh her youth away, while griping Avarice trampled on her heart-strings? She could not weep—nay, worse—she could not pray. Dark shadows came between her soul and heaven.

The little room is empty now. Mary toils there no longer. You will find her in the great house opposite: her dainty limbs clad in flowing silk; her slender fingers and dimpled arms glittering with gems: and among all that merry group, Mary's laugh rings out the merriest. Surely—surely, this is better than to toil, weeping, through the long weary days in the little darkened room.

Is it, Mary?

There is a ring at the door of the great house. A woman glides modestly in; by her dress, she is a widow. She has opened a small school in the neighborhood, and in the search for scholars has wandered in here. She looks about her. Her quick, womanly instinct sounds the alarm. She is not among the good and pure of her sex. But she does not scorn them. No; she looks upon their blighted beauty, with a Christ-like pity; she says to herself, haply some word of mine may touch their hearts. So, she says, gently, "Pardon me, ladies, but I had hoped to find scholars here; you will forgive the intrusion, I know; for though you are not mothers, you have all *had* mothers."

Why is Mary's lip so ashen white? Why does she tremble from head to foot, as if smitten by the hand of God? Why do the hot tears stream through her jeweled fingers? Ah! Mary. That little dark room, with its toil, its gloom, its *innocence*, were Heaven's own brightness now, to your tortured spirit.

Pitilessly the slant rain rattled against the window panes awnings creaked and flapped, and the street lamps flickered in the strong blast: full-freighted omnibuses rolled over the muddy pavements: stray pedestrians turned up their coat-collars, grasped their umbrellas more tightly, and made for the nearest port. A woman, half-blinded by the long hair which the fury of the wind had driven across her face, drenched to the skin with the pouring rain — shoeless, bonnetless, *homeless*, leans unsteadily against a lamp-post, and in the maudlin accents of intoxication curses the passers-by. A policeman's strong grasp is laid upon her arm, and she is hurried, struggling, through the dripping streets, and pushed into the nearest "station house." Morning dawns upon the wretched, forsaken outcast. She sees it not. Upon those weary eyes only the resurrection morn shall dawn.

No more shall the stony-hearted shut, in her imploring face, the door of hope; no more shall gilded sin, with Judas smile, say, "Eat, drink, and be merry;" no more shall the professed followers of Him who said, "Neither do I condemn thee," say to the guilt-stricken one, "Stand aside — for I am holier than thou." No, none may tempt, none may scorn, none may taunt her more. A pauper's grave shall hide poor Mary and her shame.

God speed the day when the Juggernaut wheels of Avarice shall no longer roll over woman's dearest hopes; when thousands of doors, now closed, shall be opened for starving Virtue to earn her honest bread; when he who would coin her tears and groans to rear his palaces, shall become a hissing and a by-word, wherever the sacred name of Mother shall be honored.

"WHO LOVES A RAINY DAY?"

The bored editor; who, for one millennial day, in slippered feet, controls his arm chair, exchanges, stove, and inkstand; who has time to hunt up delinquent subscribers; time to decipher hieroglyphical manuscripts; time to make a bonfire of bad poetry; time to kick out lozenge boys and image venders; time to settle the long-standing quarrel between Nancy, the type-setter, and Bill, the foreman, and time to write complimentary letters to himself for publication in his own paper, and to get up a new humbug prospectus for the dear, confiding public.

Who loves a rainy day?

The little child of active limb, reprieved from bench, and book, and ferule; between whom and the wire-drawn phiz of grim propriety, those friendly drops have drawn a misty vail; who is now free to laugh, and jump, and shout, and ask the puzzling question — free to bask in the sunny smile of her, to whom no sorrow can be trivial that brings a cloud over that sunny face, or dims the brightness of that merry eye.

Who loves a rainy day?

The crazed clergyman, who can face a sheet of paper, uninterrupted by dyspeptic Deacon Jones, or fault-finding brother

Grimes; or cautious Mr. Smith; or the afflicted Miss Zelia Zephyr, who, for several long years, has been "unable to find out the path of duty;" or the zealous old lady Bunce, who hopes her pastor will throw light on the precise locality fixed upon in the future state for idiots, and those heathen who have never seen a missionary.

Who loves a rainy day?

The disgusted clerk, who, lost in the pages of some care-beguiling volume, forgets the petticoat destiny which relentlessly forces him to unfurl endless yards of tinsel lace and ribbon, for lounging dames, with empty brains and purses, whose "chief end" it seems to be to put him through an endless catechism.

Who loves a rainy day?

The tidy little housewife, who, in neat little breakfast-cap and dressing-gown, overlooks the short-comings of careless cook and house-maid; explores cupboards, cellars, pantries, and closets; disembowels old bags, old boxes, old barrels, old kegs, old firkins; who, with her own dainty hand, prepares the favorite morsel for the dear, absent, toiling husband, or, by the cheerful nursery fire, sews on the missing string or button, or sings to soothing slumbers a pair of violet eyes, whose witching counterpart once stole her girlish heart away.

Who loves a rainy day?

I do! Let the rain fall; let the wind moan; let the leaf less trees reach out their long attenuated fingers and tap against my casement: pile on the coal; wheel up the arm-chair; all hail loose ringlets and loose dressing-robe. Not a blessed son or daughter of Adam can get here to-day! Unlock the old writing desk; overlook the old letters. There is a bunch tied with a ribbon blue as the eyes of the writer. Matrimony quenched their brightness long time ago.

> Irish *help* (?) and crying babies,
> I grieve to say, are 'mong the may-be's!

And here is a package written by a despairing Cœlebs — once intensely interested in the price of hemp and prussic acid; now the rotund and jolly owner of a princely house, a queenly wife, and six rollicksome responsibilities. Query: whether the faculty ever dissected a *man* who had died of a "broken heart?"

Here is another package. Let the fire purify them; never say you *know* your friend till his tombstone is over him.

What Solomon says "handwriting is an index of character?" Give him the cap and bells, and show him those bold pen-marks. They were traced by no Di Vernon! Let me sketch the writer: — A blushing, smiling, timid, loving little fairy, as ever nestled near a true heart; with a step like the fall of a snow-flake, and a voice like the murmur of a brook in June. Poor little Katie! she lays her cheek now to a little cradle sleeper's, and starts at the distant footstep, and trembles at the muttered curse, and reels under the brutal blow, and, woman-like — loves on!

And what have we here? A sixpence with a ribbon in it! Oh, those Saturday and Wednesday afternoons, with their hoarded store of nuts and candy — the broad, green meadow, with its fine old trees — the crazy old swing, and the fragrant tumble in the grass — the wreath of oak leaves, the bunch of wild violets, the fairy story book, the little blue jacket, the snowy shirt-collar, the curly, black head, with its soft, blue eyes. Oh, first love, sugar-candy, torn aprons, and kisses! where have ye flown?

What is this? only a pressed flower; but it tells me of a shadowy wood — of a rippling brook — of a bird's song — of a mossy seat — of whispered leaf-music — of dark, soul-lit eyes — of a voice sweet, and low, and thrilling — of a vow never broken till death chilled the lips that made it. Little need to look at the pictured face that lies beside me. It haunts me sleeping or waking. I shall see it again — life's trials passed.

A CONSCIENTIOUS YOUNG MAN.

"There is no object in nature so beautiful as a conscientious young man."—
[*Exchange.*

Well; I've seen the "Sea-Dog," and Thackeray; and Tom Thumb and Kossuth; the "Bearded Lady" and Father Matthew; the whistling Canary, and Camille Urso; the "white negro," and Mrs. Stowe; "Chang and Eng," and Jenny Lind; and Miss Bremer, and Madame Sontag. I have been to the top of the State House, made the tour of the "Public Garden," and crossed the "Frog Pond." I've seen Theodore Parker, and a locomotive. I've ridden in an omnibus, heard a Fourth-of-July oration, and I once saw the sun rise; but I never, *never* never saw "a conscientious young man."

If there is such an "organization" on the periphery of this globe, I should like to see him. If he *is*, *where* is he? Who owns him? Where did they raise him? What does he feed on? For whom does he vote? On what political platform do his conscientious toes rest? Does he know the difference between a Whig and a Democrat? between a "Hunker" and a "Barnburner?" between a "hard-shell" and a "soft-shell?" between a "uniform national currency" and a "sound constitutional currency?" Does he have chills, or a fever, when he sees a bonnet! Does he look at it out of the sides of his eyes, like a bashful, barn-yard bantam, or dare he not look at all? Does he show the "white feather," or crow defiance? Does he "go to roost" at sun-down? and does he rest on an aristocratic perch? I'm all alive to see the specimen. My opera-glass is poised. Will he be at the World's Fair? Might I be permitted to shake hands with, and congratulate him! I pause for a reply.

CITY SCENES AND CITY LIFE

NUMBER ONE.

"Each to his taste," somebody says: so say I: so says Gotham. Look at that splendid house, with its massive doorway, its mammoth plate-glass windows, its tasteful conservatory, where the snowy Orange blossom, and clustering Rose, and crimson Cactus, and regal Passion-flower, and fragrant Heliotrope breath out their little day of sweetness. See that Gothic stable, with its faultless span of horses, and liveried coachman, and anti-republican carriage, whose coat of arms makes our National Eagle droop his fearless pinions. Then cast your eye on that tumble-down, wooden grocery adjoining, sending up its reeking fumes of rum, onions, and salt fish, into patrician nostrils! Go where you will in New York, you see the same strong contrasts. Feast your eyes on beauty, and a skeleton startles you at its side. Lazarus sitteth ever at the Gate of Dives.

Here is a primary school: what a host of little ragged urchins are crowding in! Suppose I step in quietly among them. Now, they take their places in seats terraced off one above another, so that each little face is distinctly visible. What a pretty sight! and how Nature loves to compensate! sending beauty to the hovel, deformity to the hall. There 's a boy, now, in that ragged jacket, who is a study for an artist. See his broad, ample forehead; mark how his dark eyes glow: and that little girl at his side, whose chestnut curls droop so gracefully over her soft-fringed eyes and dimpled shoulders. And that dream-child in yonder corner, with blue-veined, transparent temples, whose spiritual eyes even now can see that fadeless shore to which bright angels beckon him. Deal gently with him — he is passing away!

Here comes the teacher, brisk, angular, and sharp-voiced. Heaven pity the children! She 's a human icicle—pastboard-y and proper! I already experience a mental shiver. Now she comes up and says, (apologetically to my new satin cloak,) "You see, madam, these are *only* poor children." The toadying creature! Lucky for her that I 'm not "a committee." Can't her dull eyes recognize God's image in linsey-woolsey? Can she see no genius written on yonder broad forehead? No poetry slumbering in yonder sweet eyes? Did Franklin, Clay, and Webster study *their* alphabet in silk and velvet? She ought to be promoted to the dignity of toe-nail polisher to Queen Victoria. Now she hands me a book, in which visitors' names are inscribed, and requests me to write mine. Certainly. "Mrs. John Smith:" there it is. Hope she likes it as well as I do.

—Speaking of names, I read on a sign yesterday, that "Richard Haas:" to-day I saw, down street, that "John Haas." I 'm sure I 'm glad of it. I congratulate both those enterprising gentlemen. There goes a baker's cart, with "Ernest Flog-er" painted on the side. It is my impression that if you do it,

Ernest, "*your* cake will be dough;" 1853 being considered the millenium of "strong-minded women." Here we are, most to the Battery. "*Fanfernot* & Dulac:" that must be a chain-lightning firm. Wonder if "Fanfernot" is the *silent* partner?

Here's a man distributing tracts. Now, if he hands me one, I'll throw it down. See how meekly he picks it up, and hands me another. "That's right, friend Colporteur, I only wanted to see if you were in earnest: glad to see you so well employed."

"Yes, Ma'am," he says, much relieved, "sinners here in New York need waking up"—which sentiment I endorse, and advise him to call at the *N. Y. Tribune* office.

Down comes the rain: had I taken my umbrella, not a drop would have fallen. "I 'spect" I was born on a Friday; but as that can't be helped now, I'll step into that book-store till the shower is over. The owner politely gives me a chair, and then hands me, for my edification, the *last fashion prints!* F-a-n-n-y F-e-r-n! can it be possible that you look so frivolous? Tracts and fashion prints, both offered you in one forenoon! Wonder if there's a second-hand drab Quaker bonnet anywhere, that will subdue your "style?"

See that little minstrel in front of the store, staggering under the weight of a hand-organ. What a crowd of little beggar-boys surround him, petitioning "for *just one tune.*" Now, I wonder if the rough school that boy has been in, has hardened his heart? Has he grown prematurely worldly-wise and selfish? Will he turn gruffly away from that penniless, Tom Thumb audience, or will he give them a *gratuitous* tune? God be thanked, his childish heart yet beats warm and true under that tattered jacket. He smiles sweetly on the eager group, and strikes up "Lang Syne." Other than mortal ears are listening! That deed, unnoticed by the hurrying Broadway throng, is noted by the Recording Angel. "Inas much as ye have done it unto one of the least of these, ye have done it unto Me."

Sunshine again! dripping awnings and sloppy pavements. There's a man preaching an out-door temperance sermon: what a bungling piece of work he makes of it! If he would lend me that pro tem barrel-pulpit I'd astonish *him*, and take the feather out of "Miss Lucy Stone's" bonnet.

Let us cross the Park. There's an Irishman seated on the withered grass, with his spade beside him, leaning wearily against that leafless tree. I wonder is he ill? I must walk that way and speak to him. What a sudden change comes over his rough face! it looks quite beautiful. Why do his eyes kindle? Ah, I see: a woman approaches from yonder path; now she seats herself beside him, on the grass, and drawing the cover from a small tin kettle, she bends over the steaming contents, and says, with a smile, that is a perfect heart-warmer, "*Dear* Dennis!" Oh, what a wealth of love in those two simple words; what music in that voice! Who says human nature is *all* depravity? Who says this earth is but a charnel-house of withered hopes? Who says the "Heart's Ease" springs never from the rock cleft? Who says it is only on *patrician* soil the finer feelings struggle into leaf and bud and blossom? No — no — that humble, faithful creature has trav eled weary miles with needful food, that "Dennis" may waste no unnecessary time from labor. And there they sit, side by side, happy and blessed in each other, deaf to the ceaseless tide of business and pleasure flowing past, blind to the supercilious gaze of the pompous millionaire, the curious stare of pampered beauty, the derisive laugh of "Young America," and the little romance they have set my brain a-weaving! What a pretty episode amid all this Babel din! What a delicious little bit of nature midst this fossil hearted Gotham!

How true — how beautiful the words of Holy Writ! "Better is a dinner of herbs, *where love is*, than a stalled ox, and hatred therewith."

What an immensely tall man! he looks like a barber's pole in those serpentine pants. Why does he make those gyrations? Why does he beckon that short man to his side? Well, I declare! everything comical comes to my net! He has taken out a slip of paper, and using the short man's head for a writing-desk, is scribbling off some directions for a porter in waiting! The lamb-like non-resistance of the short man is only equalled by the cool impudence of the scribe! What a picture for Hogarth!

CITY SCENES AND CITY LIFE.

NUMBER TWO.

THE fashionables are yet yawning on their pillows. Nobody is abroad but the workies. So much the better. Omnibus drivers begin to pick up their early-breakfast customers. The dear little children, trustful and rosy, are hurrying by to school. Apple women are arranging their stalls, and slyly polishing their fruit with an old stocking. The shopkeepers are placing their goods in the most tempting light, in the store windows; and bouquet venders, with their delicious burthens, have already taken their stand on the saloon and hotel steps.

Here come that de-socialized class, the New York business men, with their hands thrust moodily into their coat pockets, their eyes buttoned fixedly down to the sidewalk, and "the almighty dollar" written legibly all over them. If the automatons would but show *some* sign of life; were it only by a whistle. I'm very sure the tune would be

"I know a—*Bank!*"

See that pretty little couple yonder, crouched upon the sidewalk? What have you there, little ones? Five little, fat, roly-poly puppies, as I live, all heads and tails, curled up in that comical old basket! And you expect to get "a dollar apiece" for them? Bless your dear little souls, Broadway is full of "puppies," who never "bring" anything but odious cigar smoke, that ever I could find out. Puppies are at a discount, my darlings. Peanuts are a safer investment.

Here we are at Trinity Church. I doubt if human lips within those walls ever preached as eloquently as those century grave-stones. How the sight of them involuntarily arrests the bounding footstep, and the half-developed plan of the scheming brain, and wakes up the slumbering immortal in our nature. How the eye turns a questioning glance from those moss-grown graves, inward — then upward to the soft, blue heavens above us. How for a brief moment the callous heart grows kindly, and we forget the mote in our brother's eye, and cease to repulse the outspread palm of charity, and recognise the claims of a common brotherhood; and then how the sweeping tide comes rolling over us, and the clink of dollars and cents drowns "the still small voice," and Eternity recedes, and Earth only seems tangible, and Mammon, and Avarice, and Folly rule the never returning hours.

Now glance over the church-yard yonder into the street below. Cholera and pestilence, what a sight! flanked on one side by the charnel-house, on the other by houses whose basements are groggeries and markets, and at whose every pane of glass may be seen a score of dirty faces: the middle of the street a quagmire of jelly-mud, four inches deep, on which are strewn, ad-infinitum, decayed potatoes and cabbage stumps, old bones and bonnets, mouldy bread, salt fish and dead kittens.

That pussy-cat New York corporation should be put on a diet of peppered thunder and gunpowder tea, and harnessed to a comet for six months. I doubt if even then the old poppies would wake up.

Do you see that piece of antiquity playing the bagpipe? He is as much a fixture as your country cousin. There he sits, through heat and cold, squeezing out those horrible sounds with his skinny elbow, and keeping time with his nervous eye-winkers. He gets up his own programme, and is his own orchestra, door-keeper and audience: nobody stops to listen, nobody fees him, nobody seems to enjoy it so hugely as himself.

Who talks about wooden nutmegs in the hearing of Gotham? Does a shower come up? Men start up as if by magic, with all-sized India rubbers for sale, and ragged little boys nudge your elbows to purchase "cheap cotton umbrellas." Does the wind veer round south? A stack of palm-leaf fans takes the place of the umbrellas. Have you the misfortune to trip upon the sidewalk? a box of Russia salve is immediately unlidded under your nose. Do you stop to arrange your gaiter boot? whole strings of boot-lacings are dangled before your astonished eyes. Do your loosened waistbands remind you of the dinner hour? before your door stands a man brandishing "patent carving knives," warranted to dissever the toughest old rooster that ever crowed over a hen harem.

Speaking of hens — see that menagerie, in one of the handsomest parts of Broadway, defaced by that blood and murder daub of a picture, representing every animal that ever flew or trotted into Noah's ark, beside a few that the good old gentleman never undertook to perpetuate. See them lashing their tails, bristling their manes, ploughing the air and tossing high above their incensed horns, that distracted gory biped, whose every individual hair is made to stand on end with horror, and his coat-tail astonishingly to perpendicularize. Countrymen stand agape while pickpockets lighten them of their purses; innocent little children, with saucer eyes, shy to the further edge of the sidewalk, and hurry home with an embryo nightmare in their frightened craniums. "Jonathan" pays his "quarter," and is astonished to find upon entering, a very tame collection of innocent beasts and beastesses, guiltless of any intention to growl, unless poked by the long pole of curiosity. Dissatisfied, he descends to the cellar, to see the elephant, who holds a sleepy levee, for all who feel inclined to pack his trunk with the apples and cake, which a shrewd stall-keeping Yankee in the corner disinterestedly advises them to buy, "just to see how the critter eats."

Well; two-headed calves, one-eyed buffaloes, skeleton ostriches, and miles of serpents, are every day matters; but yonder is an announcement that "Two Wild Men from Borneo" may be seen within. Now that interests me. "They have the faculty of speech, but are deficient in memory." Bless me, you don't mean to say that those little Hop o' my Thumbs have the temerity to call themselves "*Men?*" little humbug, pocket editions. But what pretty little limbs they have, and how they shiver in this cold climate, spite of the silk and India-rubber dress they wear under those little tights. "The youngest weighs only twenty-seven, the oldest thirty-four pounds;" so the keeper says, who, forming a circle, lays one hand on the head of each, and commences his stereotyped, menagerie exordium, oblivious of commas, colons, semi-colons, periods or breath; adding at the close, that the Wild Men will now shake hands with any child who may be present, but will *always bite an adult*." Nothing like a barrier to make femininity leap over. I'm bent upon having the first "adult" shake. The keeper says, "Better not, Ma'am," (showing a scar on his finger,) "they bit that een-a-most to the bone." Of course, snapping at masculinity, is no proof to me of their unsusceptibility to feminine evangelization; on the contrary. So, taking a cautious patrol around the interesting little savages, I hold out my hand. Allah be praised! they take it, and my five digits still remain at the service of printers and publishers!

CITY SCENES AND CITY LIFE.

NUMBER THREE.

WHAT a never-ceasing bell-jingling, what a stampede of servants, what a continuous dumping down of big trunks; what transits, what exits, what a miniature world is a hotel! Panorama-like, the scene shifts each hour; your vis-a-vis at breakfast, supping, ten to one, in the Rocky Mountains. How delightful your unconsciousness of what you are foreordained to eat for dinner; how nonchalantly in the morning you handle tooth-brush and head-brush, certain of a cup of hot coffee whenever you see fit to make your advent. How scientifically your fire is made, without any unnecessary tattooing of shovel, tongs and poker. What a chain-lightning answer to your bell summons; how oblivious is "No. 14" of your existence; how indifferent is "No. 25" whether you sneeze six or seven times a day; how convenient are the newspapers and letter-stamps, obtainable at the clerk's office; how digestible your food; how comfortable your bed, and how never-to-be-sufficiently-enjoyed the general let-alone-ativeness.

Avaunt, ye lynx-eyed "private boarding-houses," with your two slip-shod Irish servants; your leaden bread, leather pies, ancient fowls, bad gravies, omnium gatherum bread puddings, and salt fish, and cabbage perfumed entries; your washing-day "hashes," your ironing-day "stews," and all your other "comforts of a home" (?) not *explicitly* set forth in your advertisements.

Rat-tat, rat-tat-tat! what a fury that old gentleman seems to be in. Whoever occupies No. 40, must either be deaf or without nerves. Rat-tat! what an obstinate human! there he goes again! ah, now the door opens, and a harmless-looking clergyman glides past him, down the stairs. Too late — too late, papa — the knot is tied; no use in making a fuss. Just see that pretty little bride, blushing, crying, and clinging to her boy husband. Just remember the time, sir, when the "auld wife" at home made *you* thrill to the toes of your boots; remember how perfectly oblivious you were of guide-boards or mile-stones, when you went to see her; how you used to hug and kiss her little brother Jim, though he was the ugliest, mischievous-est little snipe in Christendom; how you used to read books for hours upside down, and how you wondered what people meant by calling the moon "cold;" how you wound up your watch half-a-dozen times a day, and had n't the slightest idea whether you were eating geese or grindstones for dinner; how affectionately you nodded to Mr. Brown, of whom her father bought his groceries; how complacently you sat out the minister's seventh-lie by her side at church; how wolfy you felt if any other piece of broadcloth approached her; how devoutly you wished you were that little bit of blue ribbon round her throat; and how, one moonlight night, when she laid her head against your vest-pattern, you ——— did n't care a mint-julep whether the tailor ever got paid for it or not! Now, just imagine her papa, stepping in and deliberately turning all *that* cream to vinegar; would n't *you* have effervesced? Certainly.

See that little army of boots in the entry outside the doors. May I need a pair of spectacles, if one of their owners has a decent foot! No. 20 turns his toes in, No. 30 treads over at the side; No. 40 has a pedestal like an elephant. Stay! — there 's a pair now — Jupiter! what a high instep! what a temper that man has! wonder if those are married boots? Heaven help *Mrs.* Boots, when her husband finds a button missing! It strikes me that I should like to *mis-mate* all those boots, and view, at a respectful distance, the young tornado in the entry, when the gong sounds!

Oh, you cunning little curly-headed, fairy-footed, dimple-limbed pet! Who is blessed enough to own you? Did you know, you little human blossom, that I was aunt to all the children in creation? Your eyes are as blue as the violets, and your little pouting lip might tempt a bee from a rose. Did mamma make you that dainty little kirtle? and papa find you that horsewhip?

"Papa is dead, and mamma is dead, too. Mamma can't see Charley any more."

God bless your sweet helplessness! creep into my arms, Charley. My darling, you are never alone!—mamma's sweet, tender eyes look lovingly on Charley out of Heaven; mamma's bright angel wings ever overshadow little Charley's head; mamma and the holy stars keep watch over Charley's slum bers. Mamma sings a sweeter song when little Charley says a prayer. Going? — well, then, one kiss; for sure I am, the angels will want you before long.

What is that? A sick gentleman, borne in on a litter, from shipboard. Poor fellow! how sunken are his great dark eyes! how emaciated his limbs! What can ail him? Nobody knows; not a word of English can he speak; and the captain is already off, too happy to rid himself of all responsibility. Lucky for the poor invalid that our gallant host has a heart warm and true. How tenderly he lifts the invalid to his room; how expeditiously he dispatches his orders for a Spanish doctor and nurse; how imploringly the sufferer's speaking eyes are fastened upon his face. Ah! Death glided in at yonder door with the sick man; his grasp is already on his heart; the doctor stands aside and folds his hands — there's no work for *him* to do; dark shadows gather round the dying stranger's eyes; he presses feebly the hand of his humane host, and gasps out the last fluttering breath on that manly heart. Strange hands are busy closing his eyes; strange hands straighten his limbs; a strange priest comes all too late to shrive the sick man's soul; strange eyes gaze carelessly upon the features, one glimpse of which were worth Golconda's mines to far-off kindred. Now the undertaker comes with the coffin. Touch him gently, man of business; lay those dark locks tenderly on the satin pillow; hear you not a far-off wail from sunny Spain, as the merry song at the vintage feast dies upon the lip of the stricken-hearted?

CITY SCENES AND CITY LIFE.

NUMBER FOUR.

BARNUM'S POULTRY SHOW.

DEFEND my ears! Do you suppose Noah had to put up with such a cackling and crowing as this, in his ark? I trust ear-trumpets are cheap, for I stand a chance of becoming as deaf as a husband, when his wife asks him for money.

I have always hated a rooster; whether from his perch, before daylight, he shrilly, spitefully, and unnecessarily, recalled me from rosy dreams to stupid realities; or when strolling at the head of his hang-dog looking seraglio of hens, he stood poised on one foot, gazing back at the meek procession with an air that said, as plain as towering crests and tail feathers could say it — "Stir a foot if you dare, till I give you the signal!" — at which demonstration, I looked instinctively about, for a big stone, to take the nonsense out of him!

Save us, what a crowd! There are more onions here than patchouli, more worsted wrappers than Brummel neck-ties, and more brogans than patent leather. Most of the visitors gaze at the perches, through barn-yard spectacles. For myself, I don't care an egg-shell, whether that old "Shanghai" knew who her grandfather was or not, or whether those "Dorkings" were ever imprudent enough to let their young affections rove from their native roost. Yankee eyes were made to be used, and the first observation mine take, is, that those gentlemen fowls seem to have reversed the order of things here in New York, being very superior in point of beauty to the feminines. Of course they know it. See them strut! There never was a masculine yet whom you could enlighten on such a point.

Now, were I a hen, (which, thank the parish register, I am not,) I would cross my claws, succumb to that tall Polander with his crested helmet of black and white feathers, and share his demonstrative perch.

Oh, you pretty little "carrier doves!" I *could* find a use for *you*. Do you ever tap-tap at the wrong window, you little snow-flakes? Have you learned the secret of soaring above the heads of your enemies? Are you impregnable to bribes, in the shape of feed?

There's an Eagle, fierce as a Hospodar. Bird of Jove! that *you* should stay caged in the tantalizing vicinity of those fat little bantams! Try the strength of your pinions, grim old fellow; call no man jailer; turn your back on Barnum, and stare the sun out of countenance!

Observe with what aristocratic nonchalance those salmon-colored pigeons sit their perch! See that ruffle of feathers about their dignified Elizabethan throats. I am not at all sure that I should have intruded into their regal presence, without being heralded by a court page.

Do you call those two moving bales of wool, sheep? Hurrah for "Ayrshire" farming! Fleece six inches deep, and the animals not half grown. Comfortable looking January-defiers, may your shearing be mercifully postponed till the dog days.

Pigs, too? petite, white and frisky; two hundred dollars a pair! P-h-e-w! and such pretty little gaiter boots to be had in Broadway! Disgusting little porkers, don't wink your pink eyes at my Jewish resolution.

Puppies for sale? long-eared and short-eared, shaggy and shaven, bobtailed—curtailed—and to be re-tailed! Spaniel terrier and embryo Newfoundland. Ho! ye unappropriated spinsters, with a superfluity of long evenings—ye forlorn bachelors, weary of solitude and boot-jacks, listen to these yelping applicants for your yearning affections, and "down with the dust."

"Nelly for sale, at twenty dollars." Poor little antelope! The gods send your soft, dark eyes an appreciative purchaser. I look into their human-like depths, and invoke for you the velvety, flower-bestrewn lawn, the silver lake, in which your graceful limbs are mirrored as you stoop to drink, the leafy shade of fret-work leaves in the panting noon-tide heat, and the watchful eye and caressing hand of some bright young creature, to whom the earth is one glad anthem, and whose sweet young life (like yours) is innocent and pure.

Avaunt, pretentious peacocks, flaunting your gaudy plumage before our sated eyes. See that beautiful "Golden Pheasant," on whose plump little body, clad in royal crimson, the sunlight lingers so lovingly. See the silky fall of those flossy, golden feathers about his arching neck. Glorious pheasant! do you know that "a thing of beauty is a joy forever?" Make your home with me, and feast my pen-weary eyes: flit before me when the sunlight of happiness is clouded in, and the gray, leaden clouds of sorrow overcast my sky; perch upon my finger; lay your soft neck to my cheek; bring me visions of a happier shore, where love is written on the rainbow's arch, heard in the silver-tripping stream, seen in the blossom-laden bough and bended blade, quivering under the weight of dewy gems, and hymned by the quiet stars, whose ever-moving harmony is unmarred by the discord of envy, hate, or soul-blasting uncharitableness. Beautiful pheasant! come, bring thoughts of beauty and peace to me!

— Loving Jenny Lind smiles upon us from yonder canvass. Would that we might hear her little Swedish chicken peep! Not a semi-quaver careth the mother-bird for the homage of the Old World or New. The artless clapping of little Otto's joyous hands, drowns all the ringing plaudits, wafted across the ocean. A Dead Sea apple is fame, dear Jenny, to a true woman's heart. Happy to have hung thy laurel wreath on Otto's little cradle.

TWO PICTURES.

You will always see Mrs. Judkins in her place at the sunrise prayer-meeting. She is secretary to the "Moral Reform," "Abolition," "Branch Colporteur and Foreign Mission" Societies. She is tract distributor, manager of an "Infant School," cuts out all the work for the Brown Steeple Sewing Circle; belongs to the "Select Female Prayer Meeting;" goes to the Friday night church meeting, Tuesday evening lecture, and Saturday night Bible Class, and attends three services on Sunday. Every body says, "What an eminent Christian is Mrs. Judkins!"

Mrs. Judkins' house and servants take care of themselves. Her little boys run through the neighborhood, peeping into grocery and provision stores, loitering at the street corners, and throwing stones at the passers-by. Her husband comes home to a disorderly house, eats indigestible dinners, and returns to his gloomy counting-room, sighing that his hard earnings are wasted, and his children neglected; and sneering at the *religion* which brings forth such questionable fruits.

Mrs. Brown is a church member. Mrs. Judkins has called upon her, and brought the tears into her mild blue eyes, by telling her that she in particular, and the church in general, have been pained to notice Mrs. Brown's absence from the various religious gatherings and societies above mentioned; that it is a matter of great grief to them, that she is so lukewarm, and does not enjoy religion as much as they do.

Mrs. Brown has a sickly infant; her husband (owing to sad reverses) is in but indifferent circumstances; they have but one inexperienced servant. All the household outgoings and incomings, must be carefully watched, and looked after. The little wailing infant is never out of the maternal arms, save when its short slumbers give her a momentary reprieve. Still, the little house is in perfect order. The table tasteful and tempting, although the bill of fare is unostentatious; the children are obedient, respectful, happy and well cared for. Morning and evening, amid her varied and pressing cares, she bends the knee in secret, to Him whom her maternal heart recognizes as "My Lord and my God." No mantle of dust shrouds the "Holy Book." The sacred *household* altar flame never dies out. Little dimpled hands are reverently folded; little lips lisping say, "Our Father." Half a day on each returning Sabbath, finds the patient mother in her accustomed place in the sanctuary. At her hearth and by her board, the holy man of God hath smiling welcome. "Her children rise up and call her blessed; her husband also, and he praiseth her;" while on high, the recording angel hath written, "*She hath done what she could.*"

FEMININE WAITERS AT HOTELS.

"Some of our leading hotel-keepers are considering the policy of employing fe male waiters."

Good news for you, poor pale-faced sempstresses! Throw your thimbles at the heads of your penurious employers; put on your neatest and *plainest* dress; see that your feet and fin gers are immaculate, and then rush *en masse* for the situation, ousting every white jacket in Yankeedom. Stipulate with your employers, for leave to carry in the pocket of your French apron, a pistol loaded with cranberry sauce, to plaster up the mouth of the first coxcomb who considers it necessary to preface his request for an omelette, with "*My dear*." It is my opinion that one such hint will be sufficient; if not, you can vary the order of exercises, by anointing him with a "HASTY plate of soup" at dinner.

Always make a moustache wait twice as long as you do a man who wears a clean, presentable lip. Should he undertake to expedite your slippers by "a fee," tell him that hotel bills are *generally* settled at the clerk's office, except by *very* verdant travelers.

Should you see a woman at the table, digging down to the bottom of the salt cellar, as if the top stratum were too plebe ian; or ordering ninety-nine messes (turning aside from each with affected airs of disgust,) or rolling up the whites of her eyes, declaring that she never sat down to a dinner-table before minus "finger glasses," you may be sure that her aristocratic blood is nourished, *at home*, on herrings and brown bread. When a masculine comes in with a white vest, flashy neck-tie, extraordinary looking plaid trousers, several yards of gold chain festooned over his vest, and a mammoth seal ring on his little finger, you may be sure that his tailor and his laundress are both on the anxious seat; and whenever you see travelers of *either* sex peregrinating the country in their "best bib and tucker," you can set them down for unmitigated "snobs," for high-bred people can't afford to be so extravagant!

I dare say you 'll get sick of so much pretension and humbug. Never mind; it is better than to be stitching yourselves into a consumption over six-penny shirts; you 'll have your fun out of it. This would be a horridly stupid world, if every body were sensible. I thank my stars every day, for the share of fools a kind Providence sends in my way.

LETTER TO THE EMPRESS EUGENIA.

A Paris Letter says:—Lady Montijo has left Paris for Spain. She was extremely desirous of remaining and living in the reflection of her daughter's grandeur, but Louis Napoleon, who shares in the general prejudice against step-mothers, gave her plainly to understand, that because he had married Eugenia, she must not suppose he had married her whole family. She was allowed to linger six weeks, to have the *entree* of the Tuileries, and to see her movements chronicled in the *Pays*. She has at last left us, and the telegraph mentions her arrival at Orleans, on her way to the Peninsula.

There Teba! did not I say you would need all those two-thousand-franc pocket-handkerchiefs before your orange wreath had begun to give signs of wilting? Why did you let your mamma go, you little simpleton? Before Nappy secured your neck in the matrimonial noose, you should have had it put down, in black and white, that Madame Montijo was to live with you till — the next revolution, if you chose to have her. Now you have struck your colors, of course everything will "go by the board." I tell you Teba, that a fool is the most unmanageable of all beings. He is as dogged and perverse as a broken-down donkey. You can neither goad nor coax him into doing anything he should do, or prevent his doing what he should not do. You will have to leave Nappy and come over here; — and then everybody will nudge somebody's elbow and say, "That is Mrs. Teba Napoleon, who does not live with her husband." And some will say it is your fault; and others will say 'tis his; and all will tell you a world more about it, than *you* can tell *them.*

Then, Mrs. Samuel Snip (who has the next room to yours, who murders the king's English most ruthlessly, and is not quite certain whether Barnum or Christopher Columbus discovered America,) will have her Paul Pry ear to the keyhole of your door about every other minute, (except when her husband is on duty,) to find out if you are properly employed;—and no matter what Mrs. Snip learns, or even if she does not learn anything, she will be pretty certain to report, that, in her opinion, you are "no better than you should be." If you dress well (with your splendid form and carriage you could not but seem well-dressed) she will "wonder how you got the means to do it"; prefacing her remark with the self-evident truth that, "to be sure, it is none of her business."

If you let your little Napoleon get out of your sight a minute, somebody will have him by the pinafore and put him through a catechism about his mamma's mode of living and how she spends her time. If you go to church, it will be "to show yourself;" if you stay at home, "you are a publican and a sinner." Do what you will, it will all be wrong: if you do nothing, it will be still worse. Our gentlemen (so called) knowing that you are defenceless and taking it for granted that your name is "Barkis," will all stare at you; and the women will dislike and abuse you just in proportion as the opposite sex admire you. Of course you will sweep past them all, with that magnificent figure of yours, and your regal chin up in the air, quietly attending to your own business, and entirely unconscious of their pigmy existence.

MUSIC IN THE NATURAL WAY.

How often, when wedged in a heated concert room, annoyed by the creaking of myriad fans, and tortured optically, by the glare of gas-light, have I, with a gipsey longing, wished that the four walls might be razed, leaving only the blue sky over my head, that the tide of music might unfettered flow over my soul.

How often, when dumb with delight, in the midst of some scene of surpassing natural beauty, have I silently echoed the poet's words:

"Give me music, or I die."

My dream was all realized at a promenade concert at Castle Garden, last night. Shall I ever forget it? That glorious expanse of sea, glittering in the moonbeams; the little boats gliding smoothly over its polished surface; the cool, evening zephyr, fanning the brow wooingly; the music — soothing — thrilling — then quickening the pulse and stirring the blood, like the sound of a trumpet; then, that rare boon, a companion, who had the good taste to be *dumb*, and not disturb my trance.

There was one drawback. After the doxology, I noticed

some matter-of-fact wretches devouring ice creams. May no priest be found to give them absolution. I include, also, in this anathema, those ever-to-be-avoided masculines, who, then and there, puffed cigar smoke in my face, and the moon's.

FOR LADIES THAT "GO SHOPPING."

MATRIMONY and the toothache *may* be survived, but of all the evils feminity is heir to, defend me from a shopping excursion. But, alas! bonnets, shoes and hose will wear out, and shop-keepers will chuckle over the sad necessity that places the unhappy owners within their dry-goods clutches. Felicitous Mrs. Figleaf! why taste that Paradisaical apple?

Some victimised females frequent the stores where soiled and damaged goods are skillfully announced as selling at an "immense sacrifice," by their public-spirited and disinterested owners. Some courageously venture into more elegant estab lishments, where the claim of the applicant to notice, is measured by the costliness of her apparel, and where the clerks poise their eye-glass at any plebeian shopperess bold enough to inquire for silk under six dollars a yard. Others, still, are tortured at the counter of some fussy old bachelor, who always ties up, with distressing deliberation, every parcel he takes down for inspection, before he can open another, and moves round to execute your orders as if Mt. Atlas were fastened to his heels; or perhaps get petrified at the store of some snap-dragon old maid, whose victims serve as escape-valves for long years of bile, engendered by Cupid's oversights. Meanwhile, the vexed question is still unsolved, Where can the penance of shopping be performed with the least possible wear and tear of patience and prunella? The answer seems to me to be contained in six letters—"Stewart's."

"*Stewart's?*" I think I hear some old lady exclaim, dropping her knitting and peering over her spectacles; "Stewart's! yes, if you have the mines of California to back you." Now I have a profound respect for old ladies, as I stand self-pledged to join that respectable body on the advent of my very first gray hair; still, with due deference to their catnip and pennyroyal experience, I conscientiously repeat—"*Stewart's.*"

You may stroll through his rooms free to gaze and admire, without being annoyed by an impertinent clerk dogging your footsteps; you can take up a fabric, and examine it, without being bored by a statement of its immense superiority over every article of the kind in the market, or without being deafened by a detailed account of the enormous sums that the mushroom aristocracy have considered themselves but *too* happy to expend, in order to secure a dress from that very desirable, and altogether unsurpassed, and unsurpassable, piece of goods!

You can independently say that an article does not exactly suit you, though your husband may not stand by you with a drawn sword. You will encounter no ogling, no impertinent cross-questioning, no tittering whispers, from the quiet, well-bred clerks, who attend to their own business and allow you to attend to yours.

'Tis true that you may see at Stewart's, cobweb laces an inch or two wide, for fifty or one hundred dollars a yard, which many a brainless butterfly of fashion is supremely happy in sporting: but at the very next counter you may suit yourself, or your country cousin, to a sixpenny calico, or a shilling de laine; and, what is better, be quite as sure that her verdant queries will be as respectfully answered as if liveried Pompey stood waiting at the door to hand her to her carriage.

You can go into the silk department, where, by a soft descending light, you will see dinner dresses that remind you of a shivered rainbow, for *passé* married ladies who long since ceased to celebrate their birth-days, and who keep their budding daughters carefully immured in the nursery: or, at the same counter, you can select a modest silk for your minister's wife, at six shillings a yard, that will cause no heart-burnings in the most Argus-eyed of Paul Pry parishes.

Then if you patronise those ever-to-be-abominated and always-to-be-shunned nuisances called parties, where fools of both sexes gather to criticise their host and hostess, and cut up characters and confectionary, you can step into that little room from which day-light is excluded, and select an evening dress, *by gas-light*, upon the effect of which you can, of course, depend, and to which artistic arrangement many a New York belle has probably owed that much prized possession — her "last conquest."

Now, if you please, you can go into the upholstery-room and furnish your nursery windows with a cheap set of plain linen curtains; or you can expend a small fortune in regal crimson, or soft-blue damask drapery, for your drawing-room; and without troubling yourself to thread the never-ending streets of Gotham for an upholsteress, can have them made by competent persons in the upper loft of the building, who will also drape them faultlessly about your windows, should you so desire.

Now you can peep into the cloak room, and bear away on your graceful shoulders a six, twenty, thirty, or four hundred dollar cloak, as the length of your husband's purse, or your own fancy (which in these degenerate days amounts to pretty much the same thing) may suggest.

Then there is the wholesale department, where you will see shawls, hosiery, flannels, calicoes, and de laines, sufficient to stock all the nondescript country stores, to say nothing of city consumption.

Now, if you are not weary, you can descend (under ground) into the carpet department, from whence you can hear the incessant roll of full-freighted omnibuses, the ceaseless tramp of myriad restless feet, and all the busy train of out-door life made audible in all the dialects of Babel. Here you can see every variety of carpet, from the homespun, unpretending straw, oil cloth, and Kidderminster, to the gorgeous Brussels and tapestry, (above whose traceried buds and flowers the daintiest foot might well poise itself, loth to crush,) up to the regal Axminster, of Scottish manufacture, woven without seam, and warranted, in these days of late suppers and tobacco smoking, to *last a life-time.*

Emerging from this subterranean region, you will ascend into daylight, and reflecting first upon all this immense outlay, and then upon the frequent and devastating conflagrations in New

York, inquire with solicitude, Are you *insured?* and regret to learn that there is too much risk to effect an *entire* insurance, although Argus-eyed watchmen keep up a night-and-day patrol throughout the handsome building.

MODERN IMPROVEMENTS.

"Modern improvements?" I wonder where they are? Perhaps it is the fashionable cloaks, that take leave of their shivering owners at the hips; or the long skirts, whose muddy trains every passing pedestrian pins to the sidewalk; or the Lilliputian bonnets, that never a string in shop-dom can keep within hailing distance of the head; or the flowing sleeves, through which the winter wind plays around the arm-pits; or the break-neck, high-heeled boots, which some little, dumpy feminine has introduced to gratify her *rising* ambition, and render her tall sisters hideous; or the gas-lit, furnace-heated houses, in which the owners' eyes are extinguished, and their skins dried to a parchment; or, perhaps, it is the churches, of such cathedral dimness, that the clergyman must have candles at noonday, and where the congregation are forbidden to express their devotion by singing, and forced to listen to the trills and quavers of some scientific stage mountebank; or perhaps 'tis the brazen irreverence with which Young America jostles aside gray-headed Wisdom: perhaps the comfortless, forsaken fireside of the "strong-minded woman:" perhaps, the manly gossip, whose repetition of some baseless rumor dims the bright eyes of defenceless innocence with tears of anguish: perhaps the schools, where a superficial show of brilliancy on exhibition days, is considered the ne plus ultra of teaching: perhaps it is the time-serving clergyman, whose tongue is fettered by a monied clique: perhaps, the lawyers who lie — under a mistake! — perhaps it is the doctor, whom I saw yesterday at Aunt Jerusha's sick-room, a little thing with bits of feet, and mincing voice, and lily-white hands, and perfumed moustache. I wanted to inquire what ailed Jerusha, so I waited to see him. I wanted to ask him how long it would take him to cure her, and if he preferred pills to powders, blisters to plasters, oat-meal to barley-gruel, wine-whey to posset, arrow-root to farina, and a few such little things, you know. He stared at me over his dicky, as if I had been an unevangelized kangaroo; then he sidled up to Jerusha, pryed open her mouth, and said "humph" — in Latin. Then he crossed his legs, and rolled up the whites of his eyes at the ceiling, as if he expected some Esculapian hand writing on the wall to enlighten him as to the seat of Aunt Jerusha's complaint. Then, he drew from his pocket a box with a whole army of tiny bottles; and uncorking two of them he nipped out a little white speck from each, which he dissolved in four quarts of water, and told Jerusha "to take a drop of the water once in eight hours." Tom Thumb and Lilliput! he might as well have tried to salt the Atlantic Ocean with a widower's tear! He should be laid gently on a lily leaf, and consigned to the first stray zephyr.

Ah, you should have seen our good, old-fashioned Dr. Jalap; with a fist like a sledge-hammer, a tramp like a war-horse, and a laugh that would puzzle an echo. He was n't penurious of *his* physic: *he* did n't care a pin how much he put down your throat — no, nor the apothecary either. He pill-ed and potioned, and emetic-ed, and blistered, and plastered, till you were so transparent, that even John Mitchell (and he's the shortest-sighted being alive) could have seen through you. And then he braced you up with Iron and Quinine, till your muscles were like whip-cords, and your hair in a bristle of kinks. He was human-like, too; he did n't stalk in as if Napoleon and the Duke of Wellington were boiled down to make his grandfather. No; he 'd just as lief sit down on a butter-firkin as on a velvet lounge. He 'd pick up Aunt Esther's knitting-needles, and talk to grandpa about Bunker Hill, and those tee-totally discomfrizzled, bragging British, and offer grandma a pinch of snuff, and trot the baby, and stroke the cat, and go to the closet and eat up the pickles and doughnuts, and make himself useful generally. *He* did n't have to stupefy his patients with ether, so that they need n't find out how clumsily he operated. No; it was quite beautiful to see him take a man's head between his knees, and drag his double teeth out. He did n't write a prescription for molasses and water, in High Dutch: he did n't tell you that you were booked for the river Styx, and he was the only M. D. in creation who could annihilate the ferryman waiting to row you over. He did n't drive through the town with his horse and gig, at break-neck speed, just as meeting was out, as if life and death were hanging on his profitless chariot wheels: he did n't stick up over his door— "*at home between nine and ten,*" as if that consecrated hour were *all* he could bestow upon a clamorous public, when he was angling in vain for a patient every hour in the twenty-four; nor did he give little boys shillings to rush into church, and call him out in the middle of the service. No: Dr. Jalap was not a "modern improvement."

THE OLD MERCHANT WANTS A SITUATION.

"An elderly gentleman, formerly a well-known merchant, wishes a situation; he will engage in any respectable employment not too laborious." —*New York Daily Paper.*

I don't know the old man. I never saw him on 'change, in a fine suit of broadcloth, leaning on his gold-headed cane; while brokers, and insurance officers, and presidents of banks raised their hats deferentially, and the crowd respectfully made way for him. I never kept account of the enormous taxes he annually paid the city, or saw his gallant ships ploughing the blue ocean with their costly freight, to foreign ports. I never saw him in his luxurious home, taking his quiet siesta, lulled by the liquid voice of his fairy daughter. No: nor did I hear the auctioneer's hammer in that home, nor see the red flag floating, like a signal of distress, before the door. I did n't read the letter that recalled his only boy from college, or see the humbled family, as they passed, shrinking, over the threshold, into poor lodgings, whose landlord coarsely stipulated for "a week's rent in advance."

"Any occupation not *too laborious.*" How mournfully the old man's words fall upon the ear! Life to commence anew, with the silver head, and bent form, and faltering step, and palsied hand of age! With the first ray of morning light, that hoary head must be lifted from an unquiet pillow, to encounter the drenching rain, and driving sleet, and piercing cold. No reprieve from that wearisome ledger, for the throbbing brow and dimmed eye. Beardless clerks make a jest of "the old boy;" superciliously repeating, in his sensitive ear, their mutual master's orders. With them he meekly receives his weekly pittance; sighing, as he counts it over, to think of the few comforts it will bring to the drooping hearts at home. Foot-weary, he travels through the crowded streets; his threadbare coat, and napless hat, and dejected face, all unnoticed by the thriving young merchant, whom the old man helped to his present prosperous business position. The birth-days of his delicate daughter come and go, all unmarked by the joy-bestowing gift. With trouble and exposure, sickness comes at last: then, the tardy foot, and careless, professional touch of the callous-hearted dispensary doctor: then, the poor man's hearse stands before the door; then winds unheeded through busy streets, to the "Potter's field," while his former cotemporaries take up the daily paper, and sipping their wine, say carelessly, as if *they* had a quit-claim from sorrow, "Well, Old Smith, the broken-down millionaire, is dead."

Ah, there are tragedies of which editors and printers little dream, woven in their daily advertising sheets: the office boy feeds the fire with many a tear-blotted manuscript, penned by trembling fingers, all unused to toil.

A MOVING TALE.

The Smiths have just been moving. They always move "for the last time," on the first of May. "Horrid custom!" exclaims Smith, wiping the perspiration from his brow, and pulling up his depressed dickey. "How my blood curdles and my bones ache, at the thought!" It was on Tuesday, the third of May, that the afflicting rite was celebrated. Cartmen — four of them — were engaged the Saturday previous, to be on hand at six o'clock on Tuesday morning, to transport the household goods from the habitation of '52–3 to that of '53–4. Smith was to pay them three dollars each — twelve dollars in all. They would not come for a mill less; Smith tried them thoroughly.

On Monday, Smith's house is turned into a sort of Bedlam, minus the beds. They are tied up, ready for the next morning's Hegira; the Smiths sleeping on the floor on Monday night. Smith can't sleep on the floor; he grows restless; he receives constant reminders from Mrs. Smith to take his elbow out of the baby's face; he has horrid visions and rolls about: therefore, he is not at all surprised, on waking at cock-crow, to find his head in the fire-place, and his hair powdered with soot. The occasion of his waking at that time, was a dream of an un-

"They met, 't was in a crowd"—
on the stairs, and Smith
"Thought that Brown would shun him,
—but he did n't!

pleasant nature. He dreamed that he had rolled off the world backwards, and lodged in a thorn-bush. Of course, such a thing was slightly improbable; but how could Smith be responsible for a dream?

On Tuesday morning, the Smiths are up with the dawn. The household being mustered, it is found that the servant girl, who had often averred that, "she lived out, just for a little exercise," had deserted her colors. The grocer on the corner politely informs Smith, (whom Mrs. S. had sent on an errand of inquiry) that, on the night previous, the servant left with him a message for her employers, to the effect that "she did n't consider moving the genteel thing, at all; and that a proper regard for her character and position in society, had induced her to get a situation in the family of a gentleman who owned the house he lived in."

This is severe: Smith feels it keenly; Mrs. Smith leans her head against her husband's vest pattern, and says "She is quite crushed," and "wonders how Smith can have the heart to whistle. But, it is always so," she remarks. "Woman is the weaker vessel, and man delights to trample on her." Smith indignantly denies this sweeping assertion, and says "he tramples on nothing;" when Mrs. Smith points to a band-box containing her best bonnet, which he has just put his foot through. Smith is silent.

The cartmen were to be on the premises at six o'clock. Six o'clock comes—half-past six—seven o'clock—but no cartmen. Here is a dilemma! The successors to the Smiths are to be on the ground at eight o'clock; and being on the ground, they will naturally wish to get into the house; which they cannot well do, unless the Smiths are out of it.

Smith takes a survey of his furniture, with a feeling of intense disgust. He wishes his cumbrous goods were reduced to the capacity of a carpet-bag, which he could pick up and walk away with. The mirrors and pianoforte are his especial aversion. The latter is a fine instrument, with an Eolian attachment. He wishes it had a sheriff's attachment; in fact, he would have been obliged to any officer who should, at that wretched moment, have sold out the whole establishment, at the most "ruinous sacrifice," ever imagined by an auctioneer's fertile "marvelousness."

—Half-past seven, and no cartmen yet. What is to be done? Ah! here they come, at last. Smith is at a loss to know what excuse they will make. Verdant Smith! *They make no excuse.* They simply tell him, with an air which demands his congratulations, that they "picked up a nice job by the way, and stopped to do it. You see," says the principal, "we goes in for all we can get, these times, and there 's no use of anybody's grumbling. Kase, you see, if one don't want us, another will; and it 's no favor for anybody to employ us a week either side the first of May." The rascal grins, as he says this; and Smith, perceiving the strength of the cartman's position, wisely makes no reply.

They begin to load. Just as they get fairly at work, the Browns (the Smiths' successors) arrive, with an appalling display of stock. Brown is a vulgar fellow, who has suddenly become rich, and whose ideas of manliness all center in bru tality. He is furious because the Smiths are not "clean gone." He "can't wait there, all day, in the street." He orders his men to "carry the things into the house," and heads the column himself with a costly rocking-chair in his arms. As Brown comes up with his rocking-chair, Smith, at the head of his men, descends, with a bureau, from the second floor.

"They met, 't was in a crowd"—

on the stairs, and Smith

"Thought that Brown would shun him,"

—but he did n't! The consequence was, they came in collision; or, rather, Smith's bureau and Brown's rocking-chair came in collision. Now, said bureau was an old-fashioned, hard-wood affair, made for service, while Brown's rocking-chair was a flimsy, showy fabric, of modern make. The meeting on the stairs occasions some squeezing, and more stumbling, and Brown suddenly finds himself and chair under the bureau, to the great injury of his person and his furniture. (Brown has since recovered, but the case of the rocking-chair is considered hopeless.) This discomfiture incenses the Browns to a high degree, and they determine to be as annoying as possible; so they persist in bringing their furniture into the house, and up stairs, as the Smiths are carrying theirs out of the house, and down stairs. Collisions are, of course, the order of the day; but the Smiths do not mind this much, as they have a great advantage, viz: *their furniture is not half so good as Brown's.* After a few smashes, Brown receives light on this point, and orders his forces to remain quiet, while the foe evacuates the premises; so the Smiths retire in peace — and much of their furniture in pieces.

The four carts form quite a respectable procession; but there is no disguising the fact that the furniture looks very shabby (and whose furniture does not look shabby, piled on carts?); so the Smiths prudently take a back street, that no one may accuse them of owning it. Smith has to carry the baby and a large mirror, which Mrs. S. was afraid to trust to the cartmen, there being no insurance on either. It being a windy day, both the mirror and Smith's hat veer to all points of the compass, while the baby grows very red in the face at not being able to possess himself of them. Between the wind, the mirror, his hat and the baby, Smith has an unpleasant walk of it.

About ten o'clock, they arrive at their new residence, and find, to their horror, that their predecessors have not begun to move. They inquire the reason. The feminine head of the family informs them, with tears in her eyes, that her husband, (Mr. Jonas Jenkins,) has been sick in Washington for five weeks; that, in consequence of his affliction, they have not been able to provide a new tenement; that she is quite unwell, and that one of her children (she has six) is ill, also; that she don't know what is to become of them, &c., &c. Smith sets his hat on the back of his head, gives a faint tug at his neck-tie and confesses himself—quenched! His furniture looks more odious every minute. He once felt much pride in it, but he feels none now: he feels only disgust. The cartmen begin to growl out that they "can't stand here all day," and request to be informed "where we shall drop the big traps." Hereupon, Smith ventures, with a ghastly attempt at a smile, to inquire of Mrs. Jenkins why she did n't tell him, when he called, on Saturday, of her inability to procure a house? To which that lady innocently replies that she did n't wish to give him any unnecessary trouble!" which reply satisfies him as to Mrs. Jenkin's claim to force of intellect.

At this juncture, Smith falls into a profound reverie. He thinks that, after all, Fourier is right—"that the Solidarity of the human race is an entity;" that "nobody can be happy, until everybody is happy." He agrees with the great philosopher, that the "series distributes the harmonies." He realizes that "society is organized (or, rather, disorganized) on a wrong basis;" that it is in an "amorphous condition," whereas it should be "crystalized." With our celebrated "down east" poet, Ethan Spike, Esq., he begins to think that,

"The etarnal bung is loose,"

and that, unless it be soon tightened, there is danger that

"All nater will be spilt.

He comes to the conclusion, finally, that "something must be done," and that speedily, to "secure a home for every family."

At this point, he is aroused by his tormenters, the cartmen, who inform him that they are in a "Barkis" state of mind, (willin') to receive their twelve dollars. Smith pays the money, and turns to examine the premises. He finds that Mrs. Jenkins has packed all her things in the back basement and the second-floor sitting-room. Poor thing! she has done her best, after all. She is in ill health; her husband is sick, and away from home; and her children are not well. God pity the unfortunate who live in cities, especially in the "moving season." But Smith is a kind-hearted man. With a few exceptions, the Smiths are a kind-hearted race — and that's probably the reason they are so numerous.

Smith puts on a cheerful countenance, and busies himself in arrranging his furniture. Mrs. Smith, kind soul, forgets the destruction of her bandbox and bonnet, and cares not how long or how loud Smith whistles. Suddenly the prospect brightens! Mrs. Jenkins' brother-in-law appears, and announces that he has found rooms for her, a little higher up town. Cartmen are soon at the door, and the Jenkinses are on their "winding way" to their new residence.

— But the Smiths' troubles are not yet over. The painters, who were to have had the house all painted the day before, have done nothing but leave their paint-pots in the hall, and a little Smithling, being of an investigating turn of mind, and hungry, withal, attempts to make a late breakfast off the contents of one of them. He succeeds in eating enough to disgust him with his bill of fare, and frighten his mamma into hysterics. A doctor is sent for: he soon arrives, and, after attending to the mother, gives the young adventurer a facetious chuck under the chin, and pronounces him perfectly safe. The parents are greatly relieved, for Willy is a pet; and they con fidently believe him destined to be President of the United States, if they can only keep paint-pots out of his way.

It takes the Smiths some ten days to get "to rights." The

particulars of their further annoyances — how the carpets did n't fit; how the cartmen "lost the pieces;" how the sofas could n't be made to look natural; how the pianoforte was too large to stand behind the parlor door, and too small to stand between the front windows; how the ceiling was too low, and the book-case too high; how a bottle of indelible ink got into the bureau by mistake and "marked" all Mrs. Smith's best dresses — I forbear to inflict on the reader. Suffice it to say, the Smiths are in "a settled state;" although their apartments give signs of the recent manifestation of a strong disturbing force — reminding one, somewhat, of a "settlement" slowly recovering from the visitation of an earthquake. Still, they are thankful for present peace, and are determined, *positively*, not to move again — until next May.

THIS SIDE AND THAT.

I AM weary of this hollow show and glitter — weary of fashion's stereotyped lay-figures — weary of smirking fops and brainless belles, exchanging their small coin of flattery and their endless genuflexions: let us go out of Broadway— somewhere, anywhere. Turn round the wheel, Dame Fortune, and show up the other side.

"The Tombs!" — we never thought to be there! nevertheless, we are not to be frightened by a grated door or a stone wall, so we pass in; leaving behind the soft wind of this Indian summer day, to lift the autumn leaves as gently as does a loving nurse her drooping child.

We gaze into the narrow cells, and draw a long breath. Poor creatures, tempted and tried. How many to whom the world now pays its homage, who sit in high places, *should* be in their stead? God knoweth. See them, with their pale faces pressed up against the grated windows, or pacing up and down their stone floors, like chained beasts. There is a little boy not more than ten years old; what has *he* done?

"Stolen a pair of shoes!"

Poor child! he never heard of "Swartout." How should he know that he was put in there not for *stealing*, *but for doing it on so small a scale?*

Hist! Do you see that figure seated in the farther corner of that cell, with his hands crossed on his knees? His whole air and dress are those of a gentleman. How came such a man as that here?

"For murder?" How sad! Ah! somewhere in the length and breadth of the land, a mother's heart is aching because she spared the rod to spoil the child.

There is a coffin, untenanted as yet, but kept on hand; for Death laughs at bolts and fetters, and many a poor wretch is borne struggling within these gloomy walls, only to be carried to his last home, while none but God may ever know at whose fireside stands his vacant chair.

And here is a woman's cell. There are two or three faded dresses hanging against the walls, and a bonnet, for which she has little use. Her friends have brought her some bits of carpeting, which she has spread over the stone floor, with her womanly love of order, (poor thing,) to make the place look *home-like*. And there is a crucifix in the corner. See, she kneels before it! May the Holy Virgin's blessed Son, who said to the sinning one, "Neither do I condemn thee," send into her stricken heart the balm of holy peace.

Who is that? No! it *cannot* be — but, yes, it is he — and what a wreck! See, he shrinks away, and a bright flush chases the marble paleness from his cheek. God bless me! That R——, should come to this! Still, Intemperance, with her thousand voices, crieth "Give! give!" and still, alas! it is the gifted, and generous, and warm-hearted, who oftenest answer the summons.

More cells? — but there is no bed in them; only a wooden platform, raised over the stone floor. It is for gutter drunkards — too foul, too loathsome to be placed upon a bed — turned in here like swine, to wallow in the same slough. Oh, how few, who, festively sipping the rosy wine, say "*my* mountain stands strong," e'er dream of such an end as this.

Look there! tread softly: angels are near us. Through the grated window the light streams faintly upon a little pallet, where, sweet as a dream of heaven, lies a sleeping babe! Over its cherub face a smile is flitting. The cell has no other occupant; angels only watch the slumbers of the prison-cradled. The place is holy. I stoop to kiss its forehead. From the crowd of women pacing up and down the guarded gallery, one glides gently to my side, saying, half proudly, half sadly, "'Tis *my* babe."

"It is *so* sweet, and pure, and holy," said I.

The mother's lip quivered; wiping away a tear with her apron, she said, in a choking voice:

"Ah, it is little the likes of you, ma'am, know how hard it is for us to get the honest bread!"

God be thanked, thought I, that there is one who "judgeth *not* as man judgeth;" who holdeth evenly the scales of justice; who weigheth against our sins the *whirlpool* of our temptations, who forgetteth never the countless struggles for the victory, ere the desponding, weary heart shuts out the light of Heaven.

MRS. ZEBEDEE SMITH'S PHILOSOPHY.

Dear me! how expensive it is to be poor. Every time I go out, my best bib and tucker has to go on. If Zebedee were worth a cool million, I might wear a coal-hod on my head, if I chose, with perfect impunity. There was that old nabob's wife at the lecture, the other night, in a dress that might have been made for Noah's great grandmother. She can afford it! Now, if it rains knives and forks, I must sport a ten dollar hat, a forty dollar dress, and a hundred dollar shawl. If I go to a concert, I must take the highest priced seat, and ride there and back, just to let "Tom, Dick and Harry" see that I can afford it. Then, we must hire the most expensive pew in the broad-aisle of a tip-top church, and give orders to the sexton not to admit any strangers into it who look snobbish. Then my little children, Napoleon Bonaparte and Donna Maria Smith, can't go to a public school, because, you know, we should n't have to pay anything.

Then, if I go shopping, to buy a paper of needles, I have to get a little chap to bring them home, because it would n't answer for me to be seen carrying a bundle through the streets. We have to keep three servants, where one might do; and Zebedee's coats have to be sent to the tailor when they need a button sewed on, for the look of the thing.

P

Then, if I go to the sea-shore, in summer, I can't take my comfort, as rich people do, in gingham dresses, loose shoes and cambric sun-bonnets. No! I have to be done up by ten o'clock in a Swiss-muslin dress, and a French cap; and my Napoleon Bonaparte and Donna Maria can't go off the piazza, because the big rocks and little pebbles cut their toes so badly through their patent kid slippers.

Then, if Zebedee goes a fishing, he dare not put on a linen coat, for the price of his reputation. No, indeed! Why, he never goes to the barn-yard without drawing on his white kids. Then he orders the most ruinous wines at dinner, and fees those white jackets, till his purse is as empty as an egg-shell. I declare, it is abominably expensive. I don't believe rich people have the least idea how much it costs poor people to live!

OPENING OF THE CRYSTAL PALACE.

Such a crowd, such a rush, such a confusion I never expect to see again. Equestrians and pedestrians; omnibuses and carriages; soldiers, civilians and *uncivil*-ians; carts and curricles; city exquisites, and country nondescripts; men on the run; women tiptoe-ing, with all sails spread; papas in a putter; fat men sweltering; lean men, with tempers as sharp as their bones, ruthlessly pushing through the crowd; musicians perspiring in tuneful agony; thermometer evidently on a spree; shirt-collars prostrate; dust everywhere; police nowhere; everybody in somebody's way; — whizz — buzz — rattle — bang — crash — smash; "Oh *dear!* where's Pa?" — "Sarah Maria, take care of your flounces." — "Get out of the way, can't you?" — "Take your cane out of my eye, will you?" — "Mr. Jones, just see the way that baby's best bonnet is jammed!" — "Hurry!" — "I *can't* hurry; somebody has trod on my skirt, and burst off the hooks; so much for not letting me wear Bloomers! What a figure I cut, to appear before the President, and no chance to apologize, Mr. Jones!"

— Well; it's eleven o'clock, and after several abortive attempts, we succeed in arresting an omnibus, labelled "for the Hippodrome and Crystal Palace." Away we go — dashing through the crowd, regardless of limbs, vehicular or human. Broadway is lined, on either side, with a dense throng of questionable looking expectants, waiting "to see the procession." Short people are at a discount; no chance for the poor wretches, strain and tiptoe it as they will. One tall man, who evidently knew the worth of his inches, seemed to think himself too valuable to be let out all at once; so, he elevated himself, jack-screw fashion, letting out one link of his vertebral column after another, until he towered above his neighbors like a pine tree among scrub oaks. What altitude he finally reached, I am unable to say, as he was still on his way up (like Jack's bean-stalk) when our omnibus passed him.

"Everything comes in use once in seven years," says the old proverb. I had often wondered of what earthly use could be the tottering brick-piles, which disfigure every block in Broadway. To-day, I was enlightened; they served admirably as points of observation for the more adventurous spectators, and each pile was covered with eager gazers. The windows overlooking Broadway were all filled with neatly dressed ladies, and as the eye swept through this magnificent thoroughfare, the rushing vehicles, the swaying, motley multitudes, the gaily dressed ladies, the waving flags and banners which floated over the more public and prominent edifices, presented an ever varying panorama, that was far from being the least attractive and impressive feature of the day. I have often thought when the people come out "to see a sight," that they themselves are far more imposing than what they came to see.

On entering the Palace, we (my companion and I) found

that all the most eligible seats were already occupied, and that what were left were reserved for some man of straw and his wife. It was no use to show one's ticket. "You must n't sit here!"—"You must n't sit there!"—"You can't stand in that place!"—"You can't go there!"—"You can't come here!"—and so the throng went forlornly about and around—old men and maidens—heads of families—clergymen—elegant ladies—all sorts of people—seeking places whereon they might rest, and finding none. We finally resolved on action, seized a couple of boxes of workmen's tools, emptied the contents on the floor, and converted the boxes into comfortable seats, in the most commanding position in the eastern gallery, notwithstanding the impertinent expostulations of the rosetted officers.

Above us was the lofty stained dome, a most imposing feature;—flags of all nations waved from the latticed balconies; beneath, the jeweled arms of ladies fair gleamed and flashed in the sunlight. Directly below us was Marochetti's equestrian statue of Washington, of colossal proportions. Years ago, dear general, you rode into my young affections on that very horse, as represented on a ninepenny printed cotton handkerchief, given me as a "reward of merit" for correctly "declining to love"—(I wish I had always declined it!) In the immediate neighborhood, our eye rested on a gigantic statue of Webster. There were his features, certainly, all correct, by line and plummet; but *where 's the expression?* It was soulless and corpse-like—it failed to magnetize me.

An hour has passed; our eyes are weary with gazing; still,

no President. The singers have taken their places—the organ has emitted one or two premonitory subterranean grumbles, and the platform is beginning to fill with lesser dignitaries. The richly-cushioned Presidential chair, has been wheeled about in the most inviting locality; a huge bouquet is placed under it by way of *bait*, but still the President does n't nibble! So we bide our time with what patience we may—though the thought of a glass of ice-water, or a cake, occasionally quenches our patience and patriotism.

Another hour has passed! Even feminine curiosity cannot exist much longer on such unsubstantial aliment as pontifical robes and empty glitter. My companion is certainly a wizard! He has conjured up some ice cream and cake:—now I shall have strength to cheer the President. Here he comes, God bless him! You won't see a sight like that out of America. The representative of a mighty nation—one of the mightiest on earth—receiving the homage of expectant thousands, standing without "star" or "order," or insignia of power, other than that with which the Almighty has stamped him. No "body guard," no hedging him in from the people. It is sublime!

—Now the Bishop reads an eloquent prayer; then follows an ode, sung to the time-honored tune of *Old Hundred*, echoing from hundreds of voices, through those deep naves, with such thrilling majesty that you feel as if wings were growing from out your shoulders, and you *must* soar; and suggesting the song of the redeemed, sung by thousands and tens of thousands, before the great White Throne.

Now the speeches commence—but as I see a whole army

of reporters, down below, I shall use their ears instead of my own, and make my escape while an omnibus is to be had. Some day, when the President is not present to eclipse them, I shall return and examine all the *chef de'oeuvres* of art here collected.

—Stay! here 's a pretty conceit I must look at, as we pass along out—a mock garden of moss and flowers, about the size of a lady's work table, from the center of which plays a fountain of eau de cologne, beneath whose drops any lady can perfume her kerchief *en passant*, a dainty invention for a boudoir. Need I say its birth-place is Paris.

There 's the statue of the Amazonian Queen, startled by the sudden spring of a tiger at her horse's throat. Hartshorn and smelling salts, *it 's alive!*—no; it is lifeless bronze, but so full of vitality and expression, it makes me shiver to look at it.

Now my eye is arrested by an imposing group of Thorwalsden, "Christ and his Apostles." It is not *my* Christ. It is not He who said, "Suffer little children to come unto me." It is not He who said to the weeping Magdalen, "Neither do I condemn thee." It is not He who raised for the meek Mary, the dead Lazarus. It is not He who, dying, cried, "Father, forgive them; they know not what they do." It is a form, stern, unbending, forbidding. My heart refuses its allegiance.

But I fear I am wearying the reader; so, let me close by saying, that what astonished me more than anything else, was the appearance of four of the most consummate *Knaves* in the world. They occupied conspicuous positions during the public exercises, and in fact, all the time I was there. Indeed, I am informed that they have been in regular attendance ever since the Palace was opened, notwithstanding they are well known, not only to the police, but to the officers of the exhibition. It is even whispered that the latter named gentlemen connive at their attendance, unblushingly bestow many attentions upon them, and will, undoubtedly, permit them to be present during the entire exhibition. That the public may know and recognize them, I will give their names: they are the North Nave, the South Nave, the East Nave, and the West Nave!

A LANCE COUCHED FOR THE CHILDREN.

You have a pretty, attractive child; she is warm-hearted and affectionate, but vivacious and full of life. With judicious management, and a firm, steady rein, she is a very lovable one. You take her with you on a visit, or to make a call. You are busy, talking with the friend you went to see. A gentleman comes in and throws himself indolently on the sofa. His eye falls upon little Kitty. He is just in the mood to be amused, and makes up his mind to banter her a little, for the sake of drawing her out. So he says —

"Jemima, dear — come here!"

The child blushes, and regards him as if uncertain whether he intended to address her. He repeats his request, with a laugh. She replies, "my name is Kitty, not Jemima," which her tormentor contradicts. Kitty looks puzzled, (just as he intended she should,) but it is only for a moment. She sees he is quizzing her. Well, Miss Kitty likes a frolic, if that is what he wants; so she gives him a pert answer — he laughs uproariously, and rattles fun round her little ears like a hail storm; Kitty has plenty of answers ready for him, and he enjoys the sport amazingly.

By-and-by, he gets weary, and says, — "There — run away

now, I'm going to read the newspaper;" but Kitty is wide awake, and has no idea of being cut short in that summary way; so she continues her Lilliputian attacks, till finally he gets up and beats a despairing retreat, muttering, "what a very *disagreeable* child."

Mamma sees it all from a distance; she does not interfere — no — for she believes in "Children's Rights." Kitty was quiet, well behaved and respectful — till the visitor undertook to quiz, and tease her, for his own amusement. He wanted a frolic — and he has had it: they *who play with children must take children's play.*

A CHAPTER ON HOUSEKEEPING.

I NEVER could see the reason why your smart housekeepers must, of necessity, be Xantippes. I once had the misfortune to be domesticated during the summer months with one of this genus.

I should like to have seen the adventurous spider that would have dared to ply his cunning trade in Mrs. Carrot's premises! Nobody was allowed to sleep a wink after daylight, beneath her roof. Even her old rooster crowed one hour earlier than any of her neighbors'. "Go ahead," was written on every broomstick in the establishment.

She gave her husband his breakfast, buttoned up his overcoat, and put him out of the front door, with his face in the direction of the store, in less time than I've taken to tell it. Then she snatched up the six little Carrots; scrubbed their faces, up and down, without regard to feelings or noses, till they shone like a row of milk pans.

"Clear the track" was her motto, washing and ironing days. She never drew a long breath till the wash-tubs were turned bottom upwards again, and every article of wearing apparel sprinkled, folded, ironed, and replaced on the backs of their respective owners. It gave me a stitch in the side to look at her!

As to her "cleaning days," I never had courage to witness one. I used to lie under an apple tree in the orchard, till she was through. A whole platoon of soldiers would n't have frightened me so much as that virago and her mop.

You should have seen her in her glory on "baking days;" her sleeves rolled up to her arm-pits, and a long, check apron swathed around her bolster-like figure. The great oven glowing, blazing, and sparkling, in a manner very suggestive, to a lazy sinner, like myself. The interminable rows of greased pie-plates; the pans of rough and ready gingerbread; the pots of pork and beans, in an edifying state of progression; and the immense embryo loaves of brown and wheaten bread. To my innocent inquiry, whether she thought the latter would "rise," she set her skinny arms akimbo, marched up within kissing distance of my face, cocked her head on one side, and asked if I thought she looked like a woman to be trifled with by a loaf of bread!" The way I settled down into my slippers, without a reply, probably convinced her that I was no longer skeptical on that point.

Saturday evening she employed in winding up everything that was unwound in the house — the old entry clock included. From that time till Monday morning, she devoted to her husband and Sabbatical exercises. All I have to say is, it is to be hoped she carried some of the fervor of her secular employ ments into those halcyon hours.

BARNUM'S MUSEUM.

It is possible that every stranger may suppose, as I did, on first approaching Barnum's Museum, that the greater part of its curiosities are on the outside, and have some fears that its internal will not equal its external appearance. But, after crossing the threshold, he will soon discover his mistake. The first idea suggested will perhaps be that the view, from the windows, of the motley, moving throng in Broadway — the rattling, thundering carts, carriages and omnibuses — the confluence of the vehicular and human tides which, from so many quarters, come pouring past the museum — is, (to adopt the language of advertisements,) " worth double the price of admission."

The visitor's attention will unquestionably be next arrested by the "Bearded Lady of Switzerland" — one of the most curious curiosities ever presented. A card, in pleasant juxtaposition to the "lady," conveys the gratifying intelligence that, " Visitors are allowed to touch the beard." Not a man in the throng lifts an investigating finger! Your penetration, Madame Clofullia, does you infinite credit. You knew well enough that your permission would be as good as a handcuff to every pair of masculine wrists in the company. For my own part, I should no more meddle with your beard, than with Mons. Clo fullia's. I see no feminity in it. Its shoe-brush aspect puts me on my decorum. I am glad you raised it, however, just to show Barnum that there is something "new under the sun," and to convince men in general that a woman can accomplish about anything she undertakes.

I have not come to New York to stifle my inquisitiveness. How did you raise that beard? Who shaves first in the morning? you, or your husband? Do you use a Woman's Rights razor? Which of you does the *strap*-ping? How does your baby know you from its father? What do you think of us, smooth-faced sisters? Do you (between you and me) prefer to patronize dress-makers, or tailors? Do you sing tenor, or alto? Are you master, or mistress of your husband's affections? — Well, at all events, it has been something in your neutral pocket to have "tarried at Jericho till your beard was grown."

— What have we here? Canova's Venus. She is exquisitely beautiful, standing there, in her sculptured graces; but where 's the Apollo? Ah, here 's a sleeping Cupid, which is better. Mischievous little imp! I 'm off before you wake!— Come we now to a petrifaction of a horse and his rider, crushed in the prehensile embrace of a monstrous serpent, found in a cave where it must have lain for ages, and upon which one's imagination might pleasantly dwell for hours.—Then, here are deputations from China-dom, in the shape of Mandarins, ladies of quality, servants, priests, &c., with their chalky complexions, huckleberry eyes and shaven polls. Here, also, is a Chinese criminal, packed into a barrel, with a hole in the lid, from which his head protrudes, and two at the sides, from whence his helpless paws depend. Poor Min Yung, you ought to reflect on the error of your ways, though, I confess, you 've not much chance to *room*-inate.

Here are snakes, insects, and reptiles of every description, corked down and pinned up, as all such gentry should be,—most of them, I perceive, labeled in the masculine gender! Then there 's a "bear," the thought of whose hug makes me utter an involuntary *pater noster*, and cling closer to the arm of my guide. I tell you what, old Bruin, as I hope to travel, I trust you 've left none of your cubs behind.

—Here is a group of Suliote chiefs, and in their midst Lord Byron, with his shirt upside down; and here is the veritable carriage that little Victoria used to ride in, before the crown of royalty fretted her fair, girlish temples. Poor little embryo queen! How many times since, do you suppose, she has longed to step out of those bejeweled robes, drop the burdens state imposes, and throw her weary limbs, with a child's careless *abandon*, on those silken cushions, free to laugh or cry, to sing or sigh.

—Then, here's a collection of stuffed birds, whose rainbow plumage has darted through clustering foliage, fostered in other latitudes than ours. Nearly every species of beings that crawl or fly, or walk, or swim, is here represented. And what hideous monsters some of them are! A "pretty kettle of fish," some of the representatives of the finny tribe would make! I once thought I would like to be buried in the ocean, but I discarded that idea before I had been in the museum an hour. I should n't want such a "scaly set" of creatures swimming in the same pond with me.

—I had nearly forgotten to mention the "Happy Family." Here are animals and birds which are the natural prey of each other, living together in such pleasant harmony as would make a quarrelsome person blush to look upon. A sleek rat, probably overcome by the oppressive weather, was gently dozing—a cat's neck supporting his sleepy head in a most pillow-ly manner. Mutual vows of friendship had evidently been exchanged and rat-ified by these natural enemies. I have not time to mention in detail the many striking instances of fraternization among creatures which have been considered each other's irreconcilable foes. Suffice it to say that Barnum and Noah are the only men on record who have brought about such a state of harmonic antagonisms, and that Barnum is the only man who has ever made money by the operation.

—Heigho! time fails us to explore all the natural wonders gathered here, from all climes, and lands, and seas, by the enterprise of perhaps the only man who could have compassed it. We turn away, leaving the greater portion unexamined, with an indistinct remembrance of what we have seen, but with a most distinct impression that the "getting up" of Creation was no ordinary affair, and wondering how it could ever have been done in six days.

A FERN REVERIE.

Dear me, I must go shopping. Shopping is a nuisance: clerks are impertinent: feminity is victimized. Miserable day, too: mud plastered an inch thick on the side walk. Well, if we drop our skirts, gentlemen cry "Ugh!" and if we lift them from the mud, they level their eye-glasses at our ankles. The true definition of a gentleman (not found in incomplete Webster) is — a biped, who, of a muddy day, is perfectly oblivious of anything but the shop signs.

Vive la France! Ingenious Parisians, send us over your clever invention — a chain suspended from the girdle, at the end of which is a gold *hand* to clasp up the superfluous length of our promenading robes; thus releasing our human digits, and leaving them at liberty to wrestle with rude Boreas for the possession of the detestable little sham bonnets, which the milliners persist in hanging on the backs of our necks.

Well, here we are at Call & Ketchum's dry-goods store. Now comes the tug of war: let Job's mantle fall on my feminine shoulders.

"Have you *blue* silk?"

Yardstick, entirely ignorant of colors, after fifteen minutes of snail-like research, hands me down a silk that is as *green* as himself.

Oh! away with these stupid masculine clerks, and give us *women*, who know by intuition what we want, to the immense saving of our lungs and leather.

Here 's Mr. Timothy Tape's establishment.

"Have you lace collars, (in points,) Mr. Tape?"

Mr. Tape looks beneficent, and shows me some *rounded* collars. I repeat my request in the most pointed manner for *pointed* collars. Mr. Tape replies, with a patronizing grin:

"Points is going out, Ma'am."

"So am I."

Dear me, how tired my feet are! nevertheless, I must have some merino. So I open the door of Mr. Henry Humbug's dry-goods store, which is about half a mile in length, and inquire for the desired article. Young Yardstick directs me to the counter, at the *extreme* end of the store. I commence my travels thitherward through a file of gaping clerks, and arrive there just ten minutes before two, by my repeater; when I am told "they are quite out of merinos; but won't Lyonnese cloth do just as well?" pulling down a pile of the same. I rush out in a high state of frenzy, and, taking refuge in the next-door neighbor's, inquire for some stockings. Whereupon the clerk inquires (of the wrong customer,) "What price I wish to pay?" Of course, I am not so verdant as to be caught in that trap; and, teetotally disgusted with the entire institution of shopping, I drag my weary limbs into Taylor's new saloon, to rest.

Bless me! what a display of gilding, and girls, and gingerbread! what a heap of mirrors! There's more than one Fanny Fern in the world. I found that out since I came in.

"What will you be pleased to have?" J-u-l-i-u-s C-æ-s-a-r! look at that white-aproned waiter pulling out his snuff-box and taking a pinch of snuff right over that bowl of white sugar, that will be handed me in five minutes to sweeten my tea! And there 's another combing his hair with a pocket-comb, over that dish of oysters.

"What will I have?" Starve me, if I'll have anything, till I can find a cleaner place than this to eat in.

Shade of old Paul Pry Boston! what do I hear? Two — (well I declare, I am not sure whether they are ladies or women; I don't understand these New York feminities. At any rate, they wear bonnets, and are telling the waiter to bring them "a bottle of Maraschino de Zara, some sponge-cake, and some brandy drops!" See them sip the cordial in their glasses, with the gusto of an old toper. See their eyes sparkle and their cheeks flush, and just hear their emancipated little tongues go. Wonder if their husbands know that they—but of course they don't. However, it is six of one and half a dozen of the other. They are probably turning down sherry cobblers, and eating oysters, at Florence's; and their poor hungry children (while their parents are dainty-izing) are coming home hungry from school, to eat a fragmentary dinner, picked up at home by a lazy set of servants.

Heigho! Ladies sipping wine in a public saloon! Pilgrim rock! hide yourself under-ground! Well, it is very shocking the number of married women who pass their time ruining their health in these saloons, devouring Parisian confectionary, and tainting their children's blood with an appetite for strong drink. Oh, what a mockery of a home must theirs be! Heaven pity the children reared there, left to the chance train ing of vicious hirelings.

APOLLO HYACINTH.

"THERE is no better test of moral excellence, than the keenness of one's sense, and the depth of one's love, of all that is beautiful." — *Donohue.*

I DON'T endorse that sentiment. I am acquainted with Apollo Hyacinth. I have read his prose, and I have read his poetry; and I have cried over both, till my heart was as soft as my head, and my eyes were as red as a rabbit's. I have listened to him in public, when he was, by turns, witty, sparkling, satirical, pathetic, till I could have added a codicil to my will, and left him all my worldly possessions; and possibly you have done the same. He has, perhaps, grasped you cordially by the hand, and, with a beaming smile, urged you, in his musical voice, to "call on him and Mrs. Hyacinth;" and you have called: but, did you ever find him "in?" You have invited him to visit you, and have received a "gratified acceptance," in his elegant chirography; but, *did he ever come?* He has borrowed money of you, in the most elegant manner possible; and, as he deposited it in his beautiful purse, he has assured you, in the choicest and most happily chosen language, that he "should never forget your kindness;" but, *did he ever pay?*

Should you die to-morrow, Apollo would write a poetical

obituary notice of you, which would raise the price of pocket-handkerchiefs; but should your widow call on him in the course of a month, to solicit his patronage to open a school, she would be told "he was out of town," and that it was "quite uncertain when he would return."

Apollo has a large circle of relatives; but his "keenness of perception, and deep love, of the beautiful" are so great, that none of them *exactly* meet his views. His "moral excellence," however, does not prevent his making the most of them. He has a way of dodging them adroitly, when they call for a reciprocation, either in a business or a social way; or, if, at any time, there is a necessity for inviting them to his house, he does it when he is at his *country* residence, where their *greenness* will not be out of place.

Apollo never says an uncivil thing — never; he prides himself on that, as well as on his perfect knowledge of human nature; therefore, his sins are all sins of omission. His tastes are very exquisite, and his nature peculiarly sensitive; consequently, he cannot bear trouble. He will tell you, in his elegant way, that trouble "annoys" him, that it "bores" him; in short, that it unfits him for life — for business; so, should you hear that a friend or relative of his, even a brother or a sister, was in distress, or persecuted in any manner, you could not do Apollo a greater injury (in his estimation) than to inform him of the fact. It would so grate upon his sensitive spirit, — it would so "annoy" him; whereas, did he not hear of it until the friend, or brother, or sister, were relieved or buried, he could manage the matter with his usual urbanity and without the slightest draught upon his exquisitely sensitive nature, by simply writing a pathetic and elegant note, expressing the keenest regret at not having known "all about it" in time to have "flown to the assistance of his dear" —— &c.

Apollo prefers friends who can stand grief and annoyance, as a rhinoceros can stand flies — friends who can bear their own troubles and all his — friends who will stand between him and everything disagreeable in life, and never ask anything in return. To such friends he clings with the most touching tenacity — as long as he can use them; but let their good name be assailed, let misfortune once overtake them, and his "moral excellence" compels him, at once, to ignore their existence, until they have been extricated from all their troubles, and it has become perfectly safe and *advantageous* for him to renew the acquaintance.

Apollo is keenly alive to the advantages of social position, (not having always enjoyed them;) and so, his Litany reads after this wise: From all questionable, unfashionable, unpresentable, and vulgar persons, Good Lord, deliver us!

SPOILED LITTLE BOY.

"Boo-hoo! — I 've eaten so — m-much bee-eef and t-turkey, that I can't eat any p-p-plum p-p-pudding!"

MISERABLE little Pitcher! Take your fists out of your eyes, and know that thousands of grown-up pinafore graduates, are in the same Slough of Despond with your epicurean Lilliputian-ship. Having washed the platter clean of every crumb of "common fixins," they are left with cloyed, but tantalizing desires, for the spectacle of some mocking "plum pudding."

"*Can't eat your pudding!*"

Why, you precious, graceless young glutton! you have the start of me, by many an *ache*-r. I expect to furnish an appetite for every "plum pudding" the fates are kind enough to cook for me, from this time till Teba Napoleon writes my epitaph.

Infatuated little Pitcher! come sit on my knee, and take a little advice. Don't you know you should only take a nibble out of each dish, and be parsimonious at that; always leaving off, be the morsel ever so dainty, before your little jacket buttons begin to tighten; while from some of the dishes, you should not even lift the cover; taking aunt Fanny's word for it, that their spicy and stimulating contents will only give you a pain under your apron. Bless your little soul, life's "bill of fare" can be spun out as ingeniously as a cobweb, if you only understand it; and then you can sit in the corner, in good digestive order, and catch your flies! But if you once get a surfeit of a dainty, it takes the form of a pill to you, ever after, unless the knowing *cuisinier* disguise it under some novel process of sugaring; and sadder still, if you exhaust yourself in the gratification of gross appetites, you will be bereft of your faculties for enjoying the pure and heavenly delights which "Our Father" has provided as a *dessert* for his children.

A "BROWN STUDY"—SUGGESTED BY BROWN VAILS.

"Why *will* ladies wear those ugly brown vails, which look like the burnt edge of a buckwheat cake? We vote for green ones."—*Exchange.*

MR. CRITIC: Why don't you hit upon something objectionable? Such as the passion which stout ladies have for wearing immense plaids, and whole stories of flounces! Such as thin, bolster-like looking females wearing narrow stripes! Such as brunettes, gliding round like ghosts, in pale blue! Such as blondes blowing out like dandelions in bright yellow! Such as short ladies swathing up their little fat necks in voluminous folds of shawls, and *shingle* women, rejoicing in strips of mantles!

Then the gentlemen!

Your stout man is sure to get into a frock coat, with baggy trowsers; your May-pole, into a long-waisted body-coat, and "continuations" unnecessarily compact; your dark man looks like an "east wind" daguerreotyped, in a light blue neck-tie; while your pink-and-white man looks as though he wanted a pitcher of water in his face, in a salmon-colored or a black one.

Now allow *me* to suggest. Your thin man should always

close the thorax button of his coat, and the last two at his waistband, leaving the intermediate open, to give what he needs —more breadth of chest. Your stout man, who has almost always a nice arm and hand, should have his coat sleeve a *perfect fit* from the elbow to the wrist, buttoning *there tightly*—allowing a nice strip of a white linen wristband below it.

I understand the architecture of a coat to a charm ; know as quick as a flash whether 't is all right, the minute I clap my eye on it. As to vests, I call myself a connoisseur. "*Stocks*" are only fit for Wall Street ! Get yourself some nice silk neckties, and ask your wife, or somebody who knows something, to longitudinize them to your jugular. Throw your colored, embroidered, and ruffled shirt-bosoms overboard ; leave your cane and cigar at home ; wear a pair of neat, *dark* gloves ; sport an immaculate pocket-handkerchief and dicky — do n't say naughty words — give us ladies the *inside* of the walk—speak of every woman as you would wish *your* mother or *your* sister spoken of, and you 'll do !

INCIDENT AT THE FIVE POINTS HOUSE OF INDUSTRY.

To be able to appreciate Mr. Pease's toils, and sacrifices, and self-denying labors at the Five Points House of Industry, one must visit the locality :—one must wind through those dirty streets and alleys, and see the wrecks of humanity that meet him at every step ;—he must see children so dirty and squalid that they scarcely resemble human beings, playing in filthy gutters, and using language that would curdle his blood to hear from *childhood's* lips ; — he should see men, "made in God's own image," brutalised beyond his power to imagine ; — he should see women (girls of not more than twenty years) reeling about the pavements in a state of beastly intoxication, without a trace of feminity in their vicious faces ; — he should pass the rum shops, where men and women are quarreling and fighting and swearing, while childhood listens and *learns !* — he should pass the second-hand clothes cellars, where hard-featured Jewish dealers swing out faded, refuse garments, (pawned by starving virtue for bread,) to sell to the needy, half-naked emigrant for his last penny ;—he should see decayed fruit and vegetables which the most ravenous swine might well root twice over before devouring, purchased as daily food by these poor creatures;—he should see *gentlemen* (?) threading these streets, not to make all this misery less, God knows, but to sever the last thread of hope to which many a tempted one is despairingly clinging.

One must see all this, before he can form a just idea of the magnitude and importance of the work that Mr. Pease has single-handed and nobly undertaken; remembering that men of wealth and influence have their own reasons for using that wealth and influence to perpetuate this modern Sodom.

One should spend an hour in Mr. Pease's house, to see the constant drafts upon his time and strength, in the shape of calls and messages, and especially the applications for relief that *his* slender purse alas! is often not able to answer;—he should see his unwearied patience and activity, admire the kind, sympathetic heart—unaffected by the toil or the frowns of temporizing theorists—ever warm, ever pitiful, giving not only "the *crumbs* from his table," but often his own meals to the hungry—his own wardrobe to the naked;—he should see *this*, and go away *ashamed* to have lived so long and done so little to help the maimed, and sick, and lame, to Bethesda's Pool.

I will relate an incident which occurred, some time since, at the House of Industry, and which serves as a fair sample of daily occurrences there.

One morning an aged lady, of respectable appearance, called at the Mission House and enquired for Mr. Pease. She was told that he was engaged, and asked if some one else would not do as well. She said, respectfully, "No; my business is with him; I will wait, if you please, till he can see me."

Mr. Pease immediately came in, when the old lady commenced her story:

"I came, sir," said she, "in behalf of a poor, unfortunate woman and three little children. She is living now" — and the tears dropped over her wrinkled face — "in a bad place in Willet-street, in a basement. There are rum shops all around it, and many drunken people about the neighborhood. She has made out to pay the rent, but has had no food for the poor little children, who have subsisted on what they could manage to beg in the day time. The landlord promised, when she hired the basement, to put a lock on the door, and make it comfortable, so that 'the Croton' need not run in; but he got his rent and then broke his promise, and they have not seen him since."

"Is the woman respectable?" enquired Mr. Pease.

"Yes—no—not exactly," said the poor old lady, violently agitated. "She was well brought up. She has a good heart, sir, but a bad head, and then trouble has discouraged her. Poor Mary — yes sir, it *must* have been the *trouble* — for I know her *heart* is good, sir. I" — tears choked the old lady's utterance. Recovering herself, she continued:

"She had a kind husband once. He was the father of her two little girls: six years ago he died, and — the poor thing — oh, sir, you don't know how dear she is to *me!*" and burying her aged face in her hands, she sobbed aloud.

Mr. Pease's kind heart interpreted the old lady's emotion,

without the pain of an explanation. In the weeping woman before him he saw the *mother* of the lost one.

Yes, she was "Mary's" mother. Poverty could not chill her love; shame and the world's scorn had only filled her with a God-like pity.

After a brief pause, she brushed away her tears and went on:

"Yes, sir; Mary was a good child to me *once;* she respected religion and religious people, and used to love to go to church, but lately, sir, God knows she has almost broke my heart. Last spring I took her home, and the three dear children; but she would not listen to me, and left without telling me where she was going. I heard that there was a poor woman living in a basement in Willet street, with three children, and my heart told me that that was my poor, lost Mary, and there I found her. But, oh, sir — oh, sir" — and she sobbed as if her heart were breaking — "*such* a place! *My* Mary, that I used to cradle in these arms to sleep, that lisped her little evening prayer at *my* knee — *my* Mary, *drunk* in that terrible place!"

She was getting so agitated that Mr. Pease, wishing to turn the current of her thoughts, asked her if she herself was a member of any church. She said yes, of the —— street Baptist Church. She said she was a widow, and had had one child beside Mary — a son. And her face lighted up as she said:

"Oh sir, he was such a *fine* lad. He did all he could to make me happy; but he thought, that if he went to California he could make money, and when he left he said 'Cheer up, dear mother; I'll come back and give my money all to *you*, and you shall never work any more.'"

"I can see him now, sir, as he stood there, with his eye kindling. Poor lad! poor lad! He came back, but it was only to die. His last words were, 'God will care for you, mother— I know it — when I'm gone to Heaven.' Oh! if I could have seen my poor *girl* die as he did, before she became so bad. Oh, sir, *won't* you take her *here?* — *won't* you try to make her good? — *can't* you make her good, sir? I *can't* give Mary up. Nobody cares for Mary now but me. Won't you try, sir?"

Mr. Pease promised that he would do all he could, and sent a person out with the old lady, to visit "Mary," and obtain particulars: he soon returned and corroborated all the old lady's statements. Mr. Pease then took a friend and started to see what could be done.

In Willet street is a rickety old wooden building, filled to overflowing with the very refuse of humanity. The basement is lighted with two small windows half under ground; and in this wretched hole lived Mary and her children. As Mr. Pease descended the steps into the room, he heard some one say, "Here he comes, grandmother! he's come — he's come!"

The door was opened. On a pile of rags in the corner lay Mary, "my Mary," as the old lady tearfully called her.

God of mercy! what a wreck of beautiful womanhood! Her large blue eyes glared with maniac wildness, under the influence of intoxication. Long waves of auburn hair fell, in tangled masses, over a form wasted, yet beautiful in its graceful outlines.

Poor, lost Mary!

"*Such* a place!" as her mother had, weeping, said. Not a table, or chair, or bedstead, or article of furniture in it, of any description. On the mantle-piece stood a beer-bottle with a half burnt candle in its nose. A few broken, dirty dishes stood upon the shelf, and a quantity of filthy rags lay scattered round the floor.

The grandmother was holding by the hand a sweet child of eight years, with large, bright eyes, and auburn hair (like poor Mary's) falling about her neck. An older girl of twelve, with a sweet, Madonna face, that seemed to light up even *that* wretched place with a beam of Heaven, stood near, bearing in her arms a babe of sixteen months, which was not so large as one of eight months should have been. Its little hands looked like bird's claws, and its little bones seemed almost piercing the skin.

The old lady went up to her daughter, saying, "Mary, dear, this is the gentleman who is willing to take you to his house, if you will try to be good."

"Get out of the room, you old hypocrite," snarled the intoxicated woman, "or I 'll —— (and she clutched a hatchet beside her) — I 'll show you! You are the worst old woman I ever knew, except the one you brought in here the other day, and she is a fiend outright. Talk to *me* about being *good!* — ha — ha" — and she laughed an idiot laugh.

"Mother," said the eldest child, sweetly laying her little hand upon her arm, — "*dear* mother, do n't, please do n't hurt grandmother. She is good and kind to us; she only wants to get you out of this bad place, where you will be treated kindly."

"Yes, dear mother, chimed in the younger sister, bending her little curly head over her, "mother, you said once you *would* go. Do n't keep us here any longer, mother. We are cold and hungry. Please get up and take us away; we are afraid to stay here, mother, dear."

"Yes, Mary," said the old lady, handing her down a faded, ragged gown, "here is your dress; put it on, wont you!"

Mary raised herself on the pile of rags on which she was lying, and pushing the eldest girl across the room, screamed out, "Get away, you impudent little thing! you are just like your old grandmother. I tell you *all*," said she, raising herself on one elbow, and tossing back her auburn hair from her broad, white forehead, "I tell you all, I *never* will go from here, *never!* I *love* this place. So many fine people come here, and we have such good times. There is a gentleman who takes care of me. He brought me some candles, last night, and he says that I shan't want for anything, if I will only get rid of these troublesome children—*my husband's* children." And she hid her face in her hands and laughed convulsively.

"You may have *them*," she continued, "just as soon as you like—baby and all! but I never will go from this place. I *love* it. A great many fine people come here to see me."

The poor old lady wrung her hands and wept, while the children clung round their grandmother, with half-averted faces, trembling and silent.

Mr. Pease said to her, "Mary, you may either go with me,

or I'll send for an officer and have you carried to the station-house. Which will you do?"

Mary cursed and raved, but finally put on the dress the old lady handed her, and consented to go with them. A carriage was soon procured, and Mary helped inside — Mr. Pease lifting in the baby and the two little girls, and away they started for the Five Points House of Industry.

"Oh, mother!" exclaimed the younger of the girls, "how very pleasant it is to ride in this nice carriage, and to get away from that dirty place; we shall be so happy now, mother; and Edith and the baby too: see, he is laughing: he likes to ride. You will love sister Edith and baby, and me, *now*, wont you, dear mother? and you wont frighten us with the hatchet any more, or hurt dear grandmother, will you?"

Arriving at Mr. Pease's house, the delight of the little creatures was unbounded. They caught hold of their mother's faded dress, saying, "Did n't we *tell* you, mother, that you would have a pleasant home here? Only see that nice garden! you did n't have a garden in Willet Street, mother!"

Reader, would you know that mother's after history?

Another "Mary" hath "bathed the Saviour's feet" with her tears, and wiped them with the hairs of her head. Her name is no longer written Mary *Magdalena*. In the virtuous home of her aged mother, she sits clothed in her right mind, "and her children rise up and call her *blessed*."

NANCY PRY'S SOLILOQUY.

I WONDER if that is the bride, over at that window? Poor thing, how I pity her! Every thing in her house so bran new and fresh and uncomfortable. Furniture smelling like a mahogany coffin; every thing set up spick and span in its place; not a picture awry; not a chair out of its orbit; not a finger mark on the window panes; not a thread on the carpet; not a curtain fold disarranged; china and porcelain set up in alphabetical order in the pantry; bureau drawers fit for a Quaker; no stockings, to mend; no strings or buttons missing; no old rag-bags to hunt over; no dresses to re-flounce, or re-tuck, or re-fashionize; not even a hook or eye absent. Sauce pans, pots, and kettles, fresh from the "furnishing house;" servants fresh; house as still as a cat-cornered mouse. Nothing stirring, nothing to do. Land of Canaan! I should think it would be a relief to her to hear the braying and roaring in Driesbach's Menagerie.

Well, there 's one consolation; in all human probability, it is a state of things that won't last long.

FOR LITTLE CHILDREN.

"I love God and every little child."—*Richter.*

I WONDER if I have any little pinafore friends among the readers of *Fern Leaves?* any little Nellys, or Katys, or Billys, or Johnnys, who ever think of Fanny? Do you know that I like children much better than grown-up people? I should so like to have a whole lap full of your bright eyes, and rosy cheeks, and dimpled shoulders, to kiss. I should like to have a good romp with you, this very minute. I don't always keep this old pen of mine scratching. If a bright cloud comes sailing past my window, I throw down my pen, toss up the casement, and drink in the air, like a gipsey. I feel just as you do, when you are pent up in school, some bright summer day, when the winds are at play, and the flowers lie languidly drooping under the blue, arching sky;—when the little butterfly poises his bright wings on the rose, too full of joy even to sip its sweets;—when the birds sing, because they can't help it, and the merry little swallow skims the ground, dips his bright wing in the lake, circles over head, and then flies, twittering, back to his cunning little brown nest, under the eaves. On such a day, *I* should like to be your school-mistress., I'd throw open the old school-room door, and let you all out under the trees. You should count the blades of grass for a sum in addition;

you should take an apple from a tree, to learn subtraction; you should give me kisses, to learn multiplication. You shouldn't go home to dinner. No: we'd all take our dinner-baskets and go into the woods; we'd hunt for violets; we'd lie on the moss under the trees, and look up at the bits of blue sky, through the leafy branches; we'd hush our breath when the little chipmunk peeped out of his hole, and watch him slily snatch the ripe nut for his winter's store. And we'd look for the shy rabbit; and the little spotted toad, with its blinking eyes; and the gliding snake, which creeps out to sun itself on the old gray rock. We'd play hide and seek, in the hollow trunks of old trees; we'd turn away from the gaudy flowers, flaunting their showy beauty in our faces, and search, under the glossy leaves at our feet, for the pale-eyed blossoms which nestle there as lovingly as a timid little fledgling under the mother-bird's wing; we'd go to the lake, and see the sober, staid old cows stand cooling their legs in the water, and admiring themselves in the broad, sheeted mirror beneath; we'd toss little pebbles in the lake, and see the circles they made, widen and widen toward the distant shore — like careless words, dropped and forgotten, but reaching to the far-off shore of eternity.

And then you should nestle 'round me, telling all your little griefs; for well I know that childhood has its griefs, which are all the keener because great, wise, grown-up people have often neither time nor patience, amid the bustling whirl of life, to stop and listen to them. I know what it is for a timid little child, who has never been away from its mother's apron string, to be walked, some morning, into a great big school-room, full of strange faces;—to see a little urchin laugh, and feel a choking lump come in your little throat, for fear he was laughing at you; —to stand up, with trembling legs, in the middle of the floor, and be told to "find big A," when your eyes were so full of tears that you could n't see anything;—to keep looking at the ferule on the desk, and wondering if it would ever come down on your hand;—to have some mischievous little scholar break your nice long slate-pencil in two, to plague you, or steal your bit of gingerbread, out of your satchel, and eat it up, or trip you down on purpose, and feel how little the hard-hearted young sinners cared when you sobbed out, "I 'll tell my mother."

I know what it is, when you have lain every night since you were born, with your hand clasped in your mother's, and your cheek cuddled up to hers, to see a new baby come and take your place, without even asking your leave;—to see papa, and grandpa, and grandma, and uncle, and aunt, and cousins, and all the neighbors, so glad to see it, when *your* heart was almost broke about it. I know what it is to have a great fat nurse (whom even mamma herself had to mind) lead you, struggling, out of the room, and tell Sally to see that you did n't come into your own mamma's room again all that day. I know what it is to have that fat old nurse sit in mamma's place at table, and cut up your potato and meat all wrong;—to have her put squash on your plate, when you *hate* squash;—to have her forget (?) to give you a piece of pie, and eat two pieces *herself;*—to have Sally cross, and Betty cross, and everybody telling you to "get out of the way;"—to have your doll's leg get loose, and nobody there to hitch it on for you; — and then, when it came night, to be put away in a chamber, all alone by yourself to sleep, and have Sally tell you that "if you wasn't good an old black man would come and carry you off;"—and then to cuddle down under the sheet, till you were half stifled, and tremble every time the wind blew, as if you had an ague fit. Yes, and when, at last, mamma came down stairs, I know how *long* it took for you to like that new baby;—how every time you wanted to sit in mamma's lap, he'd be sure to have the stomach-ache, or to want his breakfast; how he was *always* wanting something, so that mamma could n't tell you pretty stories, or build little blocks of houses for you, or make you reins to play horse with; or do any of those nice little things, that she used to be always doing for you.

To be sure, my little darlings, I know all about it. I have cried tears enough to float a steamship, about all these provoking things; and now whenever I see a little child cry, I never feel like laughing at him: for I know that often his little heart is just ready to break, for somebody to pet him. So I always say a kind word, or give him a pat on the head, or a kiss; for I know that though the little insect has but one grain to carry, he often staggers under it: and I have seen the time when a kind word, or a beaming smile, would have been worth more to me, than all the broad lands of merrie England.

www.ingramcontent.com/pod-product-compliance
Lightning Source LLC
LaVergne TN
LVHW020057110826
845151LV00001B/5

* 9 7 8 1 4 2 5 5 4 5 3 8 3 *